Pepetela and the MPLA
The Ethical Evolution of a Revolutionary Writer

LEGENDA

LEGENDA is the Modern Humanities Research Association's book imprint for new research in the Humanities. Founded in 1995 by Malcolm Bowie and others within the University of Oxford, Legenda has always been a collaborative publishing enterprise, directly governed by scholars. The Modern Humanities Research Association (MHRA) joined this collaboration in 1998, became half-owner in 2004, in partnership with Maney Publishing and then Routledge, and has since 2016 been sole owner. Titles range from medieval texts to contemporary cinema and form a widely comparative view of the modern humanities, including works on Arabic, Catalan, English, French, German, Greek, Italian, Portuguese, Russian, Spanish, and Yiddish literature. Editorial boards and committees of more than 60 leading academic specialists work in collaboration with bodies such as the Society for French Studies, the British Comparative Literature Association and the Association of Hispanists of Great Britain & Ireland.

The MHRA encourages and promotes advanced study and research in the field of the modern humanities, especially modern European languages and literature, including English, and also cinema. It aims to break down the barriers between scholars working in different disciplines and to maintain the unity of humanistic scholarship. The Association fulfils this purpose through the publication of journals, bibliographies, monographs, critical editions, and the MHRA Style Guide, and by making grants in support of research. Membership is open to all who work in the Humanities, whether independent or in a University post, and the participation of younger colleagues entering the field is especially welcomed.

ALSO PUBLISHED BY THE ASSOCIATION

Critical Texts
Tudor and Stuart Translations • New Translations • European Translations
MHRA Library of Medieval Welsh Literature

MHRA Bibliographies
Publications of the Modern Humanities Research Association

The Annual Bibliography of English Language & Literature
Austrian Studies
Modern Language Review
Portuguese Studies
The Slavonic and East European Review
Working Papers in the Humanities
The Yearbook of English Studies

www.mhra.org.uk
www.legendabooks.com

STUDIES IN HISPANIC AND LUSOPHONE CULTURES

Studies in Hispanic and Lusophone Cultures are selected and edited by the Association of Hispanists of Great Britain & Ireland. The series seeks to publish the best new research in all areas of the literature, thought, history, culture, film, and languages of Spain, Spanish America, and the Portuguese-speaking world.

The Association of Hispanists of Great Britain & Ireland is a professional association which represents a very diverse discipline, in terms of both geographical coverage and objects of study. Its website showcases new work by members, and publicises jobs, conferences and grants in the field.

Editorial Committee
Chair: Professor Trevor Dadson (Queen Mary, University of London)
Professor Catherine Davies (University of Nottingham)
Professor Sally Faulkner (University of Exeter)
Professor Andrew Ginger (University of Bristol)
Professor James Mandrell (Brandeis University, USA)
Professor Hilary Owen (University of Manchester)
Professor Christopher Perriam (University of Manchester)
Professor Philip Swanson (University of Sheffield)

Managing Editor
Dr Graham Nelson
41 Wellington Square, Oxford OX1 2JF, UK

www.legendabooks.com/series/shlc

STUDIES IN HISPANIC AND LUSOPHONE CULTURES

1. *Unamuno's Theory of the Novel*, by C. A. Longhurst
2. *Pessoa's Geometry of the Abyss: Modernity and the* Book of Disquiet, by Paulo de Medeiros
3. *Artifice and Invention in the Spanish Golden Age*, edited by Stephen Boyd and Terence O'Reilly
4. *The Latin American Short Story at its Limits: Fragmentation, Hybridity and Intermediality*, by Lucy Bell
5. *Spanish New York Narratives 1898–1936: Modernisation, Otherness and Nation*, by David Miranda-Barreiro
6. *The Art of Ana Clavel: Ghosts, Urinals, Dolls, Shadows and Outlaw Desires*, by Jane Elizabeth Lavery
7. *Alejo Carpentier and the Musical Text*, by Katia Chornik
8. *Britain, Spain and the Treaty of Utrecht 1713-2013*, edited by Trevor J. Dadson and J. H. Elliott
9. *Books and Periodicals in Brazil 1768-1930: A Transatlantic Perspective*, edited by Ana Cláudia Suriani da Silva and Sandra Guardini Vasconcelos
10. *Lisbon Revisited: Urban Masculinities in Twentieth-Century Portuguese Fiction*, by Rhian Atkin
11. *Urban Space, Identity and Postmodernity in 1980s Spain: Rethinking the Movida*, by Maite Usoz de la Fuente
12. *Santería, Vodou and Resistance in Caribbean Literature: Daughters of the Spirits*, by Paul Humphrey
13. *Reprojecting the City: Urban Space and Dissident Sexualities in Recent Latin American Cinema*, by Benedict Hoff
14. *Rethinking Juan Rulfo's Creative World: Prose, Photography, Film*, edited by Dylan Brennan and Nuala Finnegan
15. *The Last Days of Humanism: A Reappraisal of Quevedo's Thought*, by Alfonso Rey
16. *Catalan Narrative 1875-2015*, edited by Jordi Larios and Montserrat Lunati
17. *Islamic Culture in Spain to 1614: Essays and Studies*, by L. P. Harvey
18. *Film Festivals: Cinema and Cultural Exchange*, by Mar Diestro-Dópido
19. *St Teresa of Avila: Her Writings and Life*, edited by Terence O'Reilly, Colin Thompson and Lesley Twomey
20. *(Un)veiling Bodies: A Trajectory of Chilean Post-Dictatorship Documentary*, by Elizabeth Ramírez Soto

Pepetela and the MPLA

The Ethical Evolution of a Revolutionary Writer

Phillip Rothwell

LEGENDA
Studies in Hispanic and Lusophone Cultures 36
Modern Humanities Research Association
2019

Published by Legenda
an imprint of the Modern Humanities Research Association
Salisbury House, Station Road, Cambridge CB1 2LA

ISBN 978-1-78188-721-9 *(HB)*
ISBN 978-1-78188-722-6 *(PB)*

First published 2019
Paperback edition 2021

All rights reserved. No part of this publication may be reproduced or disseminated or transmitted in any form or by any means, electronic, mechanical, photocopying, recording or otherwise, or stored in any retrieval system, or otherwise used in any manner whatsoever without written permission of the copyright owner, except in accordance with the provisions of the Copyright, Designs and Patents Act 1988, or under the terms of a licence permitting restricted copying issued in the UK by the Copyright Licensing Agency Ltd, Saffron House, 6–10 Kirby Street, London EC1N 8TS, *England, or in the USA by the Copyright Clearance Center, 222 Rosewood Drive, Danvers MA 01923. Application for the written permission of the copyright owner to reproduce any part of this publication must be made by email to legenda@mhra.org.uk.*

Disclaimer: Statements of fact and opinion contained in this book are those of the author and not of the editors or the Modern Humanities Research Association. The publisher makes no representation, express or implied, in respect of the accuracy of the material in this book and cannot accept any legal responsibility or liability for any errors or omissions that may be made.

Trademark notice: Product or corporate names may be trademarks or registered trademarks, and are used only for identification and explanation without intent to infringe.

© *Modern Humanities Research Association 2019*

Copy-Editor: Richard Correll

CONTENTS

	Acknowledgements	ix
	Pepetela's Principal Works Referenced in This Book	xi
	Introduction	1
1	The Problems of History or a History of Problems	7
2	A Nation of New Men or the Age-Old Abuse of a Woman's Body	19
3	When the Writer Can Say What the Man Cannot: The Original Sin of 1977	34
4	Ideology, Nationality, Racism and Rape	49
5	The Dynamics of Girl Power or the Selective Process of Myth-Making	67
6	The 1990s: Plus Ça Change	76
7	Failed Fathers, Phallic Futures and Commodified Children: The Dehumanization of Post-War Angola	86
8	The Ethical Challenges of History	95
9	The Ethics of Forgiveness	106
10	The American Bogeyman: Empire and the Terror Cell	118
11	Denationalized Dialogism and the Primordial Thing, or Reconciling beyond the Law of Capitalism	134
12	The Bourgeoisie, the City and the Loner	143
	Afterword	161
	Bibliography	162
	Index	171

for Margaret Ann
my first teacher and my first love

ACKNOWLEDGEMENTS

Many people helped me to develop the ideas in this book. Over a decade ago, Cláudia Pazos Alonso thoughtfully challenged me to think more carefully about Pepetela's portrayal of women. We were guests of Claire Williams at a conference she organized when we all worked at different institutions. As has since happened on numerous occasions in various contexts, Claire and Cláudia's astute but encouraging probing led me to see more clearly what questions I should be asking, and how to fit together disjointed ideas. Fate subsequently conspired to bring us together at the University of Oxford. Alongside Simon Park and Gui Perdigão, I could not have more ideal and supportive colleagues. To a large extent, the cooperative spirit of Portuguese in Oxford is the great legacy of Stephen Parkinson and Thomas Earle. The latter has been the perfect predecessor — a source of wisdom and inspiration.

Both Claire and Cláudia provided detailed and invaluable feedback on various parts of this book, as did Ricardo Soares de Oliveira, whose academic knowledge of Angolan politics is second to none. His ability to articulate patterns and parallels never ceases to amaze. I thank them, as well as Alexandra Reza and Thomas Stennett, who meticulously and generously read chapters, caught slippages and inconsistencies, and helped me to tighten arguments. Thanks also to Graham Nelson for overseeing the publication of this book and to Richard Correll for his proof-reading. Any remaining flaws are entirely my own. I am also grateful to Mark Damazer for his unfailing support and encouragement.

My interest in Pepetela began with a class I took with Margaret Clarke. With her patient guidance, I struggled through my first novel in Portuguese — Pepetela's *Mayombe*. Margaret's teaching was one of the seeds of my abiding interest in Portuguese-speaking Africa and, particularly, in Pepetela. She also encouraged me to try to publish work at a relatively early stage in my career, advice for which I am very grateful. The first article I submitted to a journal happened to be about *Mayombe*. The *Luso-Brazilian Review* eventually published it, after a series of revisions that took several years to complete and taught me how arguments evolve in dialogue and over time.[1] I published a second article on Pepetela's work as part of the celebrations of fifty years of the journal.[2] Again, the feedback I received on my submission helped to develop my thinking around Pepetela in ways that went beyond what was published. I am therefore grateful to the journal's past editors and particularly its current 'lusophone Africa' editor, Luís Madureira, whose critical eye and scholarship have over many years influenced my thinking.

1. 'Unmasking Structures: The Dynamics of Power in Pepetela's *Mayombe*', *Luso-Brazilian Review*, 39.1 (2002), 121–28.
2. 'Nostalgia and Misrepresenting Jagas: Pepetela's Strategies for Dealing with Failure in *Crónicas com Fundo de Guerra* and *O Sul. O Sombreiro*', *Luso-Brazilian Review*, 50.2 (2013), 118–34.

Anna M. Klobucka, Ana Paula Ferreira, David Brookshaw, Victor K. Mendes, Hilary Owen, Raquel Ribeiro and Leonor Simas-Almeida have in different settings asked me profound questions about my readings of Pepetela, giving me the opportunity to reconsider and refine my ideas. Lara Pawson and Ana Maria Martinho are generously shared reservoirs of information about contemporary Angola and its culture. Yeon-Soo Kim and Juan José Adriasola have long expanded my theoretical horizons, with intellectual acumen and political commitment. Margarida Calafate Ribeiro always asks me how my arguments can be pushed a step further, and usually provides me with the answer too. Helder Macedo's combination of erudition and conceptualization constantly opens up new ways of reading texts for me. I am immensely grateful to all of them but I am most grateful to Beto for who he is and what he does.

P.R., Oxford, February 2019

PEPETELA'S PRINCIPAL WORKS REFERENCED IN THIS BOOK

A geração da utopia	[Generation of Utopia]
A gloriosa família	[The Glorious Family]
As aventuras de Ngunga	[Ngunga's Adventures]
Crónicas com fundo de guerra	[Chronicles with a War Backdrop]
Jaime Bunda, agente secreto	[Jaime Bunda, Secret Agent]
Jaime Bunda e a morte do americano	[Jaime Bunda and the Death of the American]
Lueji, o nascimento de um império	[Lueji, the Birth of an Empire]
Mayombe	[Mayombe]
Muana Puó	[Muana Puó]
O cão e os caluandas	[The Dog and the Luandans]
O desejo de Kianda	[The Return of the Water Spirit]
O planalto e a estepe	[The Plateau and the Steppe]
O quase fim do mundo	[The Near End of the World]
O sul. O sombreiro	[The South. The Hat]
O terrorista de Berkeley, Califórnia	[The Terrorist of Berkeley, California]
O tímido e as mulheres	[The Shy Guy and the Women]
Predadores	[Predators]
Se o passado não tivesse asas	[If the Past Didn't Have Wings]
Yaka	[Yaka]

INTRODUCTION

If we judge success by grip on political power, then the People's Movement for the Liberation of Angola, known more commonly by its Portuguese acronym, the MPLA, is one of the most successful institutions in post-imperial Africa. It began as an independence movement, committed to the overthrow of Portuguese colonialism. With time its ideological positioning shifted from the Marxist sympathies it shared with the Portuguese Communist Party, which influenced its early leadership, to an enthusiastic embrace of free-market economics.

Officially, the MPLA became a vanguard Marxist-Leninist workers' party in 1977. By the mid-1980s, the changing geo-political climate led to the leadership's profound reconsideration of its commitment to state control of the means of production. At the same time, there were sectors of Angola's powerful Creole elites pushing hard for the country to re-orientate towards a neo-liberal model. Tony Hodges describes how 'leading Luanda families felt constrained by the dominance of the state in the economy and by the official ideology and began to seek more latitude for the development of private business interests'.[1]

By the 1990s, the MPLA leadership officially converted to a whole-hearted belief in the private sector. However, as Hodges points out, 'vestiges of administrative intervention in the economy, along with weak systems of transparency and accountability, encouraged cronyism'.[2] In other words, those with ties to the Angolan president and the upper echelons of the MPLA benefited disproportionately from a distorted transition to a market economy. Former espousers of communist ideals often transformed into capitalism's champions, and guaranteed their continued privilege, safeguarded by links to the state.

For Hodges, the abandonment of Marxist-Leninism took place in an 'ideological and moral void' that produced 'a rogue form of capitalism in which a handful of prominent families, linked politically to the regime [...] exploited opportunities for self-enrichment'.[3] In the book that follows, I am only tangentially interested in the MPLA's conversion into a conglomerate of self-enriching opportunists. I am more concerned with how Angola's most prominent writer, Pepetela, dealt with that 'ideological and moral void' where once he believed in an MPLA with an intellectual vision of the common good.

Beyond his extraordinary skill as an author, Pepetela's importance lies in his role in witnessing and participating in the birth and growing pains of an independent Angola. Covering nearly six decades, his writing occupies a unique position in literary history — akin to Pêro Vaz de Caminha's letter to Manuel I of Portugal in 1500, describing the discovery of Brazil, or Fernão Lopes's role, through his fifteenth-century chronicles, in shoring up the legitimacy of the House of Aviz. More than these literary predecessors, Pepetela evolves both his aesthetic technique and his ethical understanding of the stakes for the nation of which he was a cultural midwife.

The term 'nation' is inherently problematic. It references a nebulous, often unstable, concept. Its quirks change to suit the demands of the political moment. In the context of post-colonial Africa, where the artificial frontiers inherited from the imperial order were often the result of intra-European haggling and gunboat diplomacy rather than territorial and cultural cohesion, the nation has been used as a mechanism to erase cultural difference and promote unified political authority.

The etymology of the word implies a birthright. Yet Pepetela's earlier writing makes clear that, for the MPLA, nationhood had less to do with place of birth and more to do with the disciplining of thoughts and a commitment to the revolution. Pepetela's novels endorse, interact with and interrogate the MPLA — its conceptions and actions — at various stages in the movement's history. From his perspective as a militant writer who never relinquished his critical acumen or accepted the 'ideological and moral void' into which the movement plunged, he tells the story of the MPLA — even more than the story of Angola. That ambiguous story, as distilled through over half a century of his writing, is the subject of this book.

When Pepetela began to publish as a student in colonial Lisbon, he had a clear sense of the moral repugnance of imperialism. Born in the Angolan coastal city of Benguela and enjoying a relatively comfortable white-family background, he became increasingly drawn to the MPLA. He trained as a sociologist and became a nationalist historian, having joined the independence struggle. Following the departure of the Portuguese from Angola, he served in the government of the country's first president, Agostinho Neto. He subsequently produced a vast array of fiction, commanding and experimenting with the novel genre, as well as being a leading public intellectual.

The central thesis of this book is that Pepetela's early work is marked by a moral code — based on the establishment of collective customs and mores directed through a national vanguard. The socialist vision for an independent Angola propounded in his early novels and public statements rested on the identity of a community founded on ideological adherence rather than provenance or ethnicity. In other words, Angolan 'nationhood' was consciously an ideological construct. Yet even as he preached that ideological 'morality' through his writing, he critiqued it and was painfully aware of the extent to which it replicated Christian colonial models, and oversimplified human nature. As the MPLA's utopian framework unravelled, confronted by the realities of the Cold War, a civil conflict and a covetous leadership, Pepetela underwent an ethical turn. Vanguard morality and ideological purity were replaced by the depiction of individual choices and difficult compromises.

I situate Pepetela's writing in light of key moments in Angola's history: the anti-colonial struggle; independence in 1975; the MPLA purges of 1977; the prolonged civil war; the first multiparty elections of 1992; the end of the civil war in 2002; and the elections of 2017. I offer a range of readings of many of Pepetela's principal works, exploring the aesthetic brilliance of someone who writes with the voice a flawed man. His analysis of power structures furthers an understanding of how Angola, despite its promise and immense human and natural resources, became one of the most corrupt and inequitable states in the world today.

Boaventura de Sousa Santos observed in a reflection published in Manuel Rui's *O Kaputo Camionista e Eusébio* that 'ao contrário do sociólogo, o escritor dificilmente fica sob suspeita porque só ele sabe dar conta da grande tribo dos humanos em que todos são demasiadamente humanos, labirinticamente humanos, capazes de serem tudo e o seu contrário sequencial ou simultaneamente'[4] [unlike the sociologist, only with difficulty does the writer find himself under suspicion because he alone knows how to portray the great human tribe in which all are far too human, labyrinthinely human, capable of being everything and its opposite, in sequence or simultaneously]. Pepetela is both a writer and a sociologist, and a historian too. His fiction is, in the words of Pires Laranjeira, a 'bisturi da História' [scalpel of history].[5] He brings his sociological training from six years spent in Algiers in the 1960s and his surgical reading of history repeatedly to bear on his writing. As a result, his novels are thoroughly steeped in humanism. He generally sees the good in humanity despite its many shortcomings, while revelling in its labyrinthine complexity.

Despite Sousa Santos's claim, the writer can be as suspect as the sociologist. Pepetela has blind spots, most seriously in how he portrays female characters. While being the most sophisticated of Angolan writers, his writing rests at various points on the crudest sexist assumptions and fits into a paradigm identified by Dorothée Boulanger as 'misogynist nationalist narratives'.[6] His early portrayals of women, and even some of his later ones, are an uncomfortable symptom of the unchecked fantasies of a Marxist New Man. The other major point of suspicion that will be covered in this book is the uneasy complicity Pepetela shared with some of the excesses of Agostinho Neto's regime. In their appreciations of his fiction, many literary critics remain silent about Pepetela's role in a purge of the MPLA in 1977. It is a key element in understanding his subsequent work.

Inocência Mata has published widely on Pepetela, making the sustained argument for an understanding of his fiction through his relationship with history.[7] Like Pires Laranjeira, she understands much of Pepetela's work as part of a nationalist project that sought to decolonize understandings of the past. Phyllis Peres's groundbreaking English-language scholarship also makes a compelling case for the nation-forging aspect of Pepetela's earlier novels.[8] Later scholarship by, among others, Fernando Arenas, Stephen Henighan and David Brookshaw highlights Pepetela's increasing sense of disillusionment as the utopian promises of the revolution came apart under the stress of political mediocrity.[9]

After the death of Agostinho Neto, in 1979, Pepetela became gradually more alienated from the MPLA. Nevertheless, however much he parodies and condemns Angola's post-Neto leaders in his fiction, he cannot escape being defined by and, to a certain extent, defining the movement to which he dedicated his life.

This book is divided into twelve chapters. In the first chapter, I discuss the MPLA's fraught history and the movement's relationship with history as a progressive concept. I position Pepetela as one of post-colonial Angola's 'untainted' historians

— novelists who were quickly enlisted by the MPLA to write and propagate a history of Angola in order to replace the Portuguese colonial narrative. I discuss the MPLA's cultural relationship with Europe, and its relative disregard for Africa. For the movement, under Agostinho Neto, to be Angolan was an ideological stand.

In Chapter 2, I discuss Pepetela's 1980 novel *Mayombe* and argue that it offers a prescient analysis of the MPLA's future failures. A narrative steeped in the techniques of dialogism, it demonstrates how the MPLA used discourse to assert its power, and how much its techniques resembled the colonial system it sought to replace. The Kenyan author and post-colonial theorist, Ngugi wa Thiong'o, praised the book for the attention it drew to the central political concerns of the last quarter of the twentieth century, but also critiqued Pepetela for *Mayombe*'s treatment of women. I extend that analysis to question how Pepetela uncomfortably uses women's bodies as complicit metaphors for gendered abuses of power, and in the process mirrors the patriarchal positions of the MPLA.

In Chapter 3, I discuss the events surrounding one of the most horrific episodes in the history of the MPLA: the purge and massacre of thousands of MPLA members, sanctioned by Agostinho Neto. I discuss Pepetela's involvement in the purges, including his alleged membership of a commission that reportedly sentenced opponents of the regime to death. I also discuss how his short stories were used as part of a propaganda offensive to justify the elimination of Neto's opponents within the MPLA. I argue that much of Pepetela's subsequent writing seeks to expiate his ambiguous role in the events of 1977, about which he has repeatedly been circumspect in the face of accusations from those who claim to have suffered at his hands.

In Chapter 4, I analyse Pepetela's first epic narrative, *Yaka*. I argue it is his most ideologically orthodox work, presenting Angolanness as a post-racial choice and an active commitment rather than as a tradition or territorial birth-right. Once again in his writing, women's bodies are discursively appropriated for the political realization of men.

In Chapter 5, I discuss how, stung by the criticism of his portrayal of women, Pepetela wrote *Lueji, o nascimento de um império*. Lueji remains his most powerful female characterization, and also one of his most flawed. Pepetela draws on and adapts various myths about the foundation of the Lunda Empire to produce a tale about the corrupting effects of power — even on those with the best intentions and from the previously most marginalized groups.

In Chapter 6, I discuss the novels Pepetela published in the 1990s, a decade of profound political change in Angola, triggered by the fall of the Berlin Wall and the MPLA's wholesale acquiescence to free-market rhetoric. Pepetela's work in this decade repeatedly points to the ways in which the new socio-economic system favoured by the MPLA replicated what it replaced. The discourses the MPLA leaders used may have changed, but the leaders themselves did not, nor did their dependence on a system of clientelism.

In Chapter 7, I discuss one of Pepetela's darkest novels — *Predadores*. I read it as a sharp critique of Agostinho Neto's successor as Angolan president, José Eduardo dos Santos. Ostensibly the story of a mediocre capitalist, used and then discarded by the economic system to which he subscribes, the novel is replete with thinly veiled references to Angola's then first family. Written in the aftermath of Angola's civil war, the novel raises the stark possibility of a return to conflict if the country's new oligarchs should remain unchecked.

In Chapter 8, I discuss *A gloriosa família*, another of Pepetela's epic novels. In it, the role and objectivity of history is questioned through the mute voice of an enslaved narrator. Set during the seventeenth-century Dutch occupation of Angola, the novel challenges the emerging political consensus of the 1990s about the inevitability of capitalism and liberal democracy. It provides a Marxist-inspired analysis of the coloniality underpinning the unfettered growth of market economics, thus critiquing the path adopted by the MPLA at the end of the twentieth century.

In Chapter 9, I discuss Pepetela's two satirical detective novels, *Jaime Bunda, agente secreto* and *Jaime Bunda e a morte do americano*. I explore the differences between the two works, the only novels in Pepetela's oeuvre that share protagonists. Parodies of the James Bond franchise, they were published either side of the end of the civil war, in 2001 and 2003 respectively. The later novel, I argue, expounds an ethics of forgiveness as the only means for the post-civil-war nation to move forward. Pepetela is not advocating national reconciliation but rather pleading with the nation's oligarchs to rediscover their conscience. At a time when the MPLA oligarchy had monopolized both cultural and political power in Angola, Pepetela calls on them to become ethical subjects in return for an amnesty for their grand larceny of state assets.

In Chapter 10, I discuss Pepetela's deployment of an Angolan epistemology to gaze on the global hegemony of the United States. I discuss the MPLA's ambiguous relationship with George W. Bush's administration, and Pepetela's scathing condemnation of what he portrays as a dysfunctional and paranoid empire. I also discuss the curiosity of the banning in 2016 by the regime of Pepetela's *O terrorista de Berkeley, Califórnia* from the prisons holding its political opponents.

In Chapter 11, I discuss Pepetela's only science fiction novel to date. *O quase fim do mundo* was written after the MPLA elites adopted capitalism as the law of the land. Pepetela's novel imagines a world in which the law of capitalism is suspended, and redeploys the dialogic technique that was the hallmark of his early work to allow the competing discourses of liberal democracy to engage with each other, unfettered by market forces.

In the final chapter, I discuss Pepetela's portrayal of the city as the locus of the MPLA's ideas about nationhood, ideas that always excluded conceptions of Angola beyond the urban. Drawing on the author's most recent novels, I discuss how the purported sacrifices of Pepetela's generation — and their genuinely altruistic and positive intentions — morphed into a botched national project that created a self-serving bourgeoisie, rather than abolishing it.

The MPLA became one of the most successful and enduring political forces in post-colonial Africa through a willingness to adapt to changing rhetoric while being slow to change key personnel. As a writer who once occupied a central role in the MPLA's political project, and then found the premises of that project disregarded by the movement to which he retained vestigial loyalties, Pepetela has developed a keen understanding of the unintended consequences of the well-meaning actions of those, like the author himself, who once believed in and fought for the revolutionary potential of the MPLA.

Notes to the Introduction

1. Tony Hodges, *Angola: From Afro-Stalinism to Petro-diamond Capitalism* (Bloomington: Indiana University Press, 2001), p. 12.
2. Ibid., p. 13.
3. Ibid.
4. Boaventura de Sousa Santos, 'Os sociólogos não sabem andar de boleia', in Manuel Rui, *O Kaputo Camionista e Eusébio* (Lisbon: Guerra e Paz, 2017), pp. 95–99 (p. 98).
5. Pires Laranjeira, *Ensaios afro-literários* (Lisbon: Novo Imbondeiro, 2001), p. 172.
6. Dorothée Boulanger, 'Fiction as History? Resistance, Complicities and the Intellectual History of Postcolonial Angola' (unpublished doctoral thesis, King's College London, 2017), p. 42.
7. See in particular Inocência Mata, *Ficção e história na literatura angolana: o caso de Pepetela* (Luanda: Mayamba, 2010).
8. Phyllis Peres, *Transculturation and Resistance in Lusophone African Narrative* (Gainesville: University of Florida Press, 1997).
9. Fernando Arenas, *Lusophone Africa: Beyond Independence* (Minneapolis: Minnesota University Press, 2011); David Brookshaw, 'Narration and Nation-Building: The Angolan Novels of Pepetela', in *Fiction in the Portuguese-speaking world: Essays in Memory of Alexandre Pinheiro Torres*, ed. by Charles M. Kelley (Cardiff: University of Wales Press, 2000), pp. 107–16; Stephen Henighan, '"Um James Bond Subdesenvolvido": The Ideological Work of the Angolan Detective in Pepetela's Jaime Bunda Novels', *Portuguese Studies*, 22.1 (2006), 135–52.

CHAPTER 1

The Problems of History or a History of Problems

The history of the MPLA is one that has been repeatedly recast in line with the vagaries of the moment. Christine Messiant once argued with respect to the MPLA that 'even the past is unpredictable'.[1] The MPLA was founded as a movement that sought to project a better, more equitable Angola into a future, free from the yoke of colonialism, prejudice and exploitation. Once in power, the vision they offered of that future was revealed to be utopian and an inconvenient reminder of what might have been but for the flaws of men.

Over time, the MPLA became more obsessed with regulating how tales of the past were told, turning it into 'a politically sensitive subject in Angola',[2] at the service of hegemonic power. As events veered off in unsavoury directions, and colonialism gave way to civil conflict and a bitter, long-lasting fight for total control of the state, the past — rather than the future — provided justification for the MPLA elite's hold on power despite the country's plight.

In parallel, race — a social construct that had been deployed to legitimize colonial subjugation — became evacuated of its historical freight and rendered a conceptual shield protecting a tight circle of predominantly white-looking[3] and mestizo confidants surrounding Angola's first president, Agostinho Neto. As president, he repeatedly condemned racism in Angola, but the racism to which he referred had changed with the MPLA's accession to power.

Neto was no longer primarily critiquing the subjugation of black men at the hands of a white colonizer, as he had when mobilizing the tropes of negritude in his earlier poetry. Instead, his presidential condemnations of racism were effectively a warning against those who drew attention to the privileges of his pale-skinned coterie — a group to which Pepetela belonged.

Agostinho Neto was one of the most fundamental political influences on Pepetela. The first president of Angola was, for the young writer, a true hero of the nation. Pepetela served Neto in various capacities, and was at the heart of the MPLA leadership during Neto's reign. To understand Pepetela, we need to take into account the extent to which the MPLA was his vocation, and the degree to which the movement shifted ideologically over time.

The MPLA that still occupies Pepetela's heart and soul was Neto's movement, not the organization it became under his successor as president, José Eduardo dos Santos. It was a movement that inflected the principles of communism and initially sought to apply them to the reality of an underdeveloped African state with enormous potential.

In many respects, Pepetela can be defined as a post-communist writer. His world-view is heavily informed by Marxist analysis and a conception of the progress of History. His writing laments the flaws in the application of communist ideals and their national demise, yet he never disavowed the principles which the MPLA of his youth espoused, even if, as I shall discuss throughout this book, he was always aware of their limitations.

In this chapter, I will examine the MPLA under Neto, teasing out the contradictions around race and the class struggle that characterized the movement from its early existence. Reactions to those contradictions inform Pepetela's writing to this day. The contradictions took concrete form in the frictions of Cold War politics, which provided the backdrop against which an independent Angola came into being.

The MPLA has rewritten its history several times, airbrushing out leaders who fell from grace and pushing the dates of its foundation back to claim historical precedence over alternative independence movements. The precise date of its foundation is not universally agreed, even among its founding members.[4] From the 1960s onwards, the movement enjoyed the support of progressive intellectuals in the English-speaking, French-speaking and Scandinavian worlds — 'fellow travellers' — who either overlooked or were blind to the fissures and violence that characterized the often-racialized internal politics of the movement as it progressed into power. For example, Basil Davidson, the influential historian of Africa, was a vocal and uncritical ally of the MPLA, seeing it as the only legitimate voice of the Angolan people.[5]

During the liberation struggle, writers like Don Barnett and Roy Harvey pointed to the movement's opposition to all forms of racism, and celebrated 'the political programs and practices of the MPLA' that meant 'Angolan combatants do not seek vengeance for the millions of lives taken by the Portuguese. Instead, they see their fight as a just struggle for national liberation [...] outside the narrow limits of racial prejudice'.[6] They drew on the speeches of Agostinho Neto, who during the independence war repeatedly framed the MPLA as 'part of a global struggle by Humanity to bring an end to the exploitation of man by man [sic]'.[7]

The cosmopolitan outlook and cultural training of Neto and those around him made their ideology one steeped in Marxist-Leninist notions of class struggle and also infused them with Eurocentric standards and ideals. They were fighting a Portuguese colonial regime that claimed lusotropical exceptionalism. For Salazar and his successor in Lisbon, Portuguese imperialism was qualitatively different from all other colonial projects. In part, Neto's appeal to 'a global struggle by Humanity' sought to puncture the New State's rhetoric of Portuguese exceptionalism and form strategic bonds of solidarity among the oppressed. For Neto, colonial oppression was oppression wherever it occurred.

At the same time, Neto and his allies owed much of their cultural understanding of the world to lusophone literary history. They were intensely socialized in Portuguese Communist Party circles, and avid readers of the Portuguese neo-realists like Alves Redol.[8] They were more attuned to the writings of Camões, Pessoa, Jorge Amado and Guimarães Rosa — and the possibility for resistance the words of the Portuguese and Brazilian canons provided — than they were knowledgeable of Angolan culture beyond the limited urban realms in which they circulated.[9] Their upbringing and resulting mindset may explain why they were so reticent about taking into account the racial, gendered and ethnic differences that competed for a space in the conception of the Angolan nation.

The nation they were fighting to create owed more to António Vieira's seventeenth-century utopian vision of racial harmony based on superior culture and to Marxist theories of class struggle than, for example, to the Lunda and Mbundu cultures of resistance or pan-Africanism and black affirmation. Even if there are examples from Neto's poetry of moments of negritude, the political stance he took as president of Angola was decidedly post-racial, differing enormously from Senghor's example in Senegal.

Negritude was itself an evolving concept. Senghor and Cesaire — the francophone intellectuals most associated with it — did not in reality hold a monopoly on its definition. As Alexandra Reza argues, it was very polyphonic, often linked to the journals for which African nationalist leaders, including Neto, wrote.[10] For Abiola Irele, writing in the 1960s, negritude was a 'historical phenomenon' and a 'cultural movement closely related to African nationalism', rather than a philosophical system based on 'a Negro essence'.[11]

Because of Senghor's suspicion of communism, negritude is often positioned in categorical opposition to Marxist ideas of revolution applied in Africa. In fact, as Christopher Miller has discussed, it was born more as 'an engaged corrective to these ideas'.[12] Marxist thinkers' failure to factor in race as a prevalent matrix through which power relations were also marshalled was challenged by the rise of negritude. In many of its manifestations, including in instances in Neto's poetry, negritude sought to affirm a global solidarity-in-struggle and to lobby for the abolition of current class structures. For Reza, 'negritude continued to be articulated to racially informed expressions of class politics that retained a more-than-national perspective'.[13]

Once in power, however, Neto became deeply suspicious of the mobilizing appeal of any kind of race-based rhetoric — especially one grounded in black affirmation. Race as a concept became increasingly difficult for the MPLA to negotiate. Its nationalist rivals — UNITA and the FNLA — were explicit in activating ethnicity as a trigger and rallying cry for their causes. Both movements used a discourse of 'blackness' to discriminate against white-looking and mestizo Angolans, and notions of racial origin to exclude certain ethnicities from their ranks. In contrast, the MPLA, which had always staked a claim to universalist humanism, had a cadre of white-looking leaders in positions of authority over black Angolans.

The movement explicitly rejected all forms of racism once it had claimed control of the Angolan state, and implicitly discouraged the post-independence discussion of race as a factor determining economic privilege in the new Angola they were constructing. The problem was that in choosing not to see how differences in skin hue continued to determine hierarchies (or else were a correlate of them), the movement's leadership gave the appearance of being disconnected from swathes of poorer sections of Angolan society that saw white-looking men, mestizos and 'assimilados'[14] living in the relative luxury of leadership and not carrying out any menial tasks.

The MPLA, under Neto, justified this racial discrepancy through its nature as a vanguard party, dealing with the legacies of colonialism. The educated under colonialism tended to be whiter-looking so the burden would fall on those among them who were MPLA supporters to direct the nation and train its 'New Men'. Neto, as president, would iterate and reiterate: 'obviously the Party must direct the State. The Party must direct the State'.[15] At the same time, the party was 'waging a very serious fight against all the deviations we have noted in this country',[16] and sought to homogenize as much as possible, including interpretations of history.

Internal divisions were a defining characteristic of the MPLA from its inception. Neto had been one of Amnesty International's first prisoners of conscience in the 1960s, when he was detained by the Portuguese colonial state. Amnesty's backing helped to establish his credentials as a figure of international standing. His poetry was widely translated and he was rendered a larger-than-life founding father of the Angolan nation by international allies fed an ideologically constrained version of events in Angola. Constituencies beyond and, equally importantly, from within the MPLA challenged the vision projected by Neto.

In particular, there was a critique of Neto's inner circle for being dominated by a mestizo and white-looking urban elite, with little or no understanding of rural Angola or the plight of a black underclass with no formal education. In fact, although Neto did surround himself with white-looking people, his rise to the leadership of the MPLA was, in part, because he was a 'black man', in contrast to Viriato da Cruz and Mario Pinto de Andrade, who were not as dark-skinned.[17] Neto provided a better optic for the independence movement. His post-independence, post-racial speeches were strident and rousing. In them, he repeatedly attacked the 'worst reactionaries in the world, the South African racists' and their 'Unita puppets'.[18]

In the run-up to the official Portuguese departure from Angola in 1975, a civil war broke out between three competing movements (the MPLA, UNITA and the FNLA). At the time, it was by no means clear that the MPLA would become the ruling party. In fact, in the 1960s, the FNLA's Government in Exile was exclusively recognized as the only legitimate government of Angola by the Organization for African Unity (OAU), although the OAU later modified its stance and also recognized the MPLA as a bona-fide liberation movement.[19] On the departure of the Portuguese, the MPLA seized control of Luanda, from where it drew most support, with military aid offered by Cuba, a crutch that was crucial to the MPLA's survival for the next decade, as the country became a pawn in a Cold War proxy conflict.

One of the peculiarities of retrospective impressions of the Cold War is the extent to which the variegations and differences on either side of the antagonism are often overlooked or conflated. A binary mindset sometimes characterizes the proxy conflicts that raged from the end of the Second World War to the collapse of the Berlin Wall as pugilistic flexing-at-a-distance between Moscow and Washington. Both superpowers were certainly meddling in Africa, particularly in its post-independence states, as they contended to take over the mantle of imperial influence the European colonial powers had vacated.

As Eduardo Mondlane, the first president of the Mozambican liberation movement FRELIMO, pointed out in the late 1960s, that interpretation was nurtured by the superpowers themselves, who tended to view the world in monochrome:

> Along with the rest of the developing world, African states suffer from the conflicts of the major powers, who tend to interpret events everywhere in the context of the cold war. This leads to some absurd misinterpretations. Journalists and politicians describe African affairs simply in terms of a shift to or away from one world power bloc. The West regards with excessive suspicion any departure from traditional capitalism; a communist plot is seen behind every act of nationalization, every programme for social justice.[20]

Or as Patrick Chabal puts it, discussing the challenges faced by Amílcar Cabral, the revolutionary leader of Guinea-Bissau and Cape Verde, 'to a large degree, wars of national liberation were simply viewed, in the perspective of the Cold War, as subversive communist plots, which threatened the Western world'.[21]

However, as the Angolan case demonstrates, there were often major differences of opinion and policy between the countries nominally towing Moscow's line. Most of all, the Cubans were independent agents in the global south, who dictated their own policy, and at times, clashed with their Soviet allies. According to Anatoli Adamichin, the Soviet vice-minister of foreign affairs in 1975, the USSR had no plans to assist the MPLA as the Portuguese left. He asserts, 'o contingente cubano regular apareceu em Angola sem o nosso conhecimento e muito menos sem a nossa autorização [...]. Foram eles que nos envolvera, e não nós a envolvê-los'[22] [the regular Cuban contingent turned up in Angola without our knowledge and with even less of our authorization [...]. They were the ones who got us involved, not the other way round]. In fact, the Soviet Union strongly advised Cuba to abstain from intervening in Angola or from backing the MPLA.[23] Karen Brutentz, the deputy-head of the International Committee of the Soviet Communist Party claims 'irritava e até preocupava a "desobediência" dos cubanos e, além disso, alguns receavam que eles pretendessem parecer mais revolucionários e ousados do que nós'[24] [Cuban 'disobedience' was annoying and really worrying and, to top it off, some feared they were trying to seem more revolutionary and daring than we were].

The tension between the Cubans and the Soviets would flare up in 1977, when they backed opposing factions in a power struggle at the heart of the MPLA. For Castro, 'defender a revolução angolana é defender Neto' [defending the Angolan revolution means defending Neto].[25] Castro's view predominated among a number of sympathetic Western observers, for whom Neto embodied the present and future of the Angolan nation, and to whom they ceded the authority to define its past.[26]

The 1977 power struggle led to a bloody purge in which Pepetela was, to an ambiguous degree, involved. I will discuss his complicity in more detail in the third chapter, as an 'original sin' underpinning much of his subsequent writing. For the moment, and in order to understand Pepetela as a post-communist writer, it is worth noting the extent to which communism was never the global monolith its opponents claimed or the Soviets would have liked, and that was particularly the case in Angola.

Furthermore, while geopolitics clearly played an important role in the civil war that followed independence, the hostilities were not purely a product of the Cold War, and its importance is sometimes overstated. In some ways, that particular narrative played into the hands of the MPLA who aimed to discredit UNITA as an apartheid-era South African creation, funded by the Americans.[27] If that was the whole story, the civil war should have definitively ended in the aftermath of the fall of the Berlin Wall.

Justin Pearce points out that the prevailing understanding among the international diplomatic community was that the Angolan conflict was merely a product of the Cold War. 'That same orthodoxy was the premise of the Bicesse peace accord in 1991 and the elections of 1992: an arrangement that arose not from any initiative from Angolan society but as a response by political actors outside Angola to a complex series of changes in the international balance of military and political power'.[28] However, UNITA and the MPLA had profound differences in outlook that 'pre-existed the Cold War division',[29] helping to explain how and why the country so easily fell back into an ever more vicious conflict in the 1990s, long after the former superpower foes had lost interest in proxy games of distanced destruction.

The MPLA emerged from a Creole Luanda-based elite steeped in cosmopolitanism.[30] Its early leadership was characterized by a tension between an international projection of the movement and the specificities of a highly diverse nation-in-the-making, about which many of them knew only slightly more than the colonizer. Speaking of his time spent at the Casa dos Estudantes do Império (CEI) where the future generations of independence leaders fortuitously met in the 1950s, Pepetela asserts:

> Todos nós vínhamos com uma pequena experiência de África, cada um do seu cantinho. Eu conhecia a parte centro sul de Angola. Não conhecia sequer Luanda. E foi na CEI que descobrimos várias culturas africanas, antigas e extremamente ricas. E aqueles bonecos que víamos a vender ao longo da estrada, afinal eram arte. [...] a ideia de ser africano e perceber que havia muitas áfricas, muitas culturas e que tínhamos obrigação de ajudar a desenvolver isso. E depois, claro, o aspecto da formação política.[31]

> [We all came with a little experience of Africa, each from our own little corner. I knew the mid-southern part of Angola. I didn't even know Luanda. It was in the CEI that we discovered several African cultures that were ancient and extremely rich. Those dolls we used to see being sold along the streets were actually art. [...] the idea of being African and to understand there were many Africas, many cultures and that we were obliged to help to develop this. And then, of course, there was the aspect of our political formation].

In other words, it took the intervention of an institution based in Lisbon (the CEI) to help form a consciousness of Africa and Angola in the minds of those who would go on a lead the independence struggle.

The concepts were not inherent to their mindset — a mindset that included atomized notions of locality and European cultural tastes more than pan-Africanist or even pan-Angolan ideals. Those would be born through the same cosmopolitan spirit of resistance that underpinned António Vieira's idealization of the lusophone space as somewhere where a better future could be imagined, and a narration of the past could be brought into its service.

As Alexandra Reza points out, the CEI generated a community under constant reconstruction, 'whose boundaries were always receding from view in the face of humanity as a whole'.[32] The specificities of the struggles for independence many in the CEI envisaged became embedded in wider discourses of global revolution.

While many of those who would go on to lead the MPLA had profound affinities with the culture of Portugal and little or no knowledge of the traditions of Angola's hinterland, there had been attempts to 'discover Angola' through a cultural movement called 'Vamos Descobrir Angola' [Let's Discover Angola] led by Viriato da Cruz. The movement was active from 1948. Cruz went on to become one of the founding members of the MPLA who fell foul of Neto and died in miserable conditions in exile in China in 1973. He had been eager to validate the indigenous Angolan culture he deemed to be despised or ignored under colonialism by encouraging its exploration through the writings of young Angolan intellectuals. Key to his understanding of the territory covered by the Angolan state was that it was constituted of multiple nations with distinct traditions and histories.[33] The spirit of the movement he mentored was never wholly shared by Neto and his followers who repeatedly demonstrated a vision of Angola coloured through a lens that was urban and Europeanized.

Given the provenance of the MPLA's early leadership, the movement understood the power of culture in furthering its aims. The distinction discussed by Marissa Moorman between 'nation' and 'nationalism' is very relevant to understanding what would become the predominant MPLA mindset. For Moorman, nation is a cultural formation, imbued with the sense of 'we', while nationalism is a political project. In Angola, nationalism was always privileged over the nation.[34] In other words, the cultural became a highly ideological tool for furthering specific political ends. For the MPLA under Neto, the cultural represented a nationalism that tended to more monolithic than diverse, more monolingual than polyglot, and more orthodox than dialogic.

Culture was seen in political terms by the MPLA who sought to monopolize what the nation meant. Even in the 1960s, before the MPLA had taken control of the levers of the state, there was a strong desire to enforce 'cultural unity throughout Angola'.[35] It is not uncommon as nations come into being that political power seeks to shore up its project by appealing to a unifying and unified cultural sensibility. António Vieira had been part of such a project in post-restoration Portugal — and the vision he had offered had been one of profound universalism tinged by Portuguese exceptionalism. One of the complicating factors in Angola was that the unified cultural sensibility did not pre-exist. It did not have the oldest frontiers on the continent, as Portugal often boasted, even under Spanish occupation in the seventeenth century. Angola, as Viriato da Cruz understood, was vast and diverse with multiple histories, languages and traditions.

Diversity in nationhood is not particularly uncommon but the issue was compounded in Angola by the internal divisions within the MPLA. 'Cultural unity throughout Angola' was code for accepting MPLA orthodoxy internally. It was also an excuse for purging the party and then the nation of those who did not commit to the leadership's vision. Following independence, the MPLA and UNITA rivalry grew as both competed for control of Angola. The FNLA did not survive in any meaningful way much beyond the end of colonialism, and had become a regional party heavily backed by Mobutu's Zaire. In contrast, both UNITA and the MPLA had nation-building ideas, and enjoyed considerable support from constituencies that subscribed to their very different conceptions of Angola.[36]

After UNITA's resounding military defeat in 2002, the prize of defining Angola culturally fell exclusively to the MPLA. Even those MPLA members who were increasingly uncomfortable with the party's post-Cold-War capitalist turn still subscribed to a vision that depicted the Angolan nation as the unique product of the MPLA. For example, Júlio de Almeida, for whose novel *Vaicomdeus, SARL* Pepetela wrote a preface, declared in a 2017 interview:

> O MPLA, diferente dos outros partidos, das outras organizações que se formaram durante a luta de libertação ou que estão formadas agora, o MPLA é um projecto de nação. A nação que se vem fazendo nestes últimos 40 anos é um projecto do MPLA.[37]
>
> [The MPLA, unlike other parties and organizations that were formed during the struggle for independence or that are being formed now, the MPLA is a national project. The nation that has been made for the last forty years is an MPLA project].

Almeida, who in the 1970s was known to Angolan national radio listeners as 'Comandante Juju', the host of the MPLA propaganda programme 'Ponto da Situação Político-Militar', later served as an MPLA member of parliament as well as the director of Angola's national airline, TAAG. His son, Ndalu, is better known as the writer Ondjaki. Like Pepetela, Almeida looks white. Also like Pepetela, his understanding of Angolan nationhood is intricately linked to Neto's MPLA project — the nation and the party symbiotically feeding into each other and in the process blocking or sidelining other visions and possibilities.

In the same interview, Almeida credits the MPLA with turning Portuguese into the language through which Angola is imagined and the mother tongue of the majority of the population. The imposition of the Portuguese language ran counter to the logic of the 'Vamos Descobrir Angola' movement and accepted the linguistic parameters of Portuguese colonial rule. Almeida asserts that the 'conflitos um pouco irracionais, baseados na origem tribal, na origem étnico'[38] [rather irrational conflicts, based on tribal and ethnic origins] that occur in *other* African countries are a thing of the past in Angola, thanks to the MPLA's vision of nationhood.

Almeida's position is not untypical of his generation of MPLA leaders, and it was certainly one adopted by Pepetela in his earliest novels, where tribalism is characterized as an obscurantist impediment to the nation, and the sine qua non of belonging to Angola is simply adherence to the MPLA. In other words, accepting the party ideology rather than ethnicity or place of birth defined Angolanness. Almeida's assertions about 'irrational conflicts' in other African countries are also typical of certain generation of MPLA leadership. It is not that they were racist, because they were not — at least not consciously. However, they always seemed more at ease talking to Europe, through European idioms and using European theoretical frameworks, and were not particularly attentive to Africa as a political and mobilizing concept in the way that other independence movements were.

The nation they imagined was based on European ideological principles — primarily those of Marx and Lenin. When those principles faltered, the MPLA did not cede its claim to define the nation, even if its ideological underpinnings had undergone an official volte-face. It is that discrepancy that is at the heart of Pepetela's subsequent writing. For many years following independence, international historiography and scholarship on Angola focused on nationalism rather than the nation.[39] At the same time, within Angola the recording and rediscovery of the nation's history generally lay in the hands of novelists like Pepetela who, through his writing, became the premier chronicler of the MPLA — in the way that Fernão Lopes had served the House of Aviz in Portugal following the revolution of 1385.

Pepetela occupies a privileged position vis-à-vis the MPLA. More than any other author, he has borne witness to the movement's radical changes and intransigent continuities over more than half a century of writing. While often intelligently critical of the movement's shortcomings, Pepetela was at the forefront of projecting a nation as conceived by the movement. We need to be careful here: Pepetela was never a pamphleteer and his work stands out for its literary merit. However, it is interesting to see how his ideological commitment to the movement evolved against a backdrop of Cold-War disillusionment and then post-communist disaffection. It is not simply a case of the movement moving away from where he was politically, although he clearly felt more at ease with the MPLA under Agostinho Neto's leadership than under José Eduardo dos Santos. Pepetela evolved to a clearer understanding of how human beings interact with power, and how the unavoidable distortion of our reality that we term ideology always mediates human relations. That lesson was present from his earliest publications onwards. As he experimented with form, and grew as a writer, it became both clearer and more nuanced.

A former guerrilla whose nom-de-guerre became his nom-de-plume, he was born Artur Carlos Maurício Pestana dos Santos, in Benguela in 1941, in the middle of Angola's Atlantic seaboard. He was educated in Lubango and then in Portugal, where, as already mentioned, he became a member of the Casa dos Estudantes do Império, a hive of nationalist activity unwittingly sponsored by Portugal's colonial state. The CEI had been established to bring together the best and the brightest from around Portugal's far-flung empire, and seduce them into the service of Lisbon's colonial regime. Instead, it proved to be a nurturing ground for African independence movements, whose future leaders passed through its doors, and honed not just their liberation ideology but also their communist sympathies together.

Leading members of the MPLA spent time in the CEI, including Agostinho Neto and Lúcio Lara, Neto's white-looking, mestizo deputy, often seen as leading the most powerful faction while Neto was president of Angola. While in Lisbon, these future leaders of Angola were heavily influenced by the Portuguese Communist Party. They admired the PCP's brave underground opposition to the Salazar regime, and began to equate 'mística revolucionária' [revolutionary mystique] with Marxist-Leninism, drinking from 'fontes dos clássicos marxistas'[40] [classical Marxist sources] as they developed their own anticolonial ideological positions. Pepetela fled Portugal when the Angolan war for independence broke out, in 1961, in order to avoid being drafted. After a stay in Paris, he ended up in Algiers, where he formally joined the MPLA.[41] There, he helped to found the Centre for Angolan Studies, a body that sought to document Angolan culture but was also a pivotal propaganda arm in the MPLA's international charm offensive. At the time, Algiers was a nodal point of independence movements in Africa.

Pepetela began publishing short stories while at the CEI. His writing, even when it was most ideologically impregnated by a commitment to the MPLA's political project, nearly always maintained a critical distance and pointed to patterns of power abuse that the movement and then the party and regime inherited from those they displaced.[42] As a writer, he was able to use his texts to influence the perspectives of and visions within the MPLA in a way that he could never have achieved as one of its senior members. Now seen as one the nation's 'mais-velhos', or elders, he is an author whom Raquel Ribeiro identifies as following Fidel Castro's dictate, 'within the revolution, everything; against the revolution, nothing'.[43] In other words, his critiques of the MPLA revolution and of the direction of the regime were initially valid and tolerated because they were seen as a legitimate part of praxis, pushing to improve the revolution and overcoming its failings because of a firm commitment to its cause. For Ribeiro, his position contrasts with writers like José Eduardo Agualusa, who assume critical stances from outside the parties they depict. The problem Pepetela as a writer faces is what happens when the revolution that you criticize from within, because of your firm commitment to it, gradually disappears before your eyes.

His work demonstrates that the seeds of the revolution's demise were present well before the fall of the Berlin Wall. As I shall discuss in the next chapter, the work that brought Pepetela to the attention of the literary world, *Mayombe*, shows an understanding of the revolution's failings even before the MPLA had taken the reins of power in Angola in 1975. Read attentively, it plots the fracture lines that will lead the MPLA's utopian vision to fail.

Mayombe is a novel steeped in the revolution and utterly committed to its goals of justice for all. But it is also a novel that reveals the MPLA's repetition of the Christian paradigms of the colonial past, and reduces the bodies of women to little more than metaphorical objects in the service of a national narrative that, more than any other in Portuguese-speaking Africa, sought to exclude women from the agency of real power. Purposefully or not, *Mayombe* shows us, as readers, why the MPLA became a movement focused on the justifications from and rewritings of the past and that preferred to forget the future for which it had once striven.

Notes to Chapter 1

1. Christine Messiant, '"Em Angola até o passado é imprevisível": a experiência de uma investigação sobre o nacionalismo angolano e, em particular, o MPLA: fontes, crítica, necessidade actuais de investigação', in *Actas do II seminário internacional sobre a história de Angola: construindo o passado angolano: as fontes e a sua interpretação, Luanda 4 a 9 de Agosto de 1997* (Lisbon: Comissão Nacional para as Comemorações dos Descobrimentos Portugueses, 2000), pp. 808–11.
2. Justin Pearce, *Political Identity and Conflict in Central Angola, 1975–2002* (Cambridge: Cambridge University Press, 2015), p. xi.
3. Given the complexity of the Angolan nation, as of any social group, racial categorization is an intellectually flawed exercise. However, that does not stop the perception of race being a fundamental aspect of Angolan society. I use the term white-looking (rather than white) to reflect relative perceptions of skin colour rather than biological ancestry.
4. See Jean Martial Arsene Mbah, *As rivalidades políticas entre a Frente Nacional de Libertação de Angola (FNLA) e o Movimento Popular de Liberatação de Angola (MPLA) [1961–1975]* (Luanda: Mayamba, 2010), pp. 74–76, for the various different accounts of Mário de Andrade, Lúcio Lara, Joaquim Pinto de Andrade and André Franco de Sousa. See also Carlos Pacheco, 'Em que ano realmente foi fundado o MPLA', in his *Repensar Angola* (Lisbon: Vega, 2000), pp. 63–73.
5. See Basil Davidson, *In the Eye of the Storm: Angola's People* (London: Longman, 1972).
6. Don Barnett and Roy Harvey, *The Revolution in Angola: MPLA, Life Histories and Documents* (New York: Bobbs-Merrill Company, 1972), p. xi.
7. Quoted in Barnett and Harvey, *The Revolution in Angola*, p. xi.
8. For more on the influence of the Portuguese neo-realists on Neto see Júlia Massoxi da Costa Talaia, *O neo-realismo na poética de Agostinho Neto* (Luanda: União dos Escritores Angolanos, 2009).
9. See Mário Pinto de Andrade's book-length interview with Michel Laban, *Mário Pinto de Andrade, uma entrevista* (Lisbon: João Sá da Costa, 1997), for a reflection on the literary sources on which his generation drew and their ignorance of many aspects of Angola's multiple cultures.
10. Alexandra Reza, 'African Literary Journals in French and Portuguese, 1947–1968: Politics, Culture and Form' (unpublished doctoral thesis, University of Oxford, 2018).
11. Abiola Irele, 'Negritude or Black Cultural Nationalism', *The Journal of Modern African Studies*, 3.3 (1965), 321–48 (p. 322).
12. Christopher L. Miller, 'The (Revised) Birth of Negritude: Communist Revolution and "the Immanent Negro" in 1935', *MLA*, 125.3 (2010), 743–49 (p. 747).
13. Reza, 'African Literary Journals in French and Portuguese, 1947–1968', p. 98.
14. 'Assimilado' was a preferential status under Portuguese colonial law granted to Africans who passed a series of demeaning tests to prove they were 'assimilated', as defined by the Portuguese state.
15. A. Agostinho Neto, *Speeches* (Luanda: Department of Politico-Ideological Education, Propaganda and Information, 1980), p. 56.
16. Ibid., p. 81.
17. Fernando Andressen Guimarães, *The Origins of the Angolan Civil War: Foreign Intervention and Domestic Political Conflict* (New York: St Martin's Press, 1997), p. 67.
18. Neto, *Speeches*, p. 12.
19. For more on the rivalry between the MPLA and the FNLA, see Jean Martial Arsene Mbah, op. cit.
20. Eduardo Mondlane, *The Struggle for Mozambique*, introduction by John Saul and biographical sketch by Herbert Shore (London: Zed Books, 1983), p. 198.
21. Patrick Chabal, *Amílcar Cabral: Revolutionary Leadership and People's War* (Trenton, NJ: Africa World Press, 2003), p. 83.

22. Quoted in José Milhazes, *Angola: o princípio do fim da União Soviética* (Lisbon: Vega, 2009), p. 67.
23. Ibid., p. 68.
24. Ibid.
25. Edgar Valles quoted in Dalila Cabrita Mateus and Álvaro Mateus, *Purga em Angola: o 27 de Maio de 1977* (Lisbon: Texto, 2007), p. 102.
26. Basil Davidson is among the most influential. Others include Michael Wolfers and Victoria Brittain.
27. See Linda Heywood, *Contested Power in Angola, 1840s to the Present* (Rochester, NY: University of Rochester Press, 2000) and Fernando Andresen Guimarães, Op. Cit.
28. Justin Pearce, *Political Identity*, p. 4.
29. Justin Pearce, *An Outbreak of Peace: Angola's Situation of Confusion* (Claremont, South Africa: David Philip Books, 2005), p. xv.
30. For more on the provenance and cultural background of Luanda's Creole elite see Jacopo Corrado, *The Creole Elite and the Rise of Angolan Proto-Nationalism, 1870–1920* (Amherst, NY: Cambria, 2008).
31. Hugo Jorge, 'Pepetela: o estado da cultura e literatura angolana por uma das suas maiores referências', *Rede Angolana*, 8 June 2015 <http://www.redeangola.info/especiais/cultura-foi-substituida-pelo-interesse-de-enriquecer/> [accessed 27 March 2018].
32. Alexandra Reza, 'African Anti-colonialism and the *Ultramarinos* of the *Casa dos Estudantes do Império*', *Journal of Lusophone Studies*, 1.1 (2016), 37–56 (p. 39).
33. See Carlos Serrano, 'Angola: a "Geração de 50", os jovens intelectuais e a raiz das coisas', União dos Escritores Angolanos [Web Essays] <http://www.ueangola.com/criticas-e-ensaios/item/157-angola-a-geracao-de-50-os-jovens-intelectuais-e-a-raiz-das-coisas> [accessed 27 March 2018].
34. Marissa J. Moorman, *Intonations: A Social History of Music and Nation in Luanda, Angola, from 1945 to Recent Times* (Athens: Ohio University Press, 2008), p. 11.
35. The words are Commander Spartacus Monimambu's, who headed the MPLA military commission in the 1960s, and was on its central committee. Quoted in Barnett and Harvey, *The Revolution in Angola*, p. 23.
36. Justin Pearce, *Political Identity*, p. 7.
37. Amarílis Borges, 'Grande Entrevista com Júlio de Almeida', *Rede Angola*, 17 March 2017 <http://www.redeangola.info/especiais/nossa-administracao-e-muito-mediocre/> [accessed 27 March 2018].
38. Ibid.
39. Marissa J. Moorman, *Intonations*, p. 11.
40. Jean-Michel Mabeko Tali, *Dissidências e poder de estado: o MPLA perante si próprio (1962–1977): ensaio de história política*, 2 vols (Luanda: Nzila, 2001), II, 162.
41. 'Interview with Pepetela', in *Speaking the Postcolonial Nation: Interviews with Writers from Angola and Mozambique*, ed. by Ana Mafalda Leite, Sheila Khan, Jessica Falconi and Kamila Krakowska (Oxford: Peter Lang, 2014), pp. 111–12.
42. One notable exception that we will discuss in the third chapter relates to the use of one of his stories during the events surrounding the 27 May 1977.
43. Raquel Ribeiro, 'Angola, a Nation in Pieces in José Eduardo Agualusa's *Estação das chuvas*', *Journal of Lusophone Studies*, 1.1 (2016), 57–72 (p. 61).

CHAPTER 2

❖

A Nation of New Men or the Age-Old Abuse of a Woman's Body

For Phyllis Peres, Pepetela's early works, particularly *As aventuras de Ngunga* (1972), *Muana Puó* (1978), and *Mayombe* (1980), 'optimistically posit that the nationalist liberation struggle will transform contentious voices and histories into voices of a single nation'.[1] Although two of the works were published after independence, all were written during the armed struggle at a time when Pepetela was convinced that an ideological commitment to the MPLA was the pathway to Angolanness. In *Mayombe*, the work that propelled Pepetela to the forefront of Angolan literature and the focus of this chapter, racial and tribal tensions are played out among MPLA combatants fighting in the Cabinda enclave for independence from the Portuguese. The freedom-fighters come to realize that it is their commitment to the MPLA's cause rather than their ethnic identity that defines them as Angolan.

Significantly, Pepetela invites his reader to identify the parallels that existed between apparently competing power structures, particularly those of Christianity and Marxism. He uses the complex patriarchal economy of a woman's body in the character of Ondina to portray the intellectual incongruities within the leadership of the MPLA. He also characterizes her as troublingly complicit with her own violation. Pepetela's depiction of Ondina's sexuality is open to the charge that it uncritically re-inscribes the very disturbing phallocentric fantasy that when a woman says no, she means yes — a repeated trope in Pepetela's work, as I discuss in this chapter. Ondina's body can also be read as indicative of the unstable yet efficient functioning of the MPLA power structure.

The MPLA under Neto faced many internal as well as external challenges. Neto's inner circle, which included Pepetela as one of his speechwriters and a member of his government, worried constantly about its grip on power. Neto and his allies became adept at planning for and dealing with existential threats to his leadership. I will discuss in more detail the results of those plans in the next chapter. Those Neto trusted most were conventionally educated, shared his cultural values, and were versed in theories of how power worked, including the dangers, flagged by Frantz Fanon, of colonial power structures giving way to equally iniquitous national elites. The MPLA leadership's initial commitment to a class-based analysis of exploitation was meant to be a bulwark against replicating the colonial model, and to inoculate the independent nation's leaders from falling into the trap Fanon had outlined in the case of French colonialism, of a national bourgeoisie stepping 'into the shoes of the former European settlement'.[2]

Pepetela's writing, however, demonstrates several structural flaws in the operation of that class analysis, and shows the extent to which power is, in a Foucauldian sense, 'exercised' rather than 'possessed',[3] as those leading the revolution learn the wrong lessons from the past. In other words, power, for Pepetela, is something that corrupts. It is not something tangible that can be fully controlled. Because of his understanding of how power moves in dynamic ways, Pepetela could foresee the trajectory the movement would take, even while writing at the height of the independence struggle. The post-independence MPLA would see survival not in a revolutionary spirit but in an uncomfortable alliance between pragmatic corruption and dogmatic orthodoxy. This, at least, seems to be one of the conclusions to be drawn from *Mayombe*, as I discuss in this chapter.

Mayombe remained unpublished for nine years after it was written, because an influential group within the MPLA disliked it. However, at the behest of Neto, *Mayombe* was released in 1980, shortly after his death.[4] There are several reasons why the novel provoked the higher echelons of the MPLA. It deals directly with the problem of tribalism within a movement that claimed to be based on ideology and not race. Also, as Pires Laranjeira has pointed out, Pepetela dared to question the monolithic portrayal of national heroes as supermen beyond reproach.[5] But most significantly, *Mayombe* explicitly draws parallels between the praxis of the Marxist ideology within the liberation movement and the Catholic Church that — thanks to the Concordat signed between the Vatican and Lisbon in the early days of the Salazar regime — was heavily compromised by and often conterminous with Portuguese colonialism.

The exploration and exposition of tribal tensions was of less concern to the MPLA elite than the implicit warning that the movement would repeat à la Fanon the structures of colonialism. In fact, exposing tribal tensions in the name of national unity and in order to condemn opponents was one of the tactics deployed by the MPLA leadership. The novel ends with the defeat of these tensions — a false utopia held in place by Neto's supporters as the ultimate aspiration of the true Angolan. In the words of the character of the Operations Chief, 'Lutamos, que era cabinda, morreu para salvar um kimbundo. Sem Medo, que era kikongo, morreu para salvar um kimbundo. É uma grande lição para nós, camaradas'[6] [Struggle, who was Cabinda, died to save a Kimbundu. Fearless, who was Kikongo, died to save a Kimbundu. It is a great lesson for us, comrades].[7] In contrast, the novel's revelation that power relations follow similar paradigms regardless of the ideologies in whose interests they operate undermines the straightforward assumption that the replacement for colonialism would automatically be grounded in the egalitarian concepts of the liberation movement. By delaying the novel's publication, the MPLA elites showed they were not interested in hearing they might be as bad as the colonizers they sought to replace.

Mayombe is all about uncovering hidden things. The novel opens with an act of concealment when Teoria [Theory], the mestizo teacher, hides the pain he feels from a graze. In fact, he hides many things from his comrades, the most significant of which is the anxiety he bears for being neither black nor white, but something in-between. Through Teoria, Pepetela exemplifies Angola's Creole elites, but presents them as a group subject to prejudice, and suffering from a sense of not belonging anywhere. Because he is neither black nor white, Teoria feels the need constantly to prove himself. He asserts, 'num Universo de sim ou não, branco ou negro, eu represento o talvez' (p. 16) [in a Universe of yes or no, white or black, I represent the maybe (pp. 1–2)]. Significantly, Teoria is the first character to be named in the novel. He is also the first to deliver a reflective monologue in a text replete with dialogic ceding of the narratorial voice to the various characters.

In his monologue, Teoria confesses that he bears within himself 'o inconciliável' (p. 16) [the irreconcilable (p. 1)]. At the same time, his embodiment of an ethnic anomaly in a racially codified binary order becomes for Teoria the driving force behind his efforts for nationhood. By beginning with Teoria, Pepetela gives a certain degree of primacy to the Creole position in the independence struggle. Yet, the author also demonstrates the extent to which the binary order of colonialism and certain types of anticolonialism based on tribal or racial identities produce resentment within the Creole class, typified in Teoria, who easily slips into equally spurious binary replications. Teoria asks himself, 'Sou eu que devo tornar-me em sim ou em não? Ou são os homens que devem aceitar o talvez? Face a este problema capital, as pessoas dividem-se aos meus olhos em dois grupos: os maniqueístas e os outros' (p. 16) [Am I the one who must turn me into a yes or a no? Or must men accept the maybe? In the face of this essential problem, people are divided in my view into two categories: Manichaeans and the rest (p. 2)].

Teoria thus repeats the binary logic of which he is critical. Although he realizes the iniquity of a power structure based on the arbitrariness of dichotomous racial coding, he fails to acknowledge his own imposition of a similar two-category configuration. His view of the world is as Manichaean as a Universe of yes and no. That is the lesson Teoria teaches — a lesson to be understood in theory, as his name suggests, and to be executed in praxis. For Pepetela, the MPLA must avoid the temptation to replicate the power structure of those the movement seeks to dislodge. Fanon made the danger clear. Teoria shows how theory is prone to fail in practice; how the wrong lesson is often learned from oppressors by those who go on to punish others as a result of replicating ingrained paradigms rather than abolishing them.

Mayombe, the place, is characterized by concealment. It is for this reason that Teoria chose to be there. The place is mysterious and equated with silence. It has a peculiarly symbiotic relationship with the guerrillas in its midst. They respect it; it conceals them — both physically and psychologically from their inner secrets. The second chapter of the novel begins with a description of how Mayombe works for them and with them. At the same time, it becomes their mother-by-proxy. Their base is described as 'parida pelo Mayombe' (p. 79) [born of Mayombe (p. 51)] in an archetypal metaphor overdeployed by a generation of anticolonial poets who equated motherhood with African land.[8]

In Pepetela's novel, the eerie Mayombe seems to be a mother who shares secrets and shapes lives. For Ana Mafalda Leite, the forest is the 'uterine begetter of heroes' and 'the only true feminine presence' in the novel.[9] While it is true that the novel is extremely homosocial and male-centric in its characterizations, the character of Ondina should not be overlooked, particularly since her depiction is so problematic (as I shall discuss). She is a prototype of much that is awry with Pepetela's portrayal of women.

However, in his first novel, it seemed easier for Pepetela to paint femininity as a location rather than a sentient person. The lack of female voices with real agency underlines a major deficiency at the heart of the MPLA, a failing that it has never addressed. After more than four decades in power, the MPLA has yet to appoint a woman prime minister or foreign minister for Angola. Political roles for women are severely constrained, as they always have been. This is in sharp contrast to the other former Portuguese colonies. Guinea-Bissau furnished the first woman to be president of an African country. Mozambique has had a woman prime minister. It has also a woman foreign minister, as has São Tomé e Príncipe, which, like Cape Verde and Guinea-Bissau boasts a history of women as chairs of the national assemblies. The records of the other Portuguese-speaking African nations are far from perfect with respect to women in positions of political power, but Angola is by far the worst. Very little effort was ever made to promote women to positions of power, beyond relations of ex-President José Eduardo dos Santos, to whom I shall return. The novel *Mayombe* is a testament to the movement's early chauvinism, even at the point when it was arguing most for equality and revolutionary change.

Instead of real women with real power, womanhood is reduced to the land, at the nurturing service of Angola's future New Men. Annis Pratt has argued that the forest often operates in Western fiction as a place for retreat from the pressures of patriarchy, tapping into the stereotype of women as being at one with nature (and in contrast, men are the bearers of civilization).[10] As Kathleen Wall also points out, 'such a retreat is as likely to end in rape as in freedom from domination', as the price for rebellion against patriarchy.[11]

In *Mayombe*, the forest stands in for motherhood and femininity, and protects her children from their enemies. The soldiers' experience of and in her is formative. Under her tutelage, they learn to realize their potential. In effect, their physical presence in Mayombe is the catalyst that transforms the power structure in which they participate. Their manoeuvres and battles, their deprivations and the limits to which they push their bodies, will lead to the gradual over-writing of tribalism by an incipient allegiance to an Angolan identity. They are reborn through Mayombe. Yet their transformation comes at a narrative price — the rape of Ondina's body. The stereotypical femininity of the forest location — which reconfigures the loyalties of the men in its midst — demands a reassertion of unchecked male privilege by the end of the story.

At the same time, Sem Medo (Fearless) — who more than any other character is the man responsible for directing the soldiers' change through his example and his death — highlights the mechanisms by which the movement re-inscribes the power structures it was meant to erase. Sem Medo operates in an environment that is constantly prone to intertextual recourse to religious templates. Teoria describes having a white father as his 'pecado original' (p. 26) [original sin (p. 9)]. The same metaphor is used later to describe intellectuals' inability to be other than they are and, by Sem Medo, to describe humankind's propensity towards competition. One of Pepetela's strongest critiques of the revolution — a critique that in various forms he repeats throughout many of his novels — is that instead of abolishing religious practice, with its superstitions and dogmas, and most of all, with its structures of power based on sinfulness and virtue, Marxism became the new religion. The revolution channelled religious zeal and practice, rather than cancelling it out, and replacing it with true self-consciousness.

Sem Medo — the one true revolutionary of the novel — goes as far as to accuse his political commissar of adopting the tactics of a priest, by promising 'a vida eterna no Além, quando na Terra fazes o máximo por tornar a vida insuportável' (p. 43) [eternal life in the Hereafter, when on Earth you are doing the utmost to make life unbearable (p. 24)]. Subsequently, he berates the commissar for refusing to admit openly the true scale of the difficulties that lay ahead. Instead, according to Sem Medo, like priests who promise salvation in the next world, those responsible for political education in the movement offer a paradise so deferred that it is a 'futuro tão abstracto quanto o Paraíso cristão' (p. 131) [future as abstract as the Christian paradise (p. 96)].

This critique is truly damning. The Commissar is primarily responsible for the political education of the soldiers. He is a key component in the MPLA vanguard. Yet, the true revolutionary, Sem Medo, accuses him of spinning a dishonest metaphysical yarn that echoes the false promises of the religious agents of colonialism whose tactics and worldview he was meant to replace. Sem Medo challenges the Christian mindset he comes across repeatedly in multiple characters fighting for the MPLA in the novel. Confronted with Mundo Novo's blind faith in an orthodox Marxist model or Muatiânvua's echoing of biblical mantras, Sem Medo identifies this as the fundamental weakness and danger in outlook that persists among his comrades as a legacy of the colonial past.

The polyglottic arrangement of *Mayombe* aligns the narrator with Sem Medo's viewpoint. The narrator continually cedes control of the text to the prejudiced statements of individual characters. Phyllis Peres reads this as a means of questioning 'ideological motivations' that simultaneously 'permits a narrative self-representation of [the Angolan] nation within a type of collective discourse'.[12] Commenting on his dialectic style, Pepetela in an interview with Michel Laban sought to situate the apparent loss of authority of the writer in *Mayombe* as consistent with one of its central themes — the loss of an absolute unique truth.[13] The novel suggests that a dogmatic approach to Marxism was not the way forward as the certainties of colonialism were defeated. Such an approach would merely replace the fallacy of one truth with that of another. For Marxism to work in Africa, it had to be a living praxis that evolved with experience. The theory worked best as a guide more than a mandate. Overcoming the need for absolute certainties would, as the novel shows, be a challenge.

Over the course of his writing, Pepetela would experiment further with more complex narrative voices — from mute slaves to Angolan epistemological perspectives on America, as I shall discuss in relation to his later novels. In his early work, particularly *Mayombe*, the narrative is extremely dialogic — a near textbook replication of the techniques Bakhtin outlined as inherent to the novel.[14] Characters represent particular positions. They mouth those positions, and through somewhat stilted dialogue, thesis and antithesis are represented. There is little psychological depth. Ideas are clear and positions unambiguous. At the same time, and this is the importance of the work historically, they reflect concerns and voices — as stereotypes — from within the MPLA in the late 1960s and early 1970s. Each fighter is there for a different reason, and the novel is, in part, about them acquiring a common cause — the MPLA's Angola — beyond their limited positionalities.

In his representation of Novo Mundo, Pepetela underlined, through a negative example, his view that fighting for something together — for a new Angola — should not mean extinguishing different hues of opinion or lead to the tyranny of pure orthodoxy. This is an important point to highlight because Pepetela's position alters in his next novel, *Yaka*, as I shall discuss in Chapter 4. As I shall also discuss, *Yaka* was written after the events of 1977, while *Mayombe*, although published in 1980, was written a decade earlier.

In *Mayombe*, Novo Mundo equates diversity with bourgeois individuality. He represents those within the MPLA who push to impose an uncontested orthodoxy. The mechanisms for its defence mimic the disciplining tendencies of the Catholic Church. Sem Medo, the true revolutionary, constantly draws attentions to the parallels. For example, the party's use of 'autocrítica' [self-criticism] is, for the novel's protagonist, a legacy of the confessional. Both demand an acknowledgement by the sinner of the sin committed. Both require an act of contrition followed by absolution from a supreme authority capable of bestowing forgiveness. Crucially, both can be exploited as a means of relinquishing responsibility for actions prior to a repetition of the same deed. As the historian Malyn Newitt points out in relation to the Mozambican independence movement, Frelimo's use of public self-criticism 'is a clever and subtle political device. By allowing some areas of policy to be publicly criticised and overturned, the Frelimo leadership was able to deflect attention from other areas of policy that it did not want challenged. It also deflected any challenge from the leadership itself'.[15]

In the Angolan context portrayed in *Mayombe*, André, the corrupt official caught having sex with Ondina, understands the way in which the confessional structure of self-criticism can be turned to his personal advantage:

> Lenine teve razão ao inventar a autocrítica. Que boa coisa que é a autocrítica! Há uns burros que sempre a recusam. Ainda não descobriram o furo. Quando estiveres em maus lençóis, faz a tua autocrítica. Todos os ataques pararão imediatamente. (p. 195)

> [Lenin was right to invent self-criticism. What a fine thing self-criticism is! There are some dunces who always refuse it. They haven't yet found the loophole. When you're in a jam, make your self-criticism. All attacks will stop at once.] (pp. 147–48)

The same disciplining mechanism can function in diametrically opposite ways. It keeps the masses in line. The individual is made to feel guilty. The structure's censure is able to enter his or her mind and be verbalized in his or her own voice. Yet the confessional self-criticism can also be used, as André demonstrates, to sin and be forgiven while intending to sin again. Responsibility is absolved, and retribution is deflected. Self-criticism is, for comrades like André, a means to avoid justice.

One of the most interesting revelations made by Pepetela with regard to the difficulties he encountered trying to publish *Mayombe* was Agostinho Neto's concern over the portrayal of Ondina. The late Angolan president who, as already mentioned, facilitated the book's release, told its author, 'é um livro que retrata as coisas — e é bom começar a falar dessas coisas. Só não estou muito de acordo com os problemas morais, sobretudo a Ondina'[16] [it's a book that portrays things — and it's good to start to talk about these things. I just don't completely agree with its moral issues, especially Ondina].

In Neto's opinion, Ondina set a poor example to Angola's youth. In the novel, she has sex with three men — the Commissar, André, and Sem Medo — and it appears to be on these grounds that she was morally repugnant to the country's first president. The fact that Sem Medo sleeps with his friend's girlfriend, or that André uses his position of power to satisfy his lust, are not highlighted by Neto as a point of concern. The conclusion to be drawn is that men will be men but, as a woman, Ondina's behaviour is deemed to be inappropriate in the new Angola. The novel actually challenges this sexual inequality. Ondina is allowed to desire, and to act on her desire. Nevertheless, her body becomes a battleground for a range of masculine-coded ideologies, and reveals how the MPLA repeats the strategies of Catholic morality as a mode of control over women's bodies.

After Ondina is caught in the grass with André, a leader is sent to determine the appropriate punishment for her lapse. He is clear that the movement demands her punishment. Sem Medo puts the demand down to 'a eterna moral cristã!' (p. 178) [eternal Christian morality (p. 133)], pointing out the hypocrisy inherent in the movement's reactions to such cases. A blind eye is turned as long as discretion is maintained: 'isso é moral cristã, que se interessa pelas aparências' (p. 178) [that is Christian morality, interested in appearances (p. 134)]. Dissimulation becomes a means of control. Through pretence, the movement's members ritualistically enact a moral code to which, in practice, they do not all subscribe. However, should they refuse to enact the hypocrisy — as in the case of Ondina — the punishment must be severe and be seen to be severe. The individual can and does act contrary to the imposed moral code. This, in itself, is not particularly problematic. However, a failure to perform as if the moral code were legitimate undermines its legitimacy, and retribution must therefore be exacted.

Sem Medo questions the validity of the movement's desire to control the bodies of its members. However, his position is ambivalent. From his perspective, Ondina does, in fact, transgress, falling short of an ideal ingrained in his mind by his upbringing. As he later confesses to her, he could never accept her sexual liberation: 'eu pertenço à geração passada, aquela que foi marcada por toda a moral duma sociedade tradicionalista e cristã' (p. 265) [I belong to a past generation, that which was scarred by the total morality of a traditionalist and Christian society (p. 201)]. He is aware of the cognitive dissonance in his attitude. His intellectual position should equate sexual equality with her freedom over her own body. But his culturally inscribed patriarchal instinct prevents him from accepting that position.

After his brief affair with her, he does all that he can to return her to the Commissar. This reveals two things about Sem Medo. First, for him, the woman belongs to the man, at least in appearance. Second, given that Ondina could never be faithful in a conventional sense, he could not cope with a mere appearance and would try to change her, in the process destroying what she is. This second point demonstrates the extent to which Catholic morality has permeated the revolutionary Sem Medo's mind. Whereas André and those of his ilk are capable of using the mechanisms of morality to avoid complying with morality's dictates, Sem Medo could not be content with dissimulation: he actually and involuntarily subscribes to the content of a moral code that objectifies a woman's body, rendering it inherently exchangeable among male peers.

In some respects, the act of 'sharing' Ondina's body functions as a perverse pretext for homosocial bonding — or a metaphorical 'communion' — between the Commissar and Sem Medo. The Commissar's suspicion that Sem Medo might be gay is followed by Sem Medo's re-assertion of his virile heterosexuality as he sleeps with Ondina.[17] While ostensibly an act of mutual desire between a man and woman with her own desires, sex with Ondina is always a way for Angola's New Men to send messages to each other. Her body is a tangential marker for the resolution of their disputes and the enactment of their fantasies.

Ondina is a problematic character both within the text and extradiegetically. Not only does she demonstrate an inconsistency in Agostinho Neto's stance on equality, but she also reveals the extent to which the patriarchal aspects of Catholicism were appropriated by the Marxist New Man. Ondina's education is deemed to be one of the principal barriers between her and the Commissar. She has learnt to exceed the intellectual expectations imposed on women by society's traditions, and this undermines rather than enhances the confidence of her politically educated partner.

Like his movement's leader, the Commissar effectively excludes true sexual equality from the political discourse he peddles. This becomes the case particularly at the point when he rapes Ondina, a process used to assert his authority over her body. The horror of this scene is not lessened by his immediate repentance. In fact, it is intensified by her reaction. The rape and the Commissar's subsequent tears arouse her.[18] They fulfil her need to be dominated, a need later confessed to Sem Medo, as she makes love to him: 'É mesmo disso que preciso. Dum homem forte que me domine' (p. 228) [It's what I need. A strong man who dominates me (p. 173)].

Ondina's reaction to her rape, more than anything else, makes her portrayal both troubling and inconsistent. It marks her as complicit in the structure she contests, reduced to a passivity that the rest of her persona disputes. She is the victim of an internalized (Catholic/Marxist) power structure that casts femininity as the dominated element in a gender dyad — the obscene underside of the feminine nurturing land that produces the New Man. At the same time, her complicity reveals the complexity of that structure, as it operates around and through Ondina. She sanctions the abuse of her body yet is never fully dominated. This ambivalence is denied by the patriarchal structure, which seeks to cloak the conflictive potential of her body by reducing her to a victim of rape who retroactively consents.

Rape and violence against women is a leitmotif throughout Pepetela's writing. As I shall discuss in Chapter 4, it functions at various metaphorical levels in *Yaka*. In Pepetela's later writing, such as his 2016 depiction of the lives of street children, *Se o passado não tivesse asas*, the repeated rape of Himba and the transactional nature of exchanging sex for protection provide a nuanced depiction of the reality of life on the streets of Luanda in the twenty-first century. There is still, however, the hint that Himba grows to desire sexually what she has initially had to accept out of necessity and without giving true consent.

The problem is not so much that Pepetela portrays rape. For a writer interested in the exercise and abuse of power, rape provides an instance of that abuse at its most brutal and evident. However, Pepetela's portrayals of women's reactions to violations perpetrated against them leaves a lot to be desired. The worst instance is Ondina, although even in later examples such as the groping and penetration of Marisa's body by Lucrécio while she is sleeping and saying no in *O tímido e as mulheres* (2013),[19] Pepetela has a tendency to portray non-consensual sex involving women as something they ultimately enjoy.

The depiction of that enjoyment is when his writing falls into all the worst traps of non-reflexive patriarchy — and reveals the most fundamental problem with the Marxist New Man: his erasure of women's agency, hand in hand with the projection of his fantasies onto their bodies. As the Mozambican writer Paulina Chiziane puts it, 'quando se fala de mulher, a opinião que prevalece é a do homem — ou porque é o homem que escreve, ou porque é o homem que sugere, ou por isto e mais aquilo'[20] [when one talks of women, the opinion that predominates is that of men — either because men are writing, or because men are suggesting, or because of this, that or the other]. Even in a writer as sophisticated as Pepetela, a male fantasy of female acquiescence ultimately obscures the attempt to give women a voice, and turns the woman's body once again into something over which a man can write with impunity.

Rape has been a common trope in Western literary history since its origins in Greek mythology. *Mayombe*'s epigraph, the declaration 'vou contar a história de Ogun, o Prometeu africano' (p. 11) [I am going to relate the tale of Ogun, the African Prometheus (p. v)] situates the novel, in part, as a continuation of that history, inflecting through Ogun — the Yoruba deity who resurfaces in the Candomblé of Brazil — the Titan renegade Prometheus responsible for bringing fire and (by extension) civilization to man. As will happen in *Yaka*, Greek mythology in *Mayombe* provides the trigger for a foundational story of Angolan nationhood. Pepetela thus aligns Angolan identity as the next stage in a European-tinged story. The MPLA-defined Angola that emerges owes as much to European cultures as to those of Africa. For Victor Vitanza, rape is 'a, if not the, *hidden* founding principle for the constitution of Western cultures'.[21]

From Greek epics onwards, rape has been deployed as a trope in numerous metaphorical sleights of hand in texts that reinforce the underlying presumptions of patriarchy. For Tanya Horeck, drawing on the Anglo-American feminist Susan Brownmiller's best-selling text *Against our Will* (1975), 'rape is essential to, and constitutive of, the social bonds of patriarchy. Crucial to this thesis is the idea of rape as the primal scene of culture'.[22] In Horeck's reading of Western culture, the raped woman is 'the object over which men organize'.[23]

In the rape of Ondina's body, we see a continuation of that cultural mechanism of male organization. Her rape operates as a kind of primal scene of Angolan culture, against the backdrop of three men vying for control over her (the Commissar, Sem Medo, and André). Each man represents a different aspect of the MPLA: its dogma, its revolutionary spirit, and its corruption, respectively. The man representing political dogma — the newest of New Men — feels the need to rape his girlfriend into submission, while all three men turn Ondina into an object over which to organize their narratives, fighting for the right to narrate her body and determine her desires. Ondina's body becomes the material over which a new social contract is delineated by the New Men of Angola. She ultimately represents an uneasy alliance between political orthodoxy (the Commissar) and party corruption (André). In a peculiar inflection of Freud, the only way for them to come to terms with the primal scene of her rape at the hands of political orthodoxy is to recodify it as something that she has enjoyed.

In fact, Ondina's rape in the narrative turns her into what Laura Tanner has argued, in relation to Western culture, is 'the object rather than the subject of violence, a human being stripped of agency and mercilessly attached to a physical form that cannot be dissolved at will'.[24] If, as Sharon Stockton has argued, 'the subject of Western history — of logical and metaphysical thought, of market, industrial and imperial capitalism — exists in supreme metaphysical thought by virtue of the violable feminized other',[25] where does that leave Ondina? She begins as such a strong character in the novel with her own thoughts, will and desires, and yet she will ultimately provide, in a provocative continuation of an archetypal Western foundational narrative, the 'violable feminized other' for Angola's New Men.

As Stockton reminds us, 'we have all too long a history [...] of deploying "rape" as a textual event or image to signify something other than rape, in the meantime (and by so doing) preserving rape as a structuring component of Western culture'.[26] Pepetela, as he forges a new Angolan culture, falls back onto the same old trope. As Stockton continues, 'it is far more often the case than not [...] that rape stories do indeed direct the reader away from the materiality and gender politics of the event toward "hidden depths" and "inner meanings"'.[27] Ondina's body — metaphorized to represent an Angolan nationhood over which men fight — re-inscribes patriarchy by deflecting the true nature of her violent abuse through directing the reader to 'hidden depths' and 'inner meanings'. She also becomes the prototype for the ultimate rape-fantasy in Pepetela, namely that women enjoy being dominated. That, more than anything else, is the greatest condemnation of the way a certain class of Angolan New Man thought in the 1970s.

Despite being dated, as a novel written during the height of the colonial struggle by a writer who was still learning his craft (the dialogues are stilted and the tone at times didactic), *Mayombe* stands the test of time as a historical document that portrays the debates raging within the independence movement in the late 1960s and early 1970s. It also outlines the fault lines that would persist well after 1975. Its analysis of how power works continues to be relevant to our understanding of Angola and even human relations to this day. It provides a contemporaneous account of rifts within the MPLA and the strategies the movement undertook to paper over those ruptures — a prioritizing of ideological commitment and the discouragement of cultural diversity.

Sean Rogers argues the novel's open ending (the utopian Marxist nation is yet to be realized) illustrates a tension between 'Pepetela-the-author and Pepetela-the-MPLA-member'.[28] That tension would certainly grow as Pepetela continued to write. This was more because of changes in the position adopted by the MPLA leadership and global ideological shifts than because of a relinquishing of Pepetela's own commitment to what the MPLA originally set out to achieve. Rogers claims that *Mayombe* shows 'Pepetela understands that colonialism and its violence will live on in Angola for many years to come as a result of the damage that both it and the resistance to it have done to the citizens of the land'.[29] Implicit in Rogers's argument is that there is a certain degree of deliberateness in the violent continuities between pre- and post-independence Angola, in part due to what he terms the 'intoxification of agency', grounded in a personal desire for revenge. Violence as enacted in the novel, he claims, is rooted in either the personal (a vindictiveness against the Portuguese colonizer) or the political (a means to attain the Marxist goal). He asserts that Pepetela's 'use of Marxist discourse' restricts 'the attempt to nuance' the ambiguities between these two poles.[30] Yet, the nuance is certainly there, even in *Mayombe*, and would develop further in Pepetela's evolution as a writer. Another way of glossing Rogers's argument is that there is always a tension between the psychological and sociological, between the ethical and the moral, and between subjectivity and society.

Throughout his work, Pepetela has endeavoured to show how systems create subjectivities. We are, in his world-view, products of our societies. His Marxist-leaning sociological training nudged him towards an outlook in which people's actions can be traced back to their social conditions. In Pepetela, there is not an evil person as such but rather an unjust society that facilitates cruel actions by men (and women) against their neighbours. In his early work, that society was colonial. Later, it would become neo-liberal and globalized with Angola's wholesale adoption of free-market capitalism. However — and this is where he becomes one of the most nuanced writers with a clear grasp of the complexities of the dynamics of power — there is always an aspect beyond the merely social, even in his texts like *Mayombe*, constrained by the 'use of Marxist discourse'.

The petty jealousies and irrational dislikes, fears and hopes, as well as the lust of the soldiers thrown together in the Cabinda enclave are not merely explicable in terms of their social conditions, although these contribute. There are also the seeds of something psychological underpinning their actions. Pepetela would develop those seeds further in subsequent characterizations. His characters would become more pusillanimous. He would consign cardboard-cutout heroes like Sem Medo to the past. To be human, contains an irrational element that cannot, even in Pepetela's early work, be fully explained in terms of circumstance.

The work of Kenyan author and academic, Ngugi wa Thiong'o — whose commitment to socialism is longstanding while also evolving in light of geopolitical changes — has been read in comparison with Pepetela's.[31] Ngugi is also an appreciative critic of Pepetela, and particularly highlights the Angolan author's prescience. In a reading of *Mayombe*, Ngugi asserts 'many of the issues that confront the characters [...] bear on the fate and destiny of the country; and they anticipate with unerring clarity the problems of the post-colonial era. The forces of nationalism, democracy and socialism; the organization of power at the party and state levels, are pertinent issues for Angola and the world'.[32] Ngugi continues, 'these forces have changed the face of the 20th century; and the questions of power in a one party socialist state anticipate the current international debate occasioned by the collapse of Eastern European states in the eighties' (p. 10). For Ngugi, Pepetela's brilliance resides in his ability to foresee the many contradictions that would be involved in founding the Angolan nation, while wholeheartedly using his skills to further the project.

Ngugi, the author of *Decolonising the Mind: The Politics of Language in African Literature*, does have concerns, most particularly in regard to Pepetela's apparent 'distrust' of the use of national languages,[33] as depicted in *Mayombe*, in which Portuguese is presented as the cultural medium of unity, and the use of national languages is discouraged. Portuguese as the language of Angola was at the core of MPLA doctrine. It resonated with the cultural heritage of the movement's Creole leadership, and was seen as the only way of forging national unity against a backdrop of multiple linguistic and ethnic identities.

Ngugi finds Pepetela's depiction of women of even more concern than the neo-colonial charge of discouraging linguistic diversity in the name of national unity, implicit in *Mayombe*'s treatment of the different languages of Angola. For Ngugi, male and female roles in the national liberation struggle are 'not adequately addressed in the narrative' (p. 22). In particular, the novel offers more than it delivers, by naming an entire section after Ondina but then failing to foreground her as an integral part of the independence movement. Instead, Ondina 'simply becomes a sex object, almost a sexual measure of the prowess of those involved in the struggle. Simply put, which male can best satisfy her?' (p. 23). One could argue that Pepetela represents the reality of limited female participation in the independence struggle. There certainly were women involved.[34] The problem was, as already mentioned, they were not afforded positions in the MPLA leadership.

Pepetela's depiction of women has evolved considerably and sympathetically over the course of his work — although his repeated use of the trope of rape to metaphorize other mechanisms of power is extremely unnerving for what it implies about the darker reaches of the writer's unconscious. In *Mayombe*, a constrained 'use of Marxist discourse' with its lack of feminist sensitivities during the independence struggle can explain the patriarchal undercurrents Pepetela had yet to attempt to expunge from his writing. As Ngugi points out, Ondina is not the only woman in the novel who is objectified without much narratorial comment. Sem Medo 'who originally was a possible priest in a seminary, escapes from the contradictions of a religious life under colonial racism by taking on a woman. [...] Women then seem to function as the sexual means of men finding themselves politically' (p. 24).

Ngugi's concerns about Pepetela's depiction of women notwithstanding, he appreciates the way in which the post-independence socialist project is truly comprehended in a text actually written in 1971 before Angolan independence. *Mayombe* demonstrates the human foibles of that project but also firmly believes that socialism can come into being in a meaningful way through praxis. *Mayombe*'s prescience resides to a certain degree in who survives in the novel.

Of the three characters that vie for the affections of Ondina, who could crudely be read as representing Angola with all the patriarchal problems such a conflation implies, only two survive. They are the young political Commissar and the corrupt party official, André. At the end of the novel, the 'superhuman'[35] Sem Medo — the military commander and true revolutionary — is dead. His death suggests there is no place for a revolutionary in post-independence Angola, which will be ruled by an understanding reached between political orthodoxy (the Commissar) and an increasingly corrupt party (André).

The MPLA triangulation between revolution, political orthodoxy and corruption had at its centre until 1979 Agostinho Neto. Although he is revered as the father of the nation by many who responded to his charisma, including Pepetela, he was a polarizing figure, whose legacy is ambiguous. Recent academic work has chipped away at the benevolent image of Angola's first president.[36] He certainly had a very limited view of women's capabilities and role in the revolution. Speaking of the conditions necessary for the arrival of socialism in Angola, Neto asserted:

> We must create them [the conditions] in such a way that a youth may feel he is really advancing to a better situation; that the aged may enjoy the protection of society as a whole; that a man may feel that his future is secure, that he does not fear the future; that a woman shall not be afraid of having children, of educating her children.[37]

The message could not be clearer. Men have a future in the MPLA's Angola. Women will have children in it. Against that backdrop, Ondina is a real revolutionary. She desires. She acts on her desire. And Neto's MPLA condemns her as an affront to its morality, a morality steeped in the (Christian) past. The movement too often, it seems, opted to rename the power structures it inherited, rather than dismantle them.

As I shall discuss in the next chapter, those inherited power structures of the past — and a failure to deal with the racially coded class privileges that those in Neto's circle enjoyed — led to one of the worst episodes in the history of the MPLA. The events of 27 May 1977, and Pepetela's involvement in it, had a profound influence on him and his future writing.

Notes to Chapter 2

1. Phyllis Peres, *Transculturation and Resistance in Lusophone African Narrative* (Gainesville: University of Florida Press, 1997), p. 67.
2. Frantz Fanon, *The Wretched of the Earth*, trans. by Constance Farrington (New York: Grove Press, 2005), p. 152.
3. Michel Foucault, *Discipline and Punish: The Birth of the Prison*, trans. by Alan Sheridan (London: Penguin, 1991), p. 26.
4. See Clive Willis, '*Mayombe* and the Liberation of the Angolan', *Portuguese Studies*, 3 (1987), 205–14 (p. 208).
5. Pires Laranjeira, *Literaturas africanas de expressão portuguesa* (Lisbon: Universidade Aberta, 1995), p. 145.
6. Pepetela, *Mayombe* (Lisbon: Edições 70, 1980), p. 281. Subsequent page references given in the text.
7. Pepetela, *Mayombe*, trans. by Michael Wolfers (Oxford: Heinemann, 1996), p. 213. Subsequent page references given in the text.
8. There are multiple examples of this in *No reino de Caliban: antologia panorâmica da poesia africana de expressão portuguesa*, ed. by Manuel Ferreira, 2nd edn, 3 vols (Lisbon: Plátano, 1988).
9. Ana Mafalda Leite, 'Angola', in *The Postcolonial Literature of Lusophone Africa*, ed. by Patrick Chabal (Evanston, IL: Northwestern University Press, 1996), pp. 103–64 (p. 118).
10. Annis Pratt, *Archetypal Patterns in Women's Fiction* (Bloomington: Indiana University Press, 1982), p. 16.
11. Kathleen Wall, *The Callisto Myth from Ovid to Atwood: Initiation and Rape in Literature* (Montreal: McGill-Queen's University Press, 1988), p. 5.
12. Phyllis Peres, *Transculturation and Resistance*, p. 74.
13. Michel Laban, *Angola: encontro com escritores*, 3 vols (Porto: Fundação Eng. António de Almeida, 1991), II, 790–91.
14. See Mikhail M. Bakhtin, *The Dialogic Imagination: Four Essays*, trans. by Caryl Emerson and Michael Holquist (Austin: University of Texas Press, 1981).
15. Malyn Newitt, *A History of Mozambique* (London: Hurst, 1995), p. 544.
16. Michel Laban, *Angola: encontro com escritores*, II, 793.
17. See pages 203 and 226 of the original and pages 154 and 170–71 of the translation.
18. The rape occurs on p. 189 in the original and p. 143 in the translation.
19. Pepetela, *O tímido e as mulheres* (Lisbon: Dom Quixote, 2013), pp. 254–55.
20. Paulina Chiziane interviewed in Michel Laban, *Moçambique: encontro com escritores*, 3 vols (Porto: Fundação Eng. António de Almeida, 1991), I, 984.
21. Victor J. Vitanza, *Sexual Violence in Western Thought and Writing: Chaste Rape* (New York: Palgrave, 2011), p. xii.
22. Tanya Horeck, *Public Rape: Representing Violation in Fiction and Film* (New York: Routledge, 2004), p. 22.
23. Ibid., p. 23.
24. Laura Tanner, *Intimate Violence: Reading Rape and Torture in Twentieth-Century Fiction* (Bloomington: Indiana University Press, 1994), p. 3.
25. Sharon Stockton, *The Economics of Fantasy: Rape in Twentieth-Century Literature* (Columbus: Ohio State University Press, 2006), p. 24.
26. Ibid., p. 182.
27. Ibid.
28. Sean Rogers, 'Imagining Revenge: The Adoption of Violence by *Mayombe*'s Fighters', *Transformation: Critical Perspectives on Southern Africa*, 62 (2006), 118–29 (p. 128).

29. Ibid., p. 128.
30. Ibid., p. 124.
31. See, for example, Elda Hungwe and Chipo Hungwe, 'Nationhood and Women in Postcolonial African Literature', *CLCWeb: Comparative Literature and Culture*, 12.3 (2010), <http://docs.lib.purdue.edu/clcweb/vol12/iss3/1> [accessed 27 March 2018]; Nicholas Brown, *Utopian Generations: The Political Horizon of Twentieth-Century Literature* (Princeton, NJ: Princeton University Press, 2006).
32. Ngugi wa Thiong'o, 'Born of Violence: Pepetela's Narrative of the National Question in the Postcolonial Era', in *Transplanted Imaginaries: Literatures of New Climes*, ed. by K. T. Sunitha (Trenton, NJ: Africa World Press, 2007), 9–27 (pp. 9–10). Subsequent page references given in the text.
33. Ibid., p. 12.
34. See Margarida Paredes, *Combater duas vezes: mulheres na luta armada em Angola* (Vila do Conde: Verso da História, 2015).
35. Charles A. Nama, 'Art and Ideology in Angolan and Afro-American Fiction: Pepetela's *Mayombe* and Richard Wright's *The Long Dream*', in *On the Road to Guinea: Essays in Black Comparative Literature*, ed. by Edward O. Ako (Ibadan: Caltop Publications, 1992), pp. 20–34 (p. 25).
36. See Carlos Pacheco, *Agostinho Neto: o perfil de um ditador* (Lisbon: Vega, 2016).
37. Agostinho Neto, *Speeches*, pp. 47–48.

CHAPTER 3

When the Writer Can Say What the Man Cannot: The Original Sin of 1977

Like most writers of his stature, Pepetela cultivates a public image through interviews and talks, in which he answers a series of predictable questions, mostly related to what it means to be Angolan, and what his concerns were when he wrote a particular book at a particular moment. Over the last four decades, with ever more sophisticated novels and a wider range of styles deployed to the novel genre he commands so well, it is easy to forget that there is a person behind the writing, and like most people, he has moments in his past when he may have made mistakes he regrets. He may also have learned from those moments. If one such moment does exist for Pepetela, it is probably linked to the events around 27 May 1977, one of the ugliest days in the history of the MPLA, with far-reaching consequences for the future direction of the movement.

Its relevance to our understanding of Pepetela is that is foregrounds the complex nuances that distinguish the writer from the man, while showing how the experiences and choices of the latter inevitably feed into the concerns and obsessions of the former. In some ways, Pepetela is able to admit and explore things as a writer that he is less willing to declare as a civil person. Or more accurately, Pepetela's writing to a certain degree expresses unconscious concerns that the rational Artur Pestana may never consciously countenance or may prefer to ignore. As readers, our task is to decode those concerns.

The first novel in which such a decoding is particularly relevant is *Yaka*, published four years after *Mayombe* in 1984. It spans the eighty-five years leading up to Angolan independence in 1975. It is the first of several historical novels that Pepetela uses to comment on Angola's contemporary situation — a situation with which, as a writer and a person, he had become uneasy after the death of Agostinho Neto. Pepetela chose to leave the Angolan government and dedicate himself to his writing more fully in 1982, so that the public perception of Artur Pestana — Creole citizen and member of the political elite — became more fully aligned with Pepetela — the critical writer.[1] At some level, Pepetela took refuge in his writing because the political positions of the MPLA under dos Santos began to diverge from what he had subscribed to as an idealistic youth.

Yaka is significant because it traces the history of a colonial family — the Semedos — who will eventually sire an orthodox and committed member of the MPLA (Joel). In the course of the novel, the family's feeble and mediocre patriarch Alexandre Semedo will gain consciousness of injustice, and turn against his colonial class. Alexandre was born biting the earth in Cuvale, Angola, the son of Portuguese immigrants — and he will live just long enough to witness the birth of the Angolan nation. Alongside *As aventuras de Ngunga* [*Ngunga's Adventures: A Story of Angola*], a 1972 didactic novella that narrates the story of a young boy who joins the MPLA, *Yaka* is one of Pepetela's most ideologically bounded works. Through the depiction of a colonial dynasty, it argues strongly that ethnicity is not a determinant of belonging to the Angolan nation. The only thing that is required in order to be Angolan is a commitment to the MPLA project.

Some found the novel controversial and even questioned its Angolanness.[2] They read it as an attempt to legitimize the role of whites (including Pepetela) in the anti-colonial struggle. Pires Laranjeira challenges readings of *Yaka* that doubt Pepetela's anticolonial credentials to go and read truly 'colonial literature'.[3] The controversy points to a tension that existed from the inception of the MPLA between a national definition that rested on ideological commitment and one that took into account the territory's ethnic diversity. That tension was exacerbated by the perception that 'ideologically committed' whites and mestizos benefitted from positions of power and patronage within the Neto regime — a regime that seemed to know little about Angola's rural reality beyond an archipelago of cities centred on Luanda, where it had its power base.

These tensions surfaced at various points in Angola's history. A particularly significant event was what is often deemed an attempted coup led by Nito Alves in 1977. Whether it was a coup attempt or not depends on who relates the occurrence. Whatever the uprising was, it pitted MPLA member against MPLA member, and quickly led to a bloody purge of the party by those loyal to President Neto. Estimates vary widely of the extent of the bloodshed, with some as high as 100,000 Angolans massacred.[4] What is clear is that those supporting Nito Alves were inspired in part by dissatisfaction with the revolution's reach among poor and overwhelmingly black neighbourhoods and regions.

President Neto, who was married to a white woman, railed against the anti-white racism of the coup leaders. Nito Alves, a former member of the politburo and a minister in Neto's government, had asserted that 'no dia em que, em Angola, [...] os cidadãos varredores de rua [...] forem não só negros, mas mestiços e brancos também, o racismo desaparecerá'[5] [the day in Angola when citizens sweeping the streets are not only blacks, but mestizos and whites too, racism will be over[6]]. Nito Alves channelled a sentiment that the ideological commitment of whites (like Joel in *Yaka*) landed them with cushy jobs and left the majority in abject poverty.

Trying to understand the many tensions that surfaced during the events of 1977, and the accusations levelled against Pepetela for his involvement in them, is helpful as they mark an evolution in Pepetela's writing. *Yaka* was the first major work he wrote after 1977. In some ways, it can be read as a strong reaffirmation of loyalty to

MPLA orthodoxy as the only legitimate means to citizenship. The disillusionment present in Pepetela's subsequent work, and his increasing critique of the course taken by the MPLA leadership after the death of Neto, also bears analysis in light of his role — however limited — in 1977. In some ways, 1977 laid the groundwork for a very centralized presidency, fully exploited by Neto's successor and Pepetela's political nemesis, José Eduardo dos Santos.

The MPLA had been riven by factions since its inception. Matters came to a head in the early 1970s, when a number of wings emerged including the 'Revolta Activa' and the 'Revolta do Leste', which acted with a certain degree of autonomy during the struggle for independence. These factions, as they were known, challenged the 'dictatorship' of a single party ideology imposed by Agostinho Neto and his 'ala presidencial'. The Revolta Activa included Mário Pinto de Andrade, who had been the first president of the MPLA, and who disliked what he saw as Neto's undemocratic style. The MPLA was tenuously reunited at a conference held in Zambia, in 1974, but not before key members, including Andrade, had been forced out, and Neto's more dictatorial leadership style had been imposed on those who remained. These schisms and the way in which they were overcome left profound scars within the MPLA.

Neto's outlook was coloured by a sense that the movement needed to be disciplined if it was to defeat Portuguese colonialism and bring about a prosperous and just new nation. He also felt that the only way that Angola would be able to develop, given the general lack of formal education among the masses, was through the decisive leadership of a vanguard. Those who subsequently questioned the direction of the leadership raised the spectre of earlier 'factionalism'. They were also generally equated with 'racism' because of the sense that they despised or critiqued those in Neto's inner circle who were predominantly members of Luanda's Creole elites — whites and mestizos who had never been at the receiving end of the direct effects of colonial prejudice.

Neto was fond of arguing 'from racialism to tribalism it is only one step'.[7] The context of the statement changed as independence was achieved. The racism (or racialism as it was more commonly translated in the 1970s) of colonialism became in Neto's mindset re-codified and inverted as prejudice against the party vanguard. The critics of this vanguard offered division and factionalism, and an appeal to tribal identity that undermined what is meant to be Angolan after independence.

In large part, Pepetela began to address these concerns in *Mayombe*. He understood in the early 1970s, when he wrote the novel, the rapidity with which the racism of colonialism could transform into the prejudices of a nationalism based on exclusive and imagined tribal identities. One of the earlier incarnations of the independence movements in Angola was the UPNA (the União das Populações do Norte de Angola, or the Northern Angolan People's Union). It began as a re-assertion of Bakongo feudal monarchism, and had as little respect for southern Angolans in the Congo region as it did for Portuguese colonials there. Only later did it transform into one of the three principal movements that vied for an independent Angolan state (the FNLA). Tribal allegiances were not restricted to the UPNA. Particularly in the regions beyond Luanda, those fighting for the MPLA had often yet to form a coherent view of the Angolan nation and held the tribal prejudices explored in depth in *Mayombe*.

By the time Pepetela wrote *Yaka*, circumstances had changed. The FNLA had all but disappeared. The MPLA was widely acknowledged in the international arena as the legitimate government of Angola, despite the outbreak of a prolonged civil conflict, complicated by the Cold War dynamic. There was a concerted effort to foster a national sense of self that transcended tribal identities. And the events of 1977 had taken place, in which Pepetela had played a dubious role.

To a certain extent, much of Pepetela's subsequent writing is tainted by 1977. It acts as an original sin he needs to expiate. One of the fiercest critics of Pepetela's involvement in that year's events is the exiled Angolan historian, Carlos Pacheco. He has argued that Pepetela's role — his actions and his silences, as well as his self-justifications — can never be undone by his lacerating literary critiques of the political direction Angola went on to take:

> Reconheço haver nos seus livros uma certa beleza estética, uma contemplação e uma construção aliciante de narrativas que tanto prazer e emoção despertam nos leitores. Apesar de tudo, um imenso abismo separa as suas acções políticas do discurso literário e da componente crítica plasmada nas suas obras e, precisamente, por mistérios que me escapam não consigo entender a sua rigidez e teimosia em se negar a reconhecer o que fez no 27 de Maio.[8]
>
> [I recognize there is a certain aesthetic beauty, a thoughtfulness and a seductive construction in the narratives of his books that awakens so much pleasure and emotion in his readers. In spite of everything, an immense abyss separates his political actions from his literary discourse and from the critical component set out in his works and, more to the point, for reasons that escape me, I cannot fathom his rigidity and stubbornness in refusing to recognize what he did on 27 May.]

Another way of looking at it is that 1977 was fundamental to Pepetela's subsequent writing. It matured him as an author even if it may have diminished him as a man. Albeit at an unconscious level, he had a certain need to come to terms with what had happened during the purge. That need manifested itself in evolving ways in Pepetela's work. In the 1980s, the ghost of 1977 came out in his push through *Yaka* to recognize ideological commitment rather than race as the defining characteristic of Angolanness. At some levels, 1977 was an ideological battle to define party and national orthodoxy, a battle to which Pepetela had subscribed, and whose consequences haunted him. In subsequent works, dealing increasingly with a disillusionment with the revolution and the direction taken by the MPLA leadership under Neto's successor, there is often a hint of catharsis in which the author seeks to atone for the role he played in bringing about the conditions of possibility of an ever-more powerful executive branch post-1977.

Rumours of Pepetela's involvement in 1977 began to circulate more intensely around 2005, when those who had been victims of the purge became more vocal and accusatory. Perhaps coincidentally, in the run-up to 2005 Pepetela had published a string of novels that were unflinchingly damning of MPLA abuses of power (his Jaime Bunda parodies and *Predadores*). It is not beyond the bounds of possibility that some of the rumours were stoked by those in power, who were not averse to making their ever-more ardent critic Pepetela uncomfortable through strategic leaks about 1977 that cast the author in a negative light. Also, perhaps coincidentally, for a few years after he was challenged to explain his role in the 1977 purges, Pepetela veered away from direct critiques of the politics of the MPLA as he began to publish novels such as *O terrorista de Berkeley, Califórnia* (2007) and *O quase fim do mundo* (2008) set in contexts well removed from Angola.

While in these novels Pepetela always viewed the world through his particularly Angolan perspective — as instances of Angolan epistemology applied to different parts of the globe — he did not tackle issues of political sensitivity overtly related to the direction of Angolan society in them. Instead, Pepetela turned his attention to the relatively safe terrain of the terrorist paranoia of the George W. Bush era or the shortcomings of liberal philosophies and white supremacists.

So what exactly happened in May 1977 and how, if at all, was Pepetela compromised by it? In November 2005, Pepetela made a declaration in the Angolan weekly, *Semanário Angolense*, in which he appealed to the upper echelons of the MPLA to clear up misunderstandings circulating about his role in a commission set up by the politburo in the aftermath of the 27 May uprising. He called on the party leadership to come out 'a público defender, numa prova de lealdade, o bom-nome daqueles que o serviram desinteressadamente em todos os momentos' [in public and, as proof of loyalty, defend the good name of those who served the MPLA for no personal gain at all times].[9] He claimed the commission in which he participated merely had the role of 'seleccionar entre os depoimentos dos detidos [...] os que seriam mais elucidativos para serem transmitidos pelos órgãos de informação' [choosing from the statements of the detained [...] those that would be most clarifying to be transmitted by the information media].[10]

His appeal for the MPLA to clear his name as an act of loyalty is very revealing. He is a member of a generation and a cultural elite that truly believed in what the MPLA set out to achieve in the 1960s. It was not just about independence — although independence was non-negotiable to the movement. It was also about societal reform, service and significant revolution. At some point along the way, the movement in which he believed — even if he always critiqued it in his writing — morphed into something else that left intellectuals of his ilk with no place in it, but with a residual sense of fidelity that meant they could never completely break with the MPLA.

Their role in 1977 complicated that sense of allegiance further, because they had been required to participate in the logistics of a purge that was no longer about removing colonial overlords or overthrowing unjust economic models, but rather about disciplining and expunging comrades with legitimate concerns about the direction in which the MPLA was moving. Compromised by actions that may have made him feel uncomfortable at the time, and clearly haunted him subsequently, Pepetela has never explicitly answered the questions posed by those whose relatives were lost in the purge, or who themselves suffered the barbaric interrogations and abuse that Neto sanctioned in 1977.

In later interviews, Pepetela would deny any involvement at all in the 'comissão de lágrimas' [commission of tears] as it became known, and questioned whether such a thing had existed. 'Contam-se muitas histórias e escreve-se muita coisa falsa sobre [sic], para já não houve nenhuma Comissão das Lágrimas que eu saiba' [a lot of stories are told and many false things are written about it, to start with, there was no such commission of tears as far as I know].[11] In 2005, however, Pepetela did seem to admit to being part of such a commission, while being adamant that its only purpose was to select which reports to make public. His assertion that he knew nothing of the violent excesses of President Neto's supporters provoked a series of public rebukes from those who had suffered the consequences of 1977.

Francisca van Dunem, who would go on to be Portugal's first black minister of justice, and her brother, João, a journalist who worked for the BBC, lost their brother and his partner in the most horrific circumstances in the purge, and were forced into exile. They asked Pepetela, 'sabe ou não o cidadão Artur Pestana, ou seja o escritor Pepetela, que os cidadãos cujos depoimentos escrutinou não tiveram direito a garantias mínimas de defesa, não foram presentes a qualquer tribunal e que a maior parte deles "desapareceu", para sempre, sem que as respectivas famílias tenham sequer tido a possibilidade de lhes dar um enterro digno?' [Does Citizen Artur Pestana, or rather the writer Pepetela, know or not that the citizens whose statements he scrutinized had no right to the minimum guarantees of a legal defence, were not brought before any court and that the majority of them 'disappeared', for ever, denying their respective families any possibility of giving them a decent burial?][12]

One of the consistent accusations of those interrogated by Neto loyalists in 1977 was that the rule of law was suspended, and they were either threatened with torture or actually tortured in order to extract false confessions, in a febrile environment in which petty and personal accounts were often settled in the name of ideological orthodoxy.

Carlos Pacheco remembers a specific instance of Pepetela being present on a commission that threatened him with torture and death at the hands of the military if he did not admit to being either a CIA agent or a Russian spy. Writing in 2000, Pacheco claims 'Rui Monteiro [Manuel Rui], Pepetela e Costa Andrade (vulgo 'Ndunduma') para só referir escritores, não apareceram nessa comissão por acaso ou para fazer número. Eles estiveram lá com incumbências bem definidas e nos interrogatórios poucos se distinguiram daquilo que é o vulgar comportamento de policiais de uma ditadura' [Rui Monteiro, Pepetela and Costa Andrade (commonly known as 'Ndunduma') to name just the writers, did not appear on that commission by chance or to make up the numbers. They were there with well-defined tasks and during the interrogations few could be distinguished from the base behaviour of the police in a dictatorship].[13] Pacheco speaks at length of his own interrogation and claims:

> Rui Monteiro e Pepetela praticamente tomaram conta do 'interrogatório'. Respondi-lhes sempre que não reconhecia competência àquela comissão [...] a menos que o presidente da República os investisse de poderes para tal.

Contrafeitos, desistiram. 'Ndunduma', porém, talvez o mais encarniçado e brutal no achincalhamento e em acusações fantasiosas, ainda ameaçou com a presença de dois militares que foi buscar fora da sala, dizendo que eles me tratariam com menos complacência.[14]

[Rui Monteiro and Pepetela practically took charge of the 'interrogation'. I always answered them that I did not recognize the legitimacy of that commission [...] unless the president of the Republic had invested them with appropriate powers. Thwarted, they stopped. 'Ndunduma', however, probably the fiercest and most brutal in his scorn and in his fantasy accusations, still threatened me with the presence of two soldiers whom he went to fetch from outside the room, saying they would treat me with less indulgence].

Pacheco repeatedly protested that he had nothing to do with Nito Alves's attempted coup, if that was what it was.

Responding to Pepetela's 2005 protestation of the innocuousness of the commission and his innocent involvement in it, Pacheco sent Pepetela an open letter, first published in the Portuguese newspaper *Público*, and later greatly expanded in his collection of essays, *Angola: um gigante com pés de barro*. He accuses Pepetela of being 'um escriba sentado e submisso que sempre cortejou o príncipe e sua corte' [a sedentary and submissive scribe who always flattered the prince and his court][15] (namely Agostinho Neto). He claims the writer always 'se acomodou aos servilismos culturais do MPLA e aos fetichismos do seu regime político' [adjusted to the MPLA's cultural subservience and its political regime's fetishisms].[16]

Accusing him of keeping quiet in the face of the criminal totalitarianism of Agostinho Neto, he builds a portrait of Pepetela that resonates with Hannah Arendt's banality of evil. Pepetela was only doing his job and did not really know what was going on as he participated in a commission that was, if we are to accept his recollection, merely sifting through reports. On reading what he terms Pepetela's 'documento titubeante e tortuoso' [hesitant and tortuous document] — namely his 2005 declaration in the *Semanário Angolense* — Pacheco remains unconvinced of Pepetela's innocence, although he counts himself among those who 'espera da sua parte um gesto redentor' [are waiting for a gesture of redemption from him].[17] I suggest that much of Pepetela's subsequent writing has, in fact, been such a gesture, particularly since the events of 1977 have become ever more distant. The problem for Pacheco is Pepetela's repeated insistence on the innocuousness of the process with which he was complicit.

In an interview with the Voice of America in 2006, Pepetela challenged Pacheco's account of the latter's torture at the hands of the commission. Pepetela claimed, Carlos Pacheco 'não está a perceber o que lhe aconteceu. Não percebeu que estava perante uma Comissão que apenas decidia se valia ou não valia a pena passar para a informação. Ele não serviu e seu depoimento não passou. Se isto é interrogatório, não sei' [doesn't understand what happened to him. He did not understand that he was before a commission that just decided if he was worth passing on to the media department. He didn't fit the bill and his statement was not passed along. If that is an interrogation, I don't know].[18]

Pepetela's rather dismissive tone and vagueness contrasts starkly with Pacheco's detailed account of the fear he felt as he was interrogated by a Comissão of which Pepetela was a member on 4 June 1977, a week after the attempted coup that unleashed Neto's supporters within the MPLA. As Pacheco describes it, 'o que se viu foi uma Comissão entretida em simulacros, em actos de tortura psicológica, combinados com gritos de achincalhamento e ameaças físicas' [what was apparent was a commission busy with simulacrums, with acts of psychological torture, combined with shouts of scorn and physical threats].[19] Pacheco claims he was threatened with torture unless he admitted his treason, at which point, 'a nenhum dos presentes passou despercebido o frémito de terror que se apossou de mim e quase me paralizou' [no one there was unaware of the shudder of terror that took hold of me and almost paralyzed me].[20]

Like the Van Dunems, Pacheco claims to be shocked at the 'cinismo com que [Pepetela] tenta denegar a sua participação em tais processos torquemadescos' [cynicism with which Pepetela tries to deny his involvement in this Spanish inquisition].[21] What riles Pacheco is Pepetela's public protestation of innocence — an innocence cloaked in omission and lack of detail — and reduction of the process to something banal or even normal. For Pacheco, the commission tried to 'reduzir as vítimas a nada' [reduce its victims to nothing].[22] In one of his most pointed and directed critiques, Pacheco claims that Pepetela and the other writers who participated in the Comissão, 'não estavam ali para ouvir as vítimas, mas para as ridicularizar e condenar pelo que elas simbolizavam ideologicamente' [were not there to listen to the victims, but to ridicule them and condemn them because of what they symbolized ideologically].[23]

While Pacheco admits that Pepetela's behaviour was not the worst, compared with the other members of the commission, 'esteve lá e participou dessa alquimia de diabólicas encenações e por certo ajudou a fabricar provas falsas e "confissões" que serviam de incriminação contra tantos indivíduos' [he was there and he took part in that alchemy of diabolic play-acting and he certainly helped to fabricate false evidence and 'confessions' that served to incriminate so many individuals].[24]

Pacheco asks Pepetela directly, 'A memória do 27 de Maio não o atormenta? [...] Não se dá conta que, ao agir como agiu, V. ajudou a fazer de Angola aquilo que ela é hoje: um país injusto e violento, cujos filhos agonizam sob as garras de um regime corrupto?' [doesn't the memory of 27 May torment you? [...] Don't you realize that, acting the way you did, you helped to make Angola what it is today: a violent and unjust country, whose children agonize under the claws of a corrupt regime?].[25] Pepetela may have written *Predadores*, with its powerful critique but, for Pacheco, that does not absolve the writer of his responsibility — however peripheral — in 1977.

Pacheco has a very different public memory to Pepetela of what the role of the commission was, and how it behaved, and it is doubtful that the two versions will ever be reconciled. It is also doubtful we will ever know the truth of what went on. However, there is another aspect of Pepetela's involvement in the events of 1977 that is easier to verify objectively, and it is that aspect to which the Van Dunems refer when they say 'Pepetela pretende que não participa na repressão quem ajuda a organizar a propaganda que a "legitima", para tanto escrutinando depoimentos obtidos através de métodos de todos conhecidos e seguramente incompatíveis com padrões mínimos de humanidade' [Pepetela claims that he who helps organize the propaganda that 'legitimizes' repression does not participate in it, as he scrutinizes statements obtained through methods we all know and that are definitively incompatible with the minimum standards of humanity].[26] They allude in particular to the use of one of Pepetela's short stories in the aftermath of the 27 May, at a time when tensions were high between supporters of Nito Alves and those of President Neto.

Dalila Cabrita Mateus and Álvaro Mateus describe in some depth the circumstances that gave rise to the 27 May in their *Purga em Angola*. They make clear that supporters of Neto were moving against Nito Alves well before the events of that day. There were different opinions among Nito Alves's supporters as to whether a change of MPLA leadership was required (through a coup) or whether they merely wanted a change in the direction President Neto was taking the movement. The latter group understood what they were doing on 27 May to be a demonstration for change rather than an attempt to overthrow the president. Whether these demonstrators intended it or not, though, high profile Neto loyalists were killed, triggering a chain of events that culminated in Neto's purge of the MPLA.

Whatever Nito Alves thought he and his supporters were doing, he had become aware earlier in the year that allies of the president wanted him dealt with severely. On 11 February 1977, he finished a 143-page document, entitled 'As treze teses em minha defesa' [the thirteen theses in my defence] that he requested be circulated to key members of the MPLA, including President Neto. He claimed the purpose of the document was to 'denunciar, desmascarar e combater energeticamente a natureza reaccionária da aliança de direita e dos maoístas no seio do MPLA' [denounce, unmask and energetically fight the reactionary nature of the alliance between the right and the Maoists at the heart of the MPLA].[27]

One of the many targets of his critique is Pepetela (listed by his legal name, Artur Pestana dos Santos), whom he associates with what he deems to be Lúcio Lara's right-wing faction. Nito claims that Pepetela was part of a cabal of MPLA leaders that met frequently in the house of Júlio de Almeida (famously the radio voice of the revolution and father of Onjaki), and plotted the demise of those who did not subscribe to their own somewhat elitist view of how Angola should develop.

Mateus describes 'as treze teses em minha defesa' as 'um texto insuportavelmente dogmático' [an unbearably dogmatic text].[28] Its value for us is that it clearly codifies Pepetela in the mind of Nito Alves as a lackey in Neto's camp, intimately involved in what the former interior minister saw as intrigues to eliminate the threat that he and his ideas posed to the president's grip on power.

One of the most damning pieces of evidence against Pepetela was the publication of one of his allegorical short stories in the *Jornal de Angola*, on 21 July 1977. The story was actually written and dated two months earlier — 15 May 1977 — twelve days before the attempted coup.[29] The story is called 'A víbora da cabeça ao contrário' [the viper with a back-to-front head] and it was accompanied by a particularly inflammatory illustration of a snake whose head was that of Nito Alves. Needless to say, the snake in the narrative does not fare well. In fact, he ends up dead, as Nito Alves would too. As Mateus points out in her interpretation of the significance of Pepetela's story, and in particular of its dating:

> Nito Alves e os seus amigos estavam a ser objecto de apertada vigilância. E o Presidente tinha os seus planos.
> Repare-se que, na altura em que a história foi escrita, Nito Alves, cuja morte se anuncia, ainda era membro do Comité Central do MPLA.[30]
>
> [Nito Alves and his friends were the object of tight surveillance. And the president had his plans.
> Note that, when the story was written, Nito Alves, whose death is announced, was still a member of the MPLA Central Committee.]

In other words, President Neto was looking for an excuse to eliminate Nito Alves and his supporters, and when what he termed an attempted coup presented itself, he was ready to strike. Pepetela's story was part of a concerted effort that whipped up a frenzy of hatreds and distrusts at precisely the moment President Neto's supporters were rounding up, and often 'disappearing', their opponents. That is the most damning charge levelled against Pepetela by the Van Dunems: his work was used as part of the propaganda to instigate a bloody purge against those who disagreed with President Neto, instigating a period of fear that lasted many years.

The propaganda effort clearly predated the excuse used for the purge and its consequences. It is difficult to imagine that Pepetela did not know what was in store for a character he depicted as a rabble-rousing reptilian pretender to the presidency who, in his story, deserved to die.

One of the key arguments put forward by Neto's supporters to justify their actions was that Nito Alves was attempting a coup. Years later, when interviewed in 2008, Pepetela reflected, 'foi uma tentativa de mudar a ordem que existia [...] Será difícil chamar-lhe golpe de Estado, embora houvesse forças armadas implicadas' [it was an attempt to change the order that then existed [...] It would be difficult to call it a coup, although there were armed forces implicated in it].[31] In fairness to Pepetela, he has shown on various occasions that he is very uncomfortable with some of what followed the 27 May. What he has never done is admit publicly that he may have had a role in exacerbating the bloodshed, either through the deployment of his short stories or through his participation in the commission. Deciding which reports to publish by threatening the lives of those appearing before you, if that is what happened, is a rather strange and certainly not an innocent function.

Despite the reconciliations of 1974 in Zambia, the MPLA in 1977 was clearly still riven by factions, identified variously as right wing, left wing and Maoist. It is interesting to note that one of the peculiarities of the 1977 events was that the Soviets appeared to back Nito Alves while the Cubans remained loyal to President Neto and came to his aid in stamping out the dissent. In other words, it highlights again the complexities of Cold War politics. Cuba's official involvement in Angola would last until 1991, when Cuban military, medical and educational personnel finally departed as part of an accord that ended the South African occupation of

Namibia and foreign involvement in the Angolan civil war. There are instances in Angolan literature when Cubans are remembered warmly with nostalgia, while Soviets are presented as racist and cold.[32] But this depiction could be because the culturally sophisticated faction of the MPLA — the writers and poets whose work we most have access to — were generally aligned with Neto and his presidency, or are descendants of that particular MPLA worldview.

Pepetela has asserted that those members of the MPLA who spent time in the Soviet Union (including Neto's successor, dos Santos) returned from the experience with a clear understanding that communism would never work in Angola. In contrast, those who were sent to Cuba (and to a lesser extent to the GDR) remained committed to the revolution.[33]

Against the backdrop of the Cold War that cast the world into a system of binary understandings, the events of 1977 demonstrate how the picture in Luanda was far more complex and certainly racially charged. It also demonstrated the extent to which the MPLA was riven by internal divisions under Neto's leadership. His later speeches focused on the need for the party to 'be united, that it be one and that the tendencies that run counter to the Party be neutralised by those who are true to the Party's thinking'.[34] Post-1977, different opinions were no longer to be tolerated. Neto asserts 'not everyone can belong to the Party [...] What is necessary is for those really able to follow the orientation of our Congress and of the Central Committee to be in the Party, those who feel able to adopt the policies laid down'. In some speeches Neto identifies as the prime enemy the petty-bourgeoisie and its factionalist tendencies who want 'to take over'.[35]

Underpinning Neto's rhetoric was an excluding tendency in which a commitment to the party defined what it meant to be Angolan, but, simultaneously, the party leadership would determine who was sufficiently orthodox and developed to belong to the party. In other words, it lay in the gift of the party leadership to say who were the true Angolans.

This MPLA conception of Angolanness being in its gift developed during the 1960s when much of the leadership lived under the constraints of exile, rather than in Angola. Post-independence, this way of thinking was exacerbated by a sense of the revolution being under siege. Neto felt under attack internally as well as externally. South African troops had invaded Angolan territory following independence, and civil war destabilized the MPLA's efforts at national development. Neto saw party discipline as the only way forward, as his national project was being attacked on multiple fronts. He and his supporters felt under immense pressure and became increasingly intolerant of any form of dissent.

The MPLA, partly because of the mythical status afforded to Agostinho Neto because he was one of the first Amnesty International Prisoners of Conscience and partly because of its ideological position, enjoyed a wide degree of support among the Western intelligentsia. That community of 'fellow travellers' tended to mute any criticism or pointed analysis of the shortcomings of the MPLA once it had come to power. Their loyalty to the movement often remained even after it had adopted a predatory form of capitalism, becoming one of the most corrupt operators of clientelism anywhere in the world.

In 1977, it was still not clear that this would be the trajectory adopted by the MPLA. It was, however, very clear that something was going awry with the movement's leadership in its treatment of own membership. Despite this, a number of influential historians and commentators on Angola remained largely silent about the events of 1977, often erasing them completely from their accounts of Angolan affairs, or downplaying them as a minor coup attempt that was swiftly and judiciously squashed.

Lara Pawson's *In the Name of the People: Angola's Forgotten Massacre* is one of the most important and thorough accounts to date of the ambiguities inherent in the events of 1977. Pawson is critical of a Western conspiracy of silence among left-leaning writers and intellectuals that characterized the years of real fear among Angolans following the 27 May. One such writer who emerges in a less than favourable light in Pawson's analysis is Victoria Brittain, a journalist who worked for the *Guardian* newspaper. Pawson's attempt to interview Brittain in order to ascertain why she neglects to mention the 27 May 1977 in her 'authoritative' account of the Angolan conflict, *Death of Dignity: Angola's Civil War*, ends with Brittain fleeing down a London street, trying to escape her persistent interviewer.

In the 1990s, *Death of Dignity: Angola's Civil War* was also translated into Portuguese, and Pepetela wrote the introduction to it.[36] In it, he berates the 'chamada comunidade internacional' (p. 9) [so-called international community] for looking on 'impávida e quase serena' [undaunted and almost serene] as 'um projecto independente de afirmação nacional' (p. 9) [an independent project of national affirmation] was destroyed. That independence project 'prometia ser, se não original, pelo menos diferente dos que se registaram em outros pontos de África' (p. 9) [promised to be, if not original, at least different from those seen in other parts of Africa].

Underpinning Pepetela's argument is the MPLA vision of Angolan exceptionalism that distinguished the Angolan nation from the continent and generally gestured towards Europe in its affirmation. The MPLA drew heavily on ideological theories born in Europe. Its leadership was predominantly urban, and saw the polis as central to the national project. That national project, discussed by Pepetela in his introduction to Brittain's book, was by the late 1990s buffeted by unwelcome international interference, which revealed 'as suas fraquezas ou as dos homens que o deveriam concretizar' (p. 9) [its weaknesses and the weaknesses of the men who should have made it a reality]. Most of all, the project was, in Pepetela's words, 'inviabilizado pela vontade do Império, essa espada nuclear que sobre toda a humanidade paira, com falas mansas de liberdade e democracia, mas impondo com a mais absoluta arrogância unicamente a sua vontade e os seus interesses' (p. 9) [made unviable by the will of the Empire, that nuclear sword hovering over all humanity, with gentle talk of liberty and democracy, while imposing with absolute arrogance only its will and interests]. The abstraction and capitalization of 'Império' by Pepetela is symptomatic of an outlook that sees the world as a matrix of power relations. The Empire is no longer of one nation over another, but rather of class interests hidden behind an empty and hypocritical rhetoric of freedom and individual choice. In other words, the forces of capitalism have, for Pepetela, acted relentlessly to destroy the dream of Angolan independence.

The death of that independence project, as Pepetela saw it at the end of the 1990s, left 'um povo que perdeu grande parte do seu orgulho e a sua alma' (p. 9) [a people bereft of a great part of their pride and soul]. Rendered impotent in their own nation, with models being imposed from outside despite the country's enormous natural resources, Angola was being 'pilhada por todos os abutres que sobre ela se abateram' (p. 9) [pillaged by all the vultures crashing down on it]. Pepetela concludes, 'faltaria apenas uma conspiração para que a obra destruidora fosse completa: a do silêncio, a do esquecimento' (p. 9) [the only thing missing is a conspiracy so that this destructive work can be completed: a conspiracy of silence, of forgetting].

This is where the context in which he makes his argument becomes somewhat tricky, particularly in light of the arguments made by Lara Pawson among others about the events of 1977. Whatever purpose the 'Comissão de Lágrimas' served, as Pawson points out, it was 'nothing if not complicated, particularly given that the majority of people brought before them were black'.[37] One of Pawson's principal criticism's of Western writers, including Victoria Brittain, in regard to the events of 1977, is the way in which they avoid or downplay the role of the massacre in Angolan history, seeking to ignore it through precisely the type of conspiracy of silence and forgetting that Pepetela condemns in relation to the role of 'Empire' in destabilizing Angolan independence. In other words, Pepetela uses the introduction to a book by Victoria Brittain discussing conflicts and civil war in post-independence Angola to decry a conspiracy of silence, and yet the book he is prefacing, which begins its analysis in 1975, overlooks completely the traumatic events that afflicted the MPLA in 1977, events in which Pepetela was to some extent personally involved.

As Dorothée Boulanger points out, although those events and the subsequent repression were for decades 'national taboos' for Angola's most prominent MPLA-backing writers including Pepetela and Manuel Rui, the issue was taken up multiple times by Angolan authors 'largely considered inimical to the MPLA'.[38] Manuel dos Santos Lima, José Eduardo Agualusa and Sousa Jamba among others used their fiction to deliver damning portrayals of the violence, silence and fear that Neto's reaction to the Nito uprising produced. Yet, as Boulanger also points out, many literary critics for years overlooked these works or dismissed their literary quality as they struggled 'with the literary legacy of 27th of May'.[39] Boulanger points to the ideological inflections of leading critics of Angolan literature including Michel Laban, Inocência Mata, Russell Hamilton, and Phyllis Peres, who unconsciously or otherwise adopted positions favourable to Agostinho Neto. Most crucially, the 27 May 'brings forward the complicity of intellectuals and writers in the event itself and with postcolonial authorities generally, despite an increasingly perceptible betrayal of the ideals of the revolution by the party-state'.[40]

In his introduction to Brittain's work, Pepetela praises the way in which Brittain points to that betrayal as she outlines 'as graves falhas de quem devia concretizar o projecto de independência e evitar a consequente adulteração da situação com a corrupção quase generalizada, a incompetência, a falta de sensibilidade para os verdadeiros problemas, [...] a timidez na crítica frontal para equacionar os erros' (p. 9) [the serious failings of those who should have brought into being the independence project and avoided the subsequent adulteration of the situation with generalized corruption, incompetence, a lack of sensitivity to real problems, [...] a reluctance to speak plainly in order to think through mistakes]. In other words, Pepetela appreciates Brittain's (fairly mild) critique of the post-Neto years, in which the dreams once espoused by Neto gave way to what he perceives to be the cynicism and mediocrity of dos Santos. At the same time, he is no doubt grateful that Brittain's account remains deafeningly silent in its post-1977 complicity.

Yet, as Pacheco points out, to a certain extent, a 'país injusto e violento, cujos filhos agonizam sob as garras de um regime corrupto' [violent and unjust country, whose children agonize under the claws of a corrupt regime][41] was the product of the Neto years rather than a mere aberration of dos Santos's mandate. If we accept Pacheco's logic, the problems that Angola faces today were largely formed in the confused cauldron of the 27 May.

One is left wondering if Pepetela's decision to leave the frontline of Angolan governmental politics in the 1980s was not to some extent coloured by a sense that the events of 1977 (rather than independence in 1975) had not led to the national unity and equality he thought he was fighting for, and for which he had blood on his hands. A high price had been paid to concentrate power in the grasp of a charismatic president, Agostinho Neto. Neto died in Moscow in 1979 and was succeeded by José Eduardo dos Santos, a politician with little ideological commitment to Marxist-Leninism but highly political, despite a deceptively technocratic demeanour.

Yaka was the first major work written after Pepetela's departure from government, and, as we shall see in the next chapter, it pushes the line that ideological purity is the key to belonging in the new nation.

Notes to Chapter 3

1. In 1983, Pepetela also took up an appointment at the Agostinho Neto University, teaching sociology.
2. Luís Kandjimbo, 'Angolan Literature in the Presence of an Incipient Canon of Literatures Written in Portuguese', *Research in African Literatures*, 38.1 (Spring 2007), 9–34 (p. 15).
3. Pires Laranjeira, *Ensaios afro-literários* (Lisbon: Novo Imbondeiro, 2001), pp. 60–61.
4. Amnesty International put the number between 20,000 and 40,000. See Dalila Cabrita Mateus and Álvaro Mateus, *Purga em Angola: o 27 de Maio de 1977* (Lisbon: Texto, 2007), p. 203.
5. Nito Alves, *Discurso no comício de encerramento da campanha eleitoral para os órgãos do poder popular em Luanda, 5.7.1976* (Luanda: MPLA, 1976), pp. 27–28.
6. My translation.
7. Quoted in Don Barnett and Roy Harvey, *The Revolution in Angola: MPLA, Life Histories and Documents* (New York: Bobbs-Merrill Company, 1972), p. 33.
8. Carlos Pacheco, *Angola: um gigante com pés de barro e outras reflexões sobre a África e o mundo* (Lisbon: Vega, 2014), p. 79.
9. Pepetela quoted in 'Irmãos de José Van Dunem respondem a réplica de Pepetela' [no byline], *Semanário Angolense*, 27 November 2005 <http://www.angonoticias.com/Artigos/item/7243> [accessed 27 March 2018].
10. Quoted in Carlos Pacheco, *Angola*, p. 78.

11. '"Não houve nenhuma Comissão das Lágrimas em Angola", diz Pepetela' [Interview with João Carlos], *DW.com*, 14 May 2012 <http://www.dw.com/pt-002/não-houve-nenhuma-comissão-das-lágrimas-em-angola-diz-pepetela/a-15949744> [accessed 27 March 2018].
12. 'Irmãos de José Van Dunem respondem a réplica de Pepetela' in *Semanário Angolense*, 27 November 2005 <http://www.angonoticias.com/Artigos/item/7243> [accessed 27 March 2018].
13. Carlos Pacheco, *Repensar Angola* (Lisbon: Vega, 2000), p. 75.
14. Ibid., p. 76.
15. Carlos Pacheco, *Angola*, p. 79.
16. Ibid., p. 80.
17. Ibid.
18. Pepetela quoted in Carlos Pacheco, *Angola: um gigante com pés de barro e outras reflexões sobre a África e o mundo* (Lisbon: Vega, 2014), p. 81, footnote 17 from Voice of America interview 'Pepetela: Carlos Pacheco não percebeu o que lhe aconteceu' 28 May 2006.
19. Carlos Pacheco, *Angola*, p. 81.
20. Ibid., p. 83.
21. Ibid., p. 84.
22. Ibid., p. 86.
23. Ibid., p. 86.
24. Ibid., p. 86.
25. Ibid., p. 92.
26. 'Irmãos de José Van Dunem respondem a réplica de Pepetela', *Semanário Angolense*, 27 November 2005 <http://www.angonoticias.com/Artigos/item/7243> [accessed 27 March 2018].
27. Quoted in Mateus & Mateus, p. 68.
28. Mateus & Mateus, p. 68.
29. Ibid., p. 76.
30. Ibid., p. 78.
31. Quoted in Mateus & Mateus, p. 111. From original interview in *Notícias Magazine*, 17 February 2008.
32. See for example Ondjaki's *Bom dia, Camaradas* (Lisbon: Caminho, 2003).
33. Personal interview with the author, New Jersey, 2002.
34. A. Agostinho Neto, *Speeches* (Luanda: Department of Politico-Ideological Education, Propaganda and Information, 1980), p. 13.
35. Ibid., p. 13.
36. Victoria Brittain, *Morte da diginidade: a guerra civil em Angola*, trans. by Tânia Sofia Rocha, introduction by Pepetela (Lisbon: Dom Quixote, 1999). Subsequent page references from this translation given in the text.
37. Lara Pawson, *In the Name of the People: Angola's Forgotten Massacre* (London: I. B. Tauris, 2014), p. 200.
38. Dorothée Boulanger, 'Fiction as History? Resistance, Complicities and the Intellectual History of Postcolonial Angola' (unpublished doctoral thesis, King's College London, 2017), p. 118.
39. Ibid., p. 125.
40. Ibid., p. 152.
41. Pacheco, *Angola*, p. 92.

CHAPTER 4

Ideology, Nationality, Racism and Rape

With the publication of *Yaka*, Pepetela initiated a series of family epics. He would return to a familial narrative backdrop in various guises in *Lueji, o nascimento dum império*, *A gloriosa família* and *Predadores*.[1] The four substantial novels bear comparison because of the ways in which families are narrated. *Yaka* covers four generations of the Benguela-based Semedo clan, beginning with the birth of Alexandre Semedo towards the end of the nineteenth century and ending with Angola's independence and the family's dissipation. *Lueji* discusses the familial dynamics of the first Lunda queen. *A gloriosa família* relates the machinations of the Van Dum family, during the seventeenth-century Dutch occupation of Luanda, and finally *Predadores* tells the story of the Caposso family from the independence of Angola until the turn of the twenty-first century.

A common theme across three of these novels that starkly contrasts with the utopian heroicism of Sem Medo in *Mayombe* is the role of mediocrity. The protagonists of *Yaka*, *A gloriosa família* and *Predadores* are all mediocre, buffeted by economic and social systems they play to their advantage but with no clear, ethical vision of how to contribute to the Angolan nation. Indeed, mediocre protagonists are the norm in Pepetela after *A geração da utopia* (1992). From the blundering detective Jaime Bunda to the relentlessly ambitious Carmen in *O desejo de Kianda* (1995), ineptitude fused with small-mindedness are dominant characteristics of his leading roles.

Drawing on Elisabeth Wesseling's discussion of post-modern innovations in the historical novel,[2] Alberto Oliveira Pinto argues that *A gloriosa família* is a post-modern historical novel since it posits parallels between the time of the novel's action (the seventeenth century) and the time when it was written (the 1990s).[3] *Yaka* employs a similar though less marked strategy. *Lueji* moves between time zones mid-sentence. *Predadores*, with its anachronistic flow of time, is, in some senses, even more post-modern. In fact, Laura Padilha, drawing on Linda Hutcheon's notion of a poetics of the post-modern, argues that Pepetela is a writer who is both post-colonial and post-modern.[4] In other words, there is generally a defined political agenda in much of Pepetela's writing — one that critiques the systemic abuses of power and reveals a sense of betrayal by those who claimed to represent the people — and this agenda is aesthetically complemented by literary tropes that challenge the realist assumptions of the historical novel's form while appearing to comply with its conventions.

An aspect of the historical novel — particularly as it was written in nineteenth-century Europe — that is central to Pepetela's project is its link to nationhood. Writers like Alexandre Herculano, with novels like *Eurico, o Presbítero*, were, in part, concerned with boosting a nationalist ontology by appealing to historical narratives about Portugal's roots.[5] Pepetela is equally concerned with what it means to be Angolan in his family epics. As I shall discuss over the next few chapters, he adapts the mode of the historical novel in post-modern ways to reflect on the Angolan nation.

In this chapter, I will focus on *Yaka*, which, despite the protestations of some critics, is one of the foundational novels of Angolan literature. I will analyse how it depicts the nation in line with Agostinho Neto's message of belonging based on ideological commitment rather than geographical provenance. One of the mechanisms Pepetela uses to bolster that message is the deconstruction of the link between nationhood and territorial endogeny, particularly in his referencing of historical presences in Angola whose roots were grafted from beyond the nation's borders. As we will see, the opening authorial statement with which he prefaces the novel raises the spectre of the Jaga. They are a group to which he will return in more detail in his 2011 novel, *O sul. O sombreiro*. The complications associated with them served his ideological purposes in the 1980s.

Yaka was from the moment of its publication a contentious novel. In an article entitled 'Angolan Literature in the Presence of an Incipient Canon of Literatures Written in Portuguese' the former Angolan cultural attaché to Lisbon, Luís Kandjimbo, declares:

> with all due selectivity, the Angolan literary establishment cannot refrain from excluding from its canon those works that reflect the absence of Angolanness [...]. Such works are, for example, *Nga Muturi*, by Alfredo Troni, the works of the Portuguese poet Tomás Vieira da Cruz, Castro Soromenho's three major works of prose fiction, and Pepetela's novel *Yaka*.[6]

Kandjimbo's condemnation of *Yaka* for its supposed lack of Angolanness (or *angolanidade*) was part of a strand of critical reception that cast Pepetela's first family epic as 'uma espécie de justificação histórica e ideológica para os brancos angolanos' [a type of historical and ideological justification for white Angolans].[7] Kandjimbo's dismissal of *Yaka* was symptomatic of racially charged sensitivities about which cultural legacies could legitimately be included in what was to be considered Angolan literature. His exclusion of *Yaka* from the incipient canon challenged the Neto wing of the MPLA's dogma on racial inclusion — as the independence movement and then ruling party continuously asserted it represented all Angolans, regardless of ethnicity and cultural heritage. It also reveals the extent to which ideology and aesthetics designed subtly to convince readers of the MPLA's vanguard position were still in play in 1980s Angola.

The issue of race in *Yaka* is central — and it is complicated. In the novel, Pepetela substitutes race for ideology as a privileged marker of Angolan identity.

A clear message to emerge is that all hues, including the disproportionately white-looking vanguard that had surrounded Agostinho Neto in the 1960s and 1970s, had something important to contribute to the nation as long as they signed up to President Neto's vision. At the same time, part of the *Yaka*'s lasting appeal — transcending the post-1977 'justificação histórica e ideológica para os brancos angolanos' [historical and ideological justification for white Angolans][8] — is the way in which the novel disrupts the category of race and brings its discussion firmly into the realms of social construct and psychological forces. Rather like Justice Potter Stewart's threshold for obscenity, for characters in *Yaka*, race is something defined by the mantra 'I know it when I see it,' and the way in which they 'see it' responds to emotive rather than rational triggers.

Pepetela has on multiple occasions discussed the idea of 'angolanidade' [Angolanness], asserting that despite being a very nebulous concept, it was, at least when he wrote *Yaka*, fundamental to his literary project. In an interview originally published in 1989, five years after *Yaka* first appeared,[9] Pepetela asserts:

> No fundo, todos procuramos isso. O que é isso? Um conceito abstracto. Tenho a impressão que ninguém sabe muito bem o que é. No fundo não conseguimos até hoje teorizar, definir o que é isso de angolanidade. Isto embora esteja patente na obra dos escritores angolanos, claro. Creio que é um conceito que se vai procurar ainda durante muito tempo.[10]
>
> [Deep down, we are all looking for this. What is this? An abstract concept. I have the impression that nobody knows very well what it is. Deep down, even today, we still can't theorize it, or define what is this Angolanness. And that despite it being obvious in the work of Angolan writers, of course. I think it is a concept that will be searched for for a long time to come.]

The attempt to define what it means to be Angolan became an increasing source of disillusionment in Pepetela's work. However it was defined, it could never rest on race. Whatever 'Angola' is, its intricate links to the MPLA state — a tragic farce of corruption and malfunction — compromised it to the extent that, as we see in Pepetela's later work, there is a period in which, with novels like *O quase fim do mundo* and *O terrorista de Berkeley, Califórnia*, the author eschews completely any direct discussion of the nation.

At the time of *Yaka*'s publication, Angola had almost completed a decade of independence, undergone the trauma of the Nito Alves purges, and been plunged into an increasingly brutal civil war. In some ways, *Yaka* seeks to explain that, like the birth pangs of Alexandre Semedo, whose 'boca [...] se fechou, quando mordeu a terra'[11] ['mouth closed when he bit the earth'[12]], the formation of a national consciousness is a painful and protracted process, the origins of which are often ambiguous and ambivalent.

Alexandre's book-long quest to understand the meaning behind the Yaka statue his father, Oscar Semedo, had won through gambling, points to the difficulties in being able to accept what it means to be Angolan, at least as Pepetela then understood it. As both Pires Laranjeira and Alexandra Dias Santos point out, discussing the characterization of Alexandre Semedo's MPLA-supporting great-grandson, Joel, one reading of the novel is that adherence to the MPLA, particularly for those who came from settler families, was the sine qua non for acceptance as Angolan.[13] Angolan identity was thus an ideological position — or rather, an acquiescence to the Neto orthodoxy — rather than a tradition (however invented) or a cultural legacy. It was a wilfully induced state of mind that could be learned and it implied subservience to a party dogma. Clearly, as the ideology that officially underpinned the MPLA became bankrupt on the international stage with the fall of the Berlin Wall in 1989 and the subsequent collapse of the Soviet Union, the pillars on which 'angolanidade' had been conceived were shattered. What it meant to be Angolan, of necessity, became a much more eclectic concept.

In *Yaka*, Angolanness is somehow linked to the statue with which Alexandre Semedo tries in vain to dialogue for most of his life. There is an inscrutability to the statue that can only be decoded as Alexandre Semedo's political consciousness is raised over the course of the novel. For José Carlos Venâncio, like the mask in *Muana Puó*, the Yaka statue is the 'consciência calada da angolanidade' [silent conscience of Angolanness].[14] Pepetela asserted that the statue was 'uma espécie de símbolo da unidade nacional contra o colonizador' [a type of symbol of national unity against the colonizer] that also functions as 'a consciência muda de Alexandre Semedo' [the mute conscience of Alexandre Semedo].[15]

It takes Joel, towards the end of the novel, to decode the statue for his great-grandfather, showing that it represents the stupidity of settlers and, in fact, satirizes colonialism. In that decoding, ideology rather than tradition once again comes to the fore. Angolanness is born in resistance not as an essence waiting to be tapped. The consciousness of a committed and enlightened MPLA supporter is required to explain the meaning of the statue and, by implication, of the nation. The opening lines of the novel should have already alerted us to the strange hybridity underpinning the statue as a symbol of national unity:

> Yaka, Mbayaka, Jaga, Imbangala?
> Foram a mesma formação social (?), Nação (?) — aos antropólogos de esclarecer. Certo é que agitaram a já tremeluzente História de Angola, com as suas incursões ao Reino do Congo, na última das quais cercaram o rei numa ilha do grande rio e iam lhe cortar a cabeça, quando os portugueses intervieram para salvar a coroada cabeça, ainda não vassala. Foi o princípio do que se sabe. (p. 6)
>
> [Yaka, Mbayaka, Jaga, Imbangala?
> Were they the same social formation? Nation? The anthropologists can explain. What is certain is they stirred up the first glimmers of the history of Angola with their incursions into the Congo Kingdom, during the last of which they surrounded the king on an island in the big river and were about to cut off his head when the Portuguese intervened to save the crowned head, who was not yet a vassal. That was the beginning of what is known (p. ix).]

In conflating Yaka with the Jaga and Imbangala, Pepetela foregrounds the ethnic confusion at the heart of Angolan identity. While asserting that his novel is not about the Jaga/Yaka warriors but 'só duma estátua' (p. 6) ['only about a statue' (p. ix)], he really is saying the opposite. By beginning with a foreword in which he brings into stark relief slightly misnamed marauding warriors (Yaka for Jaga) about whom the 'inglês Battel' [sic] (p. 6) ['Englishman Battel' (p. ix)] said 'coisas de estarrecer' (p. 6) ['appalling things' (p. ix)] only to then dismiss them from the story, Pepetela is alerting his reader that something about the story of the Jaga is central to understanding his novel *Yaka*.

Pepetela's 2011 epic of the early years of Benguela, *O sul. O sombreiro*, casts a Jaga warrior in a leading role. The later novel has two predominant story lines that eventually intersect. In the first, the intrigues, misfortunes and adventures of Manuel Cerveira Pereira, the founder of Benguela, are recounted in classic Pepetela fashion, with dialogic interludes from competing viewpoints, including that of Benguela's first governor himself. Church and state plots combine to propel a narrative which demonstrates a mixture of hypocritical ambition on the part of the Portuguese, as well as offering an interesting insight into the complexities of the Portuguese court during Castile's predominance over Lisbon in the late sixteenth and first half of the seventeenth centuries.

The second strand of the tale involves Carlos Rocha, a rootless free black man, who flees Luanda, fearing his father is going to sell him into slavery to pay off his drinking debts. Rocha treks around Angola, in the company of the dreaded Jagas, biding time and building up resources in the form of salt currency, waiting for his father to die. In the course of his travels, Carlos comes across Andrew Battell, a British corsair, condemned for saying 'coisas de estarrecer' (p. 6) ['appalling things' (p. ix)] in *Yaka*'s prelude. In *O sul. O sombreiro*, Battell is caught off the coast of Brazil, and condemned to serve an indefinite term at the service of the Governor of Luanda. The English pirate has first-hand knowledge of Jaga culture. He even has a Jaga name, Kingrêje.

So, who was Andrew Battell, who makes a repeated appearance in Pepetela, particularly in two of his novels that deal with national roots? His odyssey was captured in a quaint 1901 publication entitled *The Strange Adventures of Andrew Battell of Leigh in Angola and the Adjoining Territories*, a source text towards which Pepetela points his reader in one of his characteristic italicized authorial interventions in *O sul. O sombreiro*. In fact, references to Andrew Battell of Leigh first appeared in the Vicar of Eastwood, Samuel Purchas's 1613 publication, *Purchas, his Pilgrimage*, on whose edition the 1901 volume of the *Strange Adventures*, edited by E. G. Ravenstein, and published by Hakluyt, is based. In *O sul. O sombreiro*, Carlos Rocha follows in Andrew Battell's footsteps, drawn to southern Angola by Battell's imaginings. He functions at some levels as Battell's avatar, able to act out for Pepetela the Englishman's experience of Angola through the imagined character of Carlos Rocha.

Within this myth-making setup, Pepetela takes Battell's already suspect historical source, his *Strange Adventures*, with its chapter on the 'discovery of the Gagas: their wars, man-eating; over-running countries [...] the rites and manner of life observed by the Iagges, or Gagas, which no Christian would ever know well but this author,'[16] and uses it to perpetuate and interrogate a central myth about the Jaga.

As Carlos falls in love with and impregnates a Jaga warrior, Kandalu, several competing ideological positions come to play out over her body. The myth of

Jaga culture Purchas propagated, and which took hold in the Portuguese colonial mindset, is that the Jaga, as well as being cannibals who feasted on their enemies, smothered their children at birth and then co-opted the strongest children of their vanquished enemies as their own. Despite Alfredo Margarido's studies on Jaga culture, echoed in Helder Macedo's *Partes de África*, which claim that no such child-smothering actually took place, the myth of Jaga infanticide, whose original, primary source includes the writings of Andrew Battell, took hold, and became the defining characteristic of historical depictions of the Jaga.

In Andrew Battell's original account, the Englishmen tells us, Jaga 'women are very fruitful, but they enjoy none of their children: for as soon as the woman is delivered of her child, it is presently buried quick [alive], so that there is not one child brought up in all this generation'.[17] Jagas, he continues, replenish their ranks by taking the fittest youth of the tribes they conquer and adopting them as their own. Or as Helder Macedo puts it, referring to the constantly extinguished and simultaneously replenished gene pool, 'não só não existiam mas existiam em não existir'[18] ['not only didn't they exist but they only existed by not existing'[19]]. This assertion of infanticide penetrated depictions of the Jaga for centuries and yet an alternative source, one used extensively by Pepetela in *A gloriosa família*, which I shall discuss in Chapter 8, and also consulted in the writing of O sul. O sombreiro, tells quite a different story.

António de Oliveira de Cardonega, whose *História geral das guerras angolanas* [General History of the Angolan Wars] was originally dated 1681, came to historiographical prominence as the 'first historian' of Angola when Salazar's Minister for the Colonies, Francisco José Vieira Machado, sponsored the publication of his three-volume history of the Portuguese colony in 1939. Cadornega's account of Jaga 'infanticide' is quite different from Battell's. It is less dramatic and more nuanced. In a section, entitled 'Descrevem-se os principios e antiguidade dos Iagas, seus ritos, e costumes que observão' [A description of the principles and antiquity of the Iagas, their rites, and customs they observe], Cadornega asserts:

> os ritos que seguem e observão, de matarem os filhos que nascem em seus quilombos e arrayaes, procedeo de huma senhora que tiverão ficar sem filhos, por ser esteril, a qual, sendo já velha, irritada de não ter quem lhe succedesse em o senhorio, ou pello demonio assim lhe infundir para dano de tantas almas, mandou a hum recem nascido pizar em hum pilão ou quino, que assim lhe chamão, onde pizão o milho para sua farinha, e feito em moada ou pô, o deo a todos os seus principaes vassallos a beber, fazendo com elles pacto e juramento de não consentirem mais parisse ou criasse em seus quilombos e arrayaes nenhuma criança que nelles nascesse, nem houvesse femea nelles a parisse, com pena de morte.[20]

> [the rites they follow and observe, of killing the children that are born in their *quilombos*[21] and its camps, emerged from a lady who would have remained without children, because she was barren, and who, being already old, irritated for lack of an heir to her domain, or because of the devil who thus possessed her to the detriment of so many souls, ordered a recently born infant to be crushed with a pestle or *quino*, as they call it, where they crush the grain for their flour,

and once thrashed into gruel or powder, gave him to all her leading vassals to drink, forming a pact with them and an oath never again to allow a birth or education in their *quilombos* and camps, of any child born in them, nor that any female give birth in them, on pain of death.]

Cadornega's description sounds more like a foundational myth, in which an initial sacrifice is made that prohibits future sacrifices by prohibiting certain things in order to allow for other things, with a resulting pact that protects those that follow. In this case, it is not that all Jaga children are to be slaughtered at birth, but rather that future Jaga children are to be protected from the unreasonable wrath of those in power whose sense of self-mortality puts the vulnerable at risk by being removed from the *quilombo* before they are born.

Cardonega's subsequent description shows where the myth of Jaga's exclusive appropriation of the children of conquered tribes may have originated, in misreadings of Jaga culture propagated by the likes of Andrew Battell:

> E os que nascem nas fazendas e arimos fora do quilombo, sendo já rapagotes, os trazem para o seu arrayal e os recebem nelle em som de guerra, com grande algazarra e matinada de instrumentos bellicos, como se fora entrado o seu arrayal de alguma gente inimiga.[22]

> [And those born in the farms and fields outside the *quilombo*, once they are youths, are brought to their camp and received there to the sound of war, with great fanfare and the clashing of bellicose instruments, as if their camp were entered by an enemy people.]

Jaga practice thus described becomes far more a symbolic ritual than a wholesale elimination of the Jaga gene pool. The coming of age of Jaga children is celebrated with their admission into the warrior compound as appropriated enemies rendered vassals who will go on to be great Jaga soldiers. Andrew Battell's version of the Jaga focuses on the literalization of the myth, whereas Cardornega leaves much more space open to understand the myth as myth and not history, a kind of fable that has at its root a mechanism to protect, educate and celebrate rather than to eliminate Jaga children.

Precisely who the Jaga were has long been a point of historical controversy. In many accounts they are conflated, at least in English-language historical sources, with the Imbangala, although Susan Broadhead argues it has become increasingly clear that while all the Imbangala may be considered Jaga, not all the Jaga were Imbangala.[23] The term 'Jaga', she claims, was used in sixteenth- and seventeenth-century sources to designate any group that attacked the western coast of the Kongo-Angolan region from the hinterland. At the time, they were all considered to be of the same ethnic origin.[24]

As either Imbangala or Jaga, they certainly captured the imagination of historians, lay and professional alike. The media journalist Benjamin Woolley includes an entire chapter on the Imbangala in his 2007 *Savage Kingdom: The True Story of Jamestown, 1607, and the Settlement of America*, drawing heavily on Andrew Battell to describe them as 'marauders, who would "settle themselves in any country", and live off the locals until their corn and cattle were used up. They would then move on, after looting anything they needed, including adolescent children whom they would use to replenish their numbers, their own offspring being killed at birth'.[25]

A dispute as to whether the Imbangala and the Jaga were the same group dates back at least to the 1960s, with historians debating back and forth the relationship between the two terms.[26] David Birmingham distinguishes between the 'Jaga hordes'[27] who invaded the Kongo in the 1560s, disrupting the established slave-trading networks, and an 'altogether more warlike people called the Imbangala'.[28] Like Woolley, Birmingham draws heavily on Andrew Battell's account of his time in South West Africa, asserting that these Imbangala 'did not rear their children but killed them at birth and adopted adolescents from among their defeated enemies'.[29] While Birmingham does distinguish the ethnicity of groups the Portuguese indiscriminately termed 'Jaga', he nevertheless accepts uncritically the assumptions of Battell as filtered through Purchas.

In contrast, Joseph Miller is far more cautious in his descriptions of the Jaga/Imbangala. While accepting that there is a general confusion in historical sources between the Jaga and the Imbangala, he asserts 'the so-called "Jaga" [were] famous and fearsome warriors who probably never existed in the way in which they have been described'.[30] Miller's more measured account departs from the premise that 'seventeenth-century Europeans repeatedly emphasized such superficially bizarre laws as those prohibiting the birth of children'.[31] For Miller, the laws should be understood as a mechanism to deny kinship as a social structure in the *quilombo* — refusing a matrilineal system of inherited privilege rendered the group a more effective fighting force. Most importantly for Miller:

> It is not necessary to accept the often exaggerated European stories of sexual abstinence, infanticide, and the abandonment of children in the bush to understand how these *yijila* [laws] produced the intended effect of suppressing descent as an element of social structure among the Imbangala. Births continued to occur in practice, and many children survived the formal proscriptions against their presence, but the *yijila* declared all such children illegitimate in Imbangala terms and absolutely denied them social status within the *kilombo*. Some infanticide may have taken place as the result of the low prestige of these children but, contrary to the claims of horrified and often gullible seventeenth-century missionaries, by no means all Imbangala infants died from exposure. Illegally pregnant women could circumvent the letter of the *yijila*, which specified that no children could be born *inside* the *kilombo*, by temporarily leaving the confines of the walled encampment to give birth, thus placing their infants outside the formal community of the warrior initiation society.[32]

Clearly more in agreement with Cardonega's ability to see the symbolic rather than literal meaning of the *quilombo* birth prohibition, Miller asserts:

> The metaphorical interpretation of *kilombo* rules makes Imbangala customs appear less grotesque than most writers have portrayed them. The Imbangala did not literally 'kill' their children but 'slew' them only in the sense of abolishing their lineage affiliation during the initiation rituals. This step separated them permanently (i.e. 'killed' them) from their relatives and rendered them eligible for conscription into the *kilombo* only in the sense of excluding them from the initiation rites reserved for young male warriors.[33]

Despite having drawn heavily on Cadornega in other historical novels (most notably *A gloriosa família*) and referencing him in *O sul. O sombreiro*, Pepetela opts for Battell's version of Jaga culture in his 2011 work. His source choice is intriguing, foregrounding as it does a multiply distilled seventeenth-century English imperial optic on Angola. In choosing Battell over Cardonega, Pepetela seems to fashion a narrative of female agency overcoming restrictions placed on women. The backdrop of Battell's bloodthirsty, child-sacrificing Jagas provides a contrastive setting for a novel whose plot takes it cue from Romanticism and, in the process, turns motherhood into an active choice rather than a national service.

In *O sul. O sombreiro*, Kandalu, the Jaga warrior, falls in love and because of the love she feels for Carlos, she chooses to keep her baby and flees with her lover after their child is born. Pepetela characterizes Kandalu as a strong woman with her own desires, who can break free of the collective shackles of Jaga (African) culture that curtail her rights. All she has to do is assume her individuality — an individuality coded in the tradition of a nineteenth-century European novel, through a discourse of star-crossed love as the marker of individual choice.

Despite Kandalu's impassioned defence of bride-price as respect for traditions (in her case, a slave must be provided as a meal for her family), it becomes clear that, as she falls 'in love' with Carlos, she gains maternal feelings towards her unborn child. These conflict with the cultural norms of her tribe as Pepetela portrays them. Yet, her defiance of supposed Jaga customs can also be read as another episode in a longstanding lusotropical love narrative — the myth that Portugal's colonizers were loved by those they conquered — since she is willingly complicit with Carlos, who is a descendant of the 'discoverer' of Angola (Diogo Cão). She chooses his culture over her own out of love.

Although Pepetela draws on Andrew Battell (the English fantasist) rather than Cardonega (Portugal's first historian of Angola), he ends up furnishing a tale that ambiguously resonates with Portuguese imperial mythologies — in particular those around colonized women loving their colonizers. Had Pepetela chosen Cardonega as the source for *O sul. O sombreiro*, the Jagas would not have been so completely different in their customs from their European counterparts. Cardonega could see symbolism where Battell imagined gore. In choosing Battell as the source for *O sul. O sombreiro*, Pepetela is opting for a Jaga narrative of absolute difference in a flawed effort to portray female agency.

In 1984, when Pepetela published *Yaka*, the Jaga did not serve as markers of absolute difference but rather as a metaphor for the diversity at the heart of the Angolan nation. In the preface of *Yaka*, Pepetela makes it clear how suspect Battell's account is — how filtered through the prejudices and fantasies of the British Empire. At the same time, that account took hold, providing the raw material for him to fashion in *O sul. O sombreiro* a female protagonist who rejects dubious traditions and asserts a limited form of female agency within the conventions of a nineteenth-century Romantic love story. In contrast, in *Yaka*, female agency was not yet one of Pepetela's central concerns. Instead, references to the Jaga serve the purpose of pushing exogeny and an eclectic gene pool as the very essence of Angola.

The opening lines of *Yaka* equate a multiplicity of confused sources to the origins of the Angolan nation. The various kingdoms, the Portuguese colonialists, the Jaga invaders, the Imbangala among many others, all contribute to what it will mean to be Angolan. The generalized historical mishmash is important to a hybrid understanding of Angola's origins as Pepetela reminds us when he claimed:

> Diz-se que os Bayakas talvez se possam ligar aos Jagas, aos Imbangalas, ninguém sabe. São uma espécie de formação guerreira que percorreu Angola [...] provavelmente terão deixado marcas de uma organização social, organização política que se poderia dizer comum às diferentes etnias de Angola.³⁴

> [They say that the Bayaka were perhaps linked to the Jagas, and the Imbangalas, no one knows. They are a type of warrior formation that travelled through Angola [...] and probably left vestiges of a social organization, a political organization that could be said to be common to different Angolan ethnicities.]

The Yaka statue thus becomes 'uma espécie de símbolo da unidade nacional contra o colonizador'³⁵ [a type of symbol of national unity against the colonizer]. Angolans can come from any of many groups. There is no such thing as natives to the nation, only adherents.

The novel's narrative strategy, with a variety of voices including Alexandre Semedo and the Yaka statue, foregrounds that multiplicity of sources, and in the process, demonstrates that few of them are endogenous to the land. As the novel progresses, it becomes clear that being born on Angolan soil does not make you part of Angola. To be Angolan is to accept the MPLA state — or at least what it officially fought to bring about, namely equality and solidarity. As the Jaga show, there is no such thing as 'authentic' origins to Angolanness. They, with their supposed habit of killing their own off-spring and appropriating the children of those they conquered, were the forerunner of nationalist anti-essentialism. The point is that the Jaga/Yaka, like the Portuguese settlers, came from beyond the borders of the Angolan state, and descendants from both groups (including those they 'adopted') are a legitimate part of an independent Angola, as long as they share an abhorrence of colonial practice and a commitment to the ideology of the ruling party.

The novel *Yaka* covers the 85 years of Alexandre Semedo's life, from his birth in 1890, at the time of the British Ultimatum that rocked Portuguese imperial confidence in Africa, and eventually contributed to the fall of the Portuguese monarchy, to the messy independence of Angola in 1975. Alexandre's parents were Esmeralda, a so-called 'second-class' white woman because she was not born in the metropolis, and Oscar, who arrived in the Angolan colony steeped in a discourse of freedom. Oscar gradually becomes an alcoholic; he loses his liberal ideals and turns increasingly racist as economic misfortunes make life harder for Angolan settlers. Acácio, the anarchist barber who is among the few exiles sent to Angola for their politics rather than their crimes, laments that Oscar is corrupted by his circumstances and prepared to exploit black people rather than holding true to his liberal ideals.

Oscar's descent into racism is more nuanced than the blatant and aggressive prejudice that will characterize future generations of the Semedos. He justifies his discriminatory actions paternalistically. He is prepared to cheat black people by diluting the wine they drink, but justifies the practice and is uneasy about his son's habit of cheating black customers out of cloth. For Oscar, wine is bad for black people and diluting it means 'menos veneno que se lhes dá' (p. 59) ['giving them less poison' (p. 53)], a rationale that does not extend to mismeasuring the materials they purchase. 'Incoerências dessas havia aos montes em Óscar Semedo' (p. 59) ['Oscar Semedo was full of such inconsistencies' (p. 53)] — inconsistencies that his son and grandchildren inherit in different forms, but which rotate around the ways in which they code racial difference.

Oscar bestows on his son a passion for Greek classics, manifest in the names Alexandre chooses for his children (Achilles, Orestes, Eurydice, Socrates and Helen) as well as several of his grandchildren. Underpinning those name choices is Alexandre's initial belief in predetermination, and his desire that his augustly named children escape his mediocre fate. Alexandre's great-grandchild, Joel, should have been named Ulysses, one of the greatest of classical heroes noted for his guile. Instead, he becomes Joel, a name, as Pires Laranjeira points out, that he shares with the biblical prophet who announces the Final Judgment.[36]

Joel's role is to interpret the Yaka statue and to demonstrate an unshakable commitment to the birth of an independent Angola. He fuses the notion of a final judgment based on distinguishing the good from the evil (in this particular case through their adherence to the MPLA 'gospel') and the guile necessary to bring about a new Angola (Joel's spying activities help MPLA progress in Benguela). However, before Joel's clear pro-MPLA consistency is achieved, four generations of Semedos echo each other's inconsistencies, particularly around the issue of race.

The first thing to note is the family's surname. Semedo echoes Sem Medo — except that 'medo' becomes more pronounced. The 'fearlessness' of *Mayombe*'s hero, for whom there was no space post-independence Angola, becomes a more generalized fear, characteristic of the intense mediocrity that is a fundamental trait of the Semedo clan. Throughout *Yaka*, fear is prevalent. As Acácio points out, white people are fed cannibal stories about Africans in order to make them afraid and willing to strike down a non-descript enemy — capable of taking any form, and in the context of colonial Angola, distilled into all Africans. For the barber, this use of fear has always been a ruse and one of the 'truques dos opressores' (p. 44) ['tricks of the oppressors' (p. 37)].

Acácio, the only white man who refuses to arm himself after the Bailundo rebellions that whipped up racist anxieties at the turn of the twentieth century, always understands fear as a mechanism used systemically by capitalism to limit the aspirations of those, including the white settlers, it oppresses. The economic system is the cause of suffering, not any intrinsic sense of superiority on the part of the settler community. They become more racist as their economic fortunes flounder and, to some degree, are victims of a power structure stacked against them. They become agents of oppression as a result of their systemic economic disempowerment.

Throughout much of his life, Alexandre lives in unfocused fear. It is not clear who the enemy is so that, in his misery, the non-descript face of black Africa can attract white anxiety. According to Alexandre's wife, Donana, a 'first-class' white woman who was actually a deflowered menial worker in the house of Oscar's family in Portugal, Alexandre never took any risks to grow his material worth for 'medo de perder umas migalhas' (p. 157) ['fear of losing a few crumbs' (p. 153)]. That nondescript fear leads Alexandre to declare at one point that he wants all black people exterminating:

> Enquanto houver negros viveremos no medo. [...] Não quero é viver mais no medo [...] O meu pai morreu com medo. Eu já nasci com medo. Todos esses vivem só vivem com medo. Não há ano sem revolta. Porra, já chega! (p. 101)
>
> [So long as there are blacks we'll live in fear. [...] What I don't want is to go on living in fear [...] My father died with fear. I was already born with fear. Everyone here lives only with fear. There's not a year without a revolt. Damn it, that's enough! (pp. 96–97)].

For Pepetela writing in the 1980s, fear is linked to racism — the greatest spectre to haunt Angola. Set against the backdrop of President Neto's pronouncements in the previous decade, and what became known as 'the fear' (o medo) of the post-27 May purges, the intended meanings of the fear in *Yaka* become more ambiguous. A commentary on the non-descript fear and virulent but illogical racism of mid-twentieth-century Portuguese colonialism draws unintended parallels with post-independence Angola, in which the charge of racism was directed against those who criticized President Neto's direction and his white circle, and 'fear' is what potential critics felt after the bloody example of 1977. Yet, on the surface, *Yaka* remains loyal to what Pepetela still viewed as the MPLA's legitimate project: and racism — be it in the form of colonialism or bile directed at the MPLA's (predominantly white) vanguard — can only be overcome by submission to the true tenets and teachings of the revolution.

The moment at which Alexandre declares the need to exterminate all black people because of his generalized fear is key. It bears reading alongside his previous failed attempt to seduce Njaya, the beautiful black girl he first lays eyes on at Acácio's wake. Because of Alexandre's indecisiveness, Njaya leaves the wake with the only other white attendee, Ernesto. Alexandre subsequently becomes fixated on Njaya, until a crucial scene in which he makes a pass at her but is stopped in his tracks by her response: 'Não vou gostar' (p. 98) ['I won't like it' (p. 94)]. Her plea calls to mind the words of a black friend from his youth, Tuca, who ended up serving in the Portuguese army. Tuca had been bullied into performing the doomed role of Mutu-ya-kevela in the Bailunda War games Alexandre and his friends used to play. One day, that same group of friends gang rapes a thirteen-year-old black girl in another imperial war game, a replication of Captain Calado's attack on Samacaca's village, in which the boys seek to 'vingar as mulheres brancas' (p. 47) ['avenge the white women' (p. 40)].

Alexandre takes part in the gang rape, but Tuca refuses to participate, not because the victim is black but rather because she 'não queria. Não gostou' (p. 48) ['didn't want it. She didn't like it' (p. 41)]. The echo of these words enters Alexandre's mind as he prepares to take Njaya. Significantly, he is not able to proceed with what would be the rape of Njaya. Subsequently, he calls for the extermination of all black people as the only way to avoid continued fear.

The two incidents are linked. They are part of the trajectory through which Alexandre must pass in order finally to be reconciled with the birth of an independent post-racial Angola. He will die on Angolan soil while the rest of his extensive clan, with the exception of Joel, flees in 1975. The scene in which Tuca's words immobilize Alexandre's actions highlights one of his inconsistencies: a racism linked with a fetishized desire for the black woman. The fact that she 'won't like it' completely undermines the lusotropical love-narrative, in which Portuguese males were supposedly loved by those they colonized.

At the same time, the fact that he stops, that Tuca's words lead him to desist from the thoughtless rape his childhood friends might have perpetrated against Njaya, shows that the novel is about the raising of Alexandre's consciousness, with all the back-and-forth that implies. With that in mind, his sudden turn towards aggressive racism, immediately following his colonial emasculation before Njaya, is part of the internal inconsistencies the novel seeks to play off against each other, in order to conclude, almost evangelically, that anyone can be saved (or admitted to the Angolan nation) so long as they repent of their former sins, and those of their forefathers (their racism and capitalism), and follow the orthodox strand of the MPLA faith.

For Alexandre's recuperation to be complete, his eldest son Achilles, another character in the Semedo mould, replete with inconsistencies, must be sacrificed. No salvation, in keeping with the tenets of Greek mythology and the Christian paradigm, comes without a price. Achilles knows no life other than 'esta vida de merda de branco numa terra de pretos' (p. 137) ['the lousy life of a white man in the land of blacks' (p. 134)]. He is a brawling, soccer-loving brute. As a municipal overseer who can 'dar chapadas e pontapés' (p. 128) ['hit and kick' (p. 124)], he was very efficient in 'pôr os negros a trabalhar' (p. 128) ['putting blacks to work' (p. 124). His racism is much more pronounced than that of his father and grandfather, and equally inconsistent. To be black is to be the enemy and yet Achilles energetically defends 'esse negro estreito, grande avançado-centro do Sporting' (p. 140) ['the tall thin black Sporting centre forward' Damião (p. 137)] because:

> Damião para ele não era negro, era um amigo. Negros eram esses trabalhadores matumbos e mangonheiros a quem era preciso surrar para trabalharem. Negro era o Alves, jogador do Benfica e o Jacinto, jogador do Portugal. E já partira o focinho a um sacrista branco que insultou o Damião de seu negro da merda e negra era masé a mãe do sacrista que, por sinal, até era loiro. (pp. 140–41)

> [to him Damião was not a black but a friend. Blacks were the backward and lazy workers who had to be hit at work. Alves, a Benfica player, and Jacinto, a Portugal player, were black. And he had already broken the jaw of a white bastard who had insulted Damião, calling him you bloody black, no it was the bastard's mother who was black, even though he happened to be blond.] (p. 137)

In Achilles, intolerance of racial difference becomes its most inconsistent and most violent. His characterization utterly destabilizes the concept of race while being thoroughly bound up in racial discourse. The lesson he projects to 1980s Angola is that race cannot be a valid category if even those who most vehemently and brutally enforce it so obviously, easily and randomly negate its shaky premises. Race is merely a sobriquet of exclusion, not a category on which to found a nation. It is a psychological projection rather than a physiognomy. You see the race you want to see in those you choose to oppress.

Unlike his father, Achilles enjoys the feeling of fear that periodically overwhelms the settler community, because it signals life and novelty. Learning of a supposed series of attacks by Mucabals, in which white people are portrayed as the targets, 'uma angústia agradável penetrou-o' (p. 142) ['a pleasant feeling of anxiety invaded him' (p. 138)]. For Achilles, racially coded anxieties more forcefully indicate something that is desired — something that drives him along, rather than immobilizing him in the way that racial fears had been used by Alexandre as an excuse for his inertia. He gains the opportunity to follow the logic of colonial society's racism to its conclusion, when he kills Tyenda, a Mucabal, on a hunting trip, as if he were game. As a result of this logic, Achilles is himself killed by Violanda, in retaliation.

The killing of Achilles forces another change in Alexandre's consciousness with the realization that he had brought about his son's death because of the way he had nurtured his sense of racial superiority: 'matei o Aquiles, matei o meu filho. Eduquei-o dessa maneira, de ser superior porque branco' (p. 188) ['I killed my Achilles, I killed my son. I brought him up like that, to be superior because he was white' (p. 184)]. In Pepetela's narrative from the 1980s, racism — of all kinds and with all its inconsistencies — lurks at the heart of Angola's problems.

Njaya's rejection plunges Alexandre into a virulently racist phase. He feels an acute awareness of his own mediocrity. The fragility of his masculinity is exposed. At some level, Achilles represents a bulwark for that frayed masculinity. Achilles is larger than life, brawny and impulsive, with little sensitivity. The loss of Achilles removes that bulwark. Alexandre can no longer count on any sense of male and racial privilege. His son's death forces him to confront the fallacy of the truths that have driven him. He had hoped that 'se eu não fui, seria o meu filho um herói. Herói? É isso ser herói? Matei-o, apenas' (p. 188) ['If I wasn't a hero, my son would be one. A hero? Is that being a hero? I killed him, that's all' (p. 184)]. He had projected onto his son flawed — if prevalent — notions of what it means to be a white man in colonial society. He hoped by naming him after one of the greatest heroes of Western tradition, he would rise above the contradictions of colonial masculinity to a position of superiority that could gainsay the mediocrity of his father and origins. Instead, his son turns out to be his Achilles' heal, descending into a spiralling cycle of violence and annihilation.

As is so often the case in Pepetela, sociological explanations — in this case the feeling of powerlessness among a particular underclass of Portuguese colonial settlers and a desire to change their lot without a clear sense of the wherewithal to effect any meaningful change in their insecure existences — lie behind psychological outbursts: the violence of racially inspired killings. With Achilles' death, Alexandre understands the false logic of the equation. Racial hierarchies have nothing to do with standing out. In fact, Achilles stands out most because of the loyalty he has to his friends, regardless of their ethnicity.

Achilles' son, Dionísio, becomes the extreme embodiment of his father's and grandfather's failings as a racist and as a rapist. Unlike Alexandre, he will never become self-aware enough to repent of his actions or understand them as part of a cycle that leads to nowhere good. Dionísio is involved in what are essentially two rape scenes, both of which relate to race and decadence. The first involves his cousins, Chucha and Jaimito, and begins the section of the novel entitled 'O sexo' [The Genitals]. In this section, Pepetela cedes the narrative voice to the three cousins in turn, in a strategy that Manuel Cabeleira Gomes sees as a vital protection of the omniscient narrator, ethically shielding the authorial voice from the depraved sexual conduct of an incestuous colonial family.[37]

Pepetela makes the reader work to decode who exactly is involved in this sexual encounter, dropping clues that only become clear in retrospect. First, Chucha narrates how her favourite cousin, Dionísio, followed her into a bedroom where they then had sex, until their younger cousin, Jaimito, arrived and blackmailed them by threatening to shout for the servants if he was not given his turn. Jaimito's demand filled Dionísio with hatred and impotence — the same symptoms of emasculation his grandfather Alexandre had experienced faced with Njaya's rejection.

As Chucha does not give consent and cedes to Jaimito's demand under duress, it is another example of rape in the novel. In contrast to Njaya's experience of a violent gang rape at the hands of Portuguese settler youth, Chucha ends up enjoying the intercourse more with her younger, blackmailing cousin than with Dionísio. There are echoes of Ondina's violation in *Mayombe* here. Once again, a woman is raped and realizes she enjoys it. Very problematically, Pepetela's early work tends to deploy women's bodies as metaphorical tropes subject to abuse, portraying the victim of sexual violence as either desiring or enjoying the violation. Ondina was, in some ways, the prototype that laid bare the reality of Marxist New Man's instrumental and denigrating view of women and their bodies — even at moments when the author appears to cede to those bodies a degree of agency.

In *Yaka*, Chucha's rape at the hands of Jaimito is neither violent nor consensual. Most tellingly, the rape itself is not the point of the episode. Rather, it serves to justify Dionísio's sense of humiliation. Admittedly, its incestuous overtones paint colonial society as devoid of a moral compass, but that more than anything is a result of Chucha's reaction — the physical pleasure she derives from the experience. Once again, a woman is shown to be complicit in her own rape. This time, that complicity is a means to portray colonial depravity.

As a result of his humiliation, Dionísio goes on to rape the wife of one of the Semedos's neighbours, Moma. By this point in the novel, the Semedos are effectively headed by Bartolomeu Espinha, a ruthless opportunist who marries into the family. Espinha takes advantage of simmering racial tensions to murder Moma and appropriate his land. He is a predatory capitalist willing to exploit any circumstance to accumulate wealth at the expense of others. Race, for him, is a tool enabling economic repression, through which privilege is acquired or asserted. Dionísio's particularly violent rape plays into the increasingly racialized environment Espinha foments, and harks back to the rape in which Alexandre participated in his youth, caught up in white boys' war games. In neither instance is sexual desire at stake. Instead, they are racially coded assertions of power by youths who feel emasculated by their peers.

The four instances of non-consensual sex in *Yaka* — the first two involving Alexandre, the second pair his grandson Dionísio — mirror each other structurally. In Alexandre's case, he goes from active participation in the gang-rape of a young black girl to an inability to go through with a rape because Njaya does not want to have sex, and her words echo those uttered by Tuca in the first rape. In Dionísio's case, witnessing Chucha ceding to Jaimito's demand disempowers Dionísio, and is at the forefront of his mind as he takes revenge for his frustrations on Moma's second wife. In all the cases, racial hierarchies interplay with gender hierarchies. In Alexandre's case, Njaya's eventually respected refusal to have sex with him leads to Alexandre's most vicious retreat into raw and irrational racism. In Dionísio's case, witnessing as a disempowered bystander Jaimito's sex with Chucha leads to his decision to rape Moma's wife.

What is the point of these various sex and rape scenes? Do they have any significance beyond a metaphorical reading of the colonial rape of the land? The scene involving the three cousins clearly does speak to a level of settler decadence that can only lead to their downfall. Its incestuous overtones herald an unproductive, morally bankrupt future for the majority of the Semedo clan. But once again, redemption is possible, even for the rapist — embodied in Alexandre Semedo — as long as his consciousness is raised, and he is able to become reflexive about his position within the power structure. Dionísio is a lost cause for whom there will be no place in the new Angola. Alexandre, on the other hand, belongs to the land, and will die there. But Alexandre's acceptance by the land comes with a sacrifice. That sacrifice is Achilles, his son.

Yaka is a family odyssey in which the power structures of race, sex and class interplay. Characters inherit the prejudices and repeat the mistakes of their forebears. They also demonstrate the irrationality of those prejudices in the choices they make. Despite everything, no one is beyond salvation. Ultimately, the difference between Dionísio and Alexandre is that Alexandre comes to understand the error of his ways, and pays an expiatory price for his past actions. For that reason, he belongs to the new Angola, along with his great-grandson, Joel.

Joel, who is willing to give up everything for the revolution, including his love interest Nizia, is a paradigm of ideological commitment. Alexandre is an example of repentance. They become the male pillars on which the new nation will be constructed. Women in the novel appear far less able to exercise meaningful choices and, once again, violence against them serves a tangential narrative purpose, giving the reader troubling pause for thought. The novel is also one that deconstructs the racial origins of the Angolan nation. From its initial highlighting of the muddled myths of Jaga nationhood, to its portrayal of race as a state of mind rather than an objective reality, *Yaka* drives home Agostinho Neto's vision of Angola as an ideological construct in which commitment counted over provenance.

Pepetela's next novel, published over five years after *Yaka*, is his first major work to put a woman in full control of her own actions. *Lueji, o nascimento de um império* brings out the fuller potential of *Mayombe*'s Ondina through the character of Lueji who learns what she wants and knows how to attain her goals. Ana Paula Tavares has even suggested that the powerful and independent Lueji is Pepetela's response to the 'feroz' [fierce] criticism from women of his earlier female characterizations.[38] As I shall discuss in the next chapter, *Lueji* continues and refines Pepetela's exploration of the operation of power, and speaks to an audience in 1990s Angola about the corrupting effect power has on anyone, no matter how innocent or well-intentioned their initial actions may be.

Notes to Chapter 4

1. Fabrice Schurmans reads Pepetela through the lens of the tragedy in his *O trágico do estado pós-colonial: Pius Ngandu Nkashama, Sony Labou Tansi, Pepetela* (Coimbra: CES-Almedina, 2014), linking *A gloriosa família* and *Predadores* with the *Jaime Bunda* novels because of what he sees as their depiction of the postcolonial state. *Yaka*, I would argue belongs in this group, too. While it is clearly not as overtly critical of the state (as construed and understood through the MPLA) in *Yaka* as in the later novels in this group, he clearly aims through the literary trope of the Yaka statue to show the genesis of a postcolonial understanding of the Angolan state.
2. See Elisabeth Wesseling, *Writing History as a Prophet: Postmodernist Innovations of the Historical Novel* (Amsterdam: John Benjamins, 1991).
3. Alberto Oliveira Pinto, *A oralidade no romance histórico angolano moderno: A gloriosa família de Pepetela, A casa velha das margens de Arnaldo Santos* (Lisbon: Novo Imbondeiro, 2003), p. 5.
4. Laura Cavalcante Padilha, 'Literaturas africanas e pós-modernismo: uma indagação', in her *Novos Pactos, Outras Ficções* (Porto Alegre: EDIPUCRS, 2002), p. 308.
5. Alexandre Herculano published *Eurico, o Presbítero* in 1844. As well as being at the forefront of Portuguese Romanticism, Herculano was one of Portugal's most important nineteenth-century historians.
6. Luís Kandjimbo, 'Angolan Literature in the Presence of an Incipient Canon of Literatures Written in Portuguese', *Research in African Literatures*, 38.1 (Spring 2007), 9–34 (p. 15).
7. Pires Laranjeira, 'Os clássicos africanos resistem', in his *Ensaios afro-literários* (Lisbon: Novo Imbondeiro, 2001), 22–33 (p. 29).
8. Ibid.
9. *Yaka* was first published by Ática in Brazil in 1984, and then in Angola and Portugal in 1985.
10. Interview republished in José Carlos Venâncio, *Literatura e poder na África lusófona* (Lisbon: Ministério da Educação, 1992), p. 96.
11. Pepetela, *Yaka* (São Paulo: Ática, 1984), p. 8. Subsequent page references given in the text.
12. Pepetela, *Yaka*, trans. by Marga Holness (Oxford: Heinemann, 1996), p. 3. Subsequent page references from this translation given in the text.
13. Pires Laranjeira, *Ensaios afro-literários*, p. 59; Alexandra Dias Santos, 'Nação, guerra e utopia em Pepetela (1971–1996)' (unpublished doctoral thesis, University de Lisbon, 2011), p. 133.
14. José Carlos Venâncio, *Literatura versus sociedade* (Lisbon: Palavra Africana, 1992), p. 36.
15. Interview reprinted in José Carlos Venâncio, *Literatura e poder na África lusófona* (Lisbon: Ministério da Educação, 1992), p. 97.
16. E. G. Ravenstein (ed.), *The Strange Adventures of Andrew Battell of Leigh in Angola and the Adjoining Regions, Reprinted from 'Purchas His Pilgrimes,' Edited with Notes and a Concise History of Kongo and Angola* (London: Hakluyt Society, 1901), p. 19.

17. Ibid., p. 32.
18. Helder Macedo, *Partes de África* (Lisbon: Presença, 1991), p. 165.
19. Helder Macedo, *Parts of Africa*, trans. by Phillip Rothwell (Dartmouth: LAABST, 2015), p. 193.
20. António de Oliveira de Cadornega, *História geral das guerras angolanas*, 3 vols (Lisbon: Agência Geral das Colónias, 1940–42), III, 222.
21. Gladwyn Murray Childs translates *quilombo* in the Jaga context as 'war-camp'. See her 'The Peoples of Angola in the Seventeenth Century according to Cadornega', *The Journal of African History*, 1.2 (1960), 271–79 (p. 275).
22. Ibid., p. 223.
23. Susan H. Broadhead, *Historical Dictionary of Angola*, 2nd edn (Metuchen, NJ: Scarecrow Press, 1992), p. 97.
24. Ibid., p. 98.
25. Benjamin Woolley, *Savage Kingdom: The True Story of Jamestown, 1607, and the Settlement of America* (New York: Harper Collins, 2007), p. 352.
26. The most famous configuration of the dispute was between Jan Vansina and David Birmingham, who wrote a series of articles in the *Journal of African History*, starting in 1963, challenging each other's interpretations of the Jaga/Imbangala distinction. See Linda M. Heywood and John K. Thornton, *Central Africans, Atlantic Creoles, and the Foundation of the Americas, 1585–1660* (Cambridge: Cambridge University Press, 2007), p. 94 and Paulo Jorge de Sousa Pinto, 'Em torno de um problema de identidade: os "Jaga" na história do Congo e Angola', *Mare Liberum: Revista de História dos Mares*, 18/19 (1999–2000), 193–243.
27. David Birmingham, *The Portuguese Conquest of Angola* (Oxford: Oxford University Press, 1965), p. 12.
28. Ibid., p. 17.
29. Ibid., p.18.
30. Joseph C. Miller, *Kings and Kinsmen: Early Mbundu States in Angola* (Oxford: Clarendon Press, 1976), p. xiii.
31. Ibid., p. 226.
32. Ibid., p. 226.
33. Ibid., p. 234.
34. Quoted in Venâncio, *Literatura e poder na África lusófona*, p. 97.
35. Ibid., p. 97.
36. Pires Laranjeira, *Literaturas africanas de expressão portuguesa* (Lisbon: Universidade Aberta, 1995), p. 154.
37. Manuel Cabeleira Gomes, *Literatura e estudos interculturais: uma leitura imagológica do romance YAKA de Pepetela* (Lisbon: Universidade Aberta, 1996), p. 47.
38. Ana Paula Tavares, 'Contar Histórias', in *Lendo Angola*, ed. by Laura Cavalcante Padilha and Margarida Calafate Ribeiro (Porto: Afrontamento, 2008), pp. 39–50 (p. 42).

CHAPTER 5

The Dynamics of Girl Power or the Selective Process of Myth-Making

Since his early writing in the Casa dos Estudantes do Império, Pepetela has been interested in how the dynamics of power work, and how power corrupts even those with the best of intentions. One of the story lines of his experimental 1990 novel *Lueji, o nascimento de um império* portrays an innocent young queen who assumes a leadership role, rejecting the Machiavellian strategies of her brothers only to adopt them herself over time. Lueji becomes wedded to the crown she wields on behalf of those she is meant to serve. The novel draws on the myths of the establishment of the Lunda Empire. Like all Pepetela's novels that draw on the past, it comments on the contemporaneous context in which it was written. The over-riding concern it reveals is that no one can be trusted with unchecked power, however innocuous, just or altruistic they might at first seem.

Lueji is also a novel that showcases the process of myth-making, and the political importance of how myths are constructed from fragments of history for particular purposes at particular junctures. In line with a Barthesian model of myth creation, in which an extant story is repeatedly evacuated of its contents so that it can be ideologically filled for the benefit of the context in which it is redeployed,[1] the myth of Lueji has surfaced in various guises and through various voices over the last four centuries.

As Valéria Borges Teixeira points out, prior to Pepetela's reconfiguration of Lueji's story, the Lunda queen was best known to a Portuguese-speaking audience through the *Etnographia e história tradicional dos povos da Lunda*, authored by Henrique de Carvalho,[2] a nineteenth-century colonial soldier whose worldview was coloured by the imperial prejudices of his time.[3] His account is replete with fetishistic etchings of Africans implicitly waiting to be civilized by a colonial regime in the midst of the Scramble for Africa. In other words, it has much more to do with the concerns of the Berlin Conference than with an objective historical account (if such a thing were ever possible).

Pepetela's choice of the Lueji myth as the basis for his novel stems back many years. In fact, he wanted to use the story of the Lunda queen as the basis for a novel from the 1960s, when he was working in the Centre for Angolan Studies, and helping to construct alternative, non-colonial versions of Angola's history.[4] During that undertaking, he came across multiple versions of the Lueji myth. In his novel, he adapts the myth's various strands considerably to explore in some depth the challenges faced by a woman as a leader — a concern he may have acquired in response to critiques about his depiction of Ondina in *Mayombe*.[5]

At first glance, Lueji's mythical story is not the most obvious choice from Angola's possible foundational narratives for such a project. A more famous and forceful example of a woman in a position of power is the story of Queen Ginga (or Nzinga), who featured prominently in post-independence Angola as a national heroine and example of seventeenth-century resistance to the Portuguese. There have, in fact, been multiple renditions of Ginga's story including novels by Manuel Pedro Pacavira and José Eduardo Agualusa.[6] She is also referenced as part of the melting-pot of national origins in Pepetela's preface to *Yaka*. A 2017 biography of the Mbundu queen by Linda Heywood compares her military prowess and political cunning to Elizabeth I and Catherine the Great, 'revealing how this Cleopatra of central Africa skillfully navigated — and ultimately transcended — the ruthless, male-dominated power struggles of her time'.[7]

Lueji's story is more ambivalent than Ginga's, which may help to explain Pepetela's preference for her as he fashions a narrative about the duplicitous nature of wielding power. Igor Cusack makes the point that both queens (historical and mythical) have been 'summoned to [the] task' of women placed in a 'backward look' of nationalist imaginations.[8] In contrast, he reminds us, males in nationalist narratives are projected as the future New Man, a stark dichotomy that casts women as historic material over which the male narrative of becoming can be written.

Pepetela undertakes part of that rewriting, and eschews charges that he re-inscribes the future-male/past-female binary, in part, through the form the novel takes. There are two story lines. One is four centuries in the past: the Lueji myth. The second involves a dance troop and, in particular, their lead dancer, Lu. The temporal frame of this strand is projected a decade into the future. Lu is re-enacting the story of Lueji, making it her own. The two story lines are initially distinct, with alternating sections, but gradually they become more fused as the temporal shift begins to occur mid-sentence.

Cusack reads the novel as contributing to the performative aspect of Angola's sense of self, by placing a retelling of the oral narrative accounts of the Lunda queen at the heart of its national identity and through Lu's interpretative performance of Lueji's reign. Retelling the story is part of the performative feeding into a creation of that identity. A key aspect of the future strand is how it consciously demonstrates the malleability of myths from the past. The myth of Lueji is open to Lu's artistic interpretation: she is not beholden to it but can make use of it. Likewise, Pepetela is selective in the choices he makes as he rewrites Lueji's story.

His 1990 novel is not the first time he has written about Lueji. In 1965, he was the co-author of the MPLA's *História de Angola*, and was responsible for its entry on the Lunda queen.[9] It was around this time he decided that should he ever have a daughter, he would name her Lueji, something he did when she was born in

January 1977. What intrigued him most as a writer was that, despite the multiple histories and myths in which Lueji appears, 'ninguém sabe o que se passou na Lunda naquela época, pode apenas haver conjecturas'[10] [no one knows what happened in Lunda at that time, there can only be speculation]. In other words, historical narrative is subject to imaginative leaps.

Pepetela as a writer of history in 1965 had participated in a process of recreating and reimagining Lueji as part of a conscious ideological, anti-colonial manoeuvre. By the time he published his novel, in 1990, she was no longer an instrument in the independence struggle but a potential example of female emancipation and of power's inevitably corrupting lure.

The choices Pepetela makes as he adapts the Lueji myth demonstrate his concerns in the late 1980s, when he spent over three years writing the novel. He has created his own mythology around the ordeals he endured during that process. He claims the roof over his bed collapsed during his writer's seclusion while working on *Lueji*, and also that his hands developed blisters that burst as he typed on an electric typewriter, delivering shocks to his oozing fingers. In public appearances, his reading of these trials is that the spirit of Lueji was disturbed by his delving into her past, and she wanted to make her presence felt.[11] It is doubtful that the rationalist, Marxist-trained sociologist Pepetela literally believes in the return of a myth's spirit. But as a writer, he did see the value of revisiting her story over a decade after independence, and that there was something unsettling but highly relevant about her at that particular moment in Angola's history.

For Phyllis Peres, *Lueji* is part of Pepetela's 'narrating an integral history',[12] in which the multiple ethnic identities constituting the nation have a valid contribution to make Angola's story. The fact that her story has multiple sources, often filtered through a colonizing gaze, implies for Cusack that the 'very process of adapting the various versions of the story and producing a new variant, and of recognizing in the course of the novel itself that other versions are possible, mimics what one might encounter in an oral version of the tale that is an ever-changing, evolving, ephemeral recitation of the myth'.[13] What is important for Cusack is not so much the multiple sources on which Pepetela draws — be they historical or mythical — but rather the fact that the author assists in the 'creation of a version of the myth of the origin of the modern state of Angola, as if providing a retrospective "ethnicity" for the whole nation'.[14]

Interestingly, given the strategy adopted in Pepetela's foreword in *Yaka*, in which the Angolan nation is seen to be formed of groups who originated beyond the borders of the modern state, many of the sources of the Lueji myth originate beyond Angola's frontiers, with written and oral accounts of Lueji weaving into the mythical narratives of peoples located in what is today the Democratic Republic of the Congo.[15] In other words, like the 'Yaka, Mbayaka, Jaga, Imbangala' brought to the fore at the beginning of *Yaka*, the myth of the Lunda queen has something of the exogenous about it, contributing once again to the sense that to be Angolan is not a question of provenance but more an issue of behaviour and belief. Furthermore, to be a leader in Angola, you should not have to be a man.

In most renditions of Lueji's myth, her lazy and drunk brothers are responsible for the death of her father. As Lueji tends him, he nominates her as his successor, with the understanding that she would operate as a womb, providing a son to succeed to the throne. Lueji's regency allows her to demonstrate formidable leadership skills, despite her youth. Her advisors — inherited from her father — enjoin her to marry in order to secure a stable succession, and she chooses Ilunga, the son of the king of the Luba. Lueji's decision to marry Ilunga is despite his provenance from a different tribe. In many versions of the myth, his arrival with more advanced military knowledge leads to the successful expansion of Lueji's dominions. In some versions of the myth, Lueji quickly becomes pregnant, and transfers ruling authority willingly over to Ilunga.[16] In others, she is unable to conceive children and Ilunga has to take a second wife.[17]

The myth is not particularly one of female agency (unlike Ginga's story, which is difficult not to read as an example of a woman who rises to the top against the odds), although Lueji does get a chance to rule. However, it is never in her own right but rather as a female stop-gap or placeholder between her father and her son — even if the 'son' who takes over in some versions of the myth is not actually hers. Nor is Lueji usually presented as desirous of power or ambitious. She accedes to it out of respect for her father and with the understanding that she will need his male advisors and a husband to take charge.

Pepetela's rendition of the Lueji myth challenges that depiction of a woman's womb in service of the past and the future, portraying an ambitious, complex and evolving queen who will not allow the fact that she is barren to get in the way of her authority. His challenge is not directed so much against history (as it was when he wrote about Lueji in the 1960s); rather, he targets post-independence Angola, where women continued to be excluded from positions of political power, and where the rhetoric of the revolution cast women in the role of a national matrix, whose worth was judged by the children they could bear.

Lueji marked a paradigm shift in how Pepetela crafted women characters. Several of his subsequent novels contain strong female protagonists. His 1995 *O desejo de Kianda* centres on the ambition and career of Carmina, an MPLA apparatchik, who, though disagreeable, at least portrays political power as potentially exercised by women. Like many of Pepetela's characters, she is a product of her circumstances, being forced to the take on the mantle of family leadership at an early age out of necessity, when her father dies, and her brothers reveal themselves to be inept. She then becomes the embodiment of the MPLA's transitions from paladin of Marxism to predatory free-market capitalist, as I shall discuss in the next chapter. In *Jaime Bunda e a morte do americano* (2003), Pepetela creates the character of Shirley — an African-American lesbian who serves US imperialism as a committed agent while exuding multiple labels of marginalized subalternity with a mixture of pride, expectation and cynicism. While neither characterization is particularly positive, both are complex, strong-willed and depicted as taking and owning their own decisions.

Lueji, in contrast, is a character who inspires a certain degree of sympathy in her reader, and is, to date, probably the strongest woman in Pepetela's work. Nearly all versions of the Lueji myth converge on one important point: she broke with established traditions in strategic ways (particular through her decision to marry outside her ethnicity). These choices shored up her position among the Lunda. As a result — and this is one of the key points Pepetela's novel will make — she gives birth to an empire even if she is physically unable to give birth to her successor.

In the novel, a young, innocent woman reluctantly takes the crown (or the *lukano*, as the emblem of royal prerogative — a bracelet made up of human tendons — is known) in the aftermath of the regicide of her father, Kondi, killed by her favourite older brother, Tchinguri, with whom she has had an incestuous relationship. On taking power, Lueji promises to protect traditions, and offers assurances that her possession of the *lukano* is purely transitory until she can provide an heir for Kondi. Her promise places her body at the centre of the plot — a narrative trope that echoes the deployment of Ondina's body in *Mayombe*. Lueji's worth is initially measured purely by the presumed ability of her womb to guarantee her father's perpetuity. However, she soon discovers that she enjoys the taste of power she has acquired, and becomes increasingly reluctant to cede the *lukano*. Lueji marks the point in Pepetela's work when women cease to be bounded by their biological materiality and become grounded in greater psychological depth. The portrayal of Lueji comes to transcend her embodiment. She becomes an agent of power. This transformation occurs against a backdrop of 'tradition' that, rather like MPLA rhetoric under Neto, limits female agency.

The meaning of tradition is a core theme with which the novel engages. Pepetela is interested in how traditions are used to justify actions, and how they are selected for particular purposes. For Pepetela, tradition is always something invented, and then reinvented, in a way signposted by Eric Hobsbawm and Terence Ranger in their seminal *The Invention of Tradition*.[18] Cultural production is all about the constant recreation of tradition, not its immobilization or perfect replication. For Pepetela, tradition tells us more about the moment in which the term is activated than the moment of its supposed origin. Like all origins in Pepetela, the origins of tradition are contingent and flexible. An appeal to tradition is more about inconsistencies overlooked than memories conserved or customs respected. Lueji's accession to the *lukano* signifies that process.

In the novel, the Lunda nobility, known as the Tubungo, decide to break with one of the most entrenched traditions, when they accept Lueji, a woman, as their ruler. In so doing, they are following her father Kondi's wishes and understand her position as transitory. Nevertheless, Pepetela presents the Tubungo's choice as a major disruption to their gender-normative practices. They justify their break with tradition because, paradoxically, they trust her alone to conserve tradition. In effect, they selectively deploy tradition as a soubriquet to protect their own interests against the danger a Tchinguri reign would pose for them.

The Tubungo fear Tchinguri not only because of the regicide he perpetrated, but because he has a project to eliminate their power by smashing them as a class. Lunda kings relied on their nobility to furnish them with an army. Tchinguri makes no secret of his intention to raise his own standing army. Pepetela's characterization of Tchinguri thus bestows on him all the attributes of a Machiavellian modern statesman. For Tchinguri, the only purpose of tradition is to accumulate power in the hands of the Head of State. Tradition is something in the service of power. If a tradition does not serve this purpose, it can be broken with impunity. Likewise, the elimination of potential rivals is a strategic necessity, devoid of any moral ambiguity. Tchinguri is well aware that the key to the efficient exercise of power is the king's military supremacy.

In contrast, Lueji initially subscribes to the nebulous concept of tradition, while overlooking the fact that it excludes her from holding the *lukano*. She respects her ancestors and is willing to rule in a temporary capacity in the name of the Tubungo and her deceased father. However, as the story develops, she begins to adopt the tactics suggested by her older brother, as a means of securing her position and destroying her rivals. The gradual fusion of her outlook with that of Tchinguri demonstrates the truth of her father's warning: 'o poder é um vício, adquire-se usando-o' [power is a vice, it is acquired by using it].[19]

As her taste for power grows, she reveals the degree to which she is much more than a woman's body. In some ways, the more she behaves like Tchinguri, the more she defeats Kondi's patriarchal claim over her body. Everything that Tchinguri stands for at the beginning of the novel — the destruction of the nobility, the creation of a royal army, the cynical use of tradition as a means of controlling others, meritocratic rights as opposed to aristocratic privilege, and the efficient and bureaucratic establishment of an empire — is achieved by and through Lueji by the end of the novel.

From her childhood, Lueji 'em tudo imitava o irmão mais velho' (p. 10) [imitated her eldest brother in everything]. Once in power, she follows a brand of Machiavellianism that 'lembrava Tchinguri' (p. 369) [brought Tchinguri to mind], in the words of Ndumba, a suitor whom she strategically seduces and then unceremoniously dumps once he has outlived his usefulness. Her seductiveness and the strategic use of her femininity ultimately distinguish her from her brother. Doubts about her ability to take up the *lukano* because she is a woman are dispelled on the day of her coronation by an aggressive display of femininity. 'Os seios nus de Lueji pareciam mais firmes, atirados provocantemente para a frente, se destacando do colar. O povo, antes duvidoso da força do novo chefe, viu neles um desafio que o tranquilizou' (p. 36) [Lueji's naked breasts seemed firmer, flung provocatively forward, standing out from her necklace. The people, previously doubtful of their new chief's force, saw in them a reassuring defiance]. From that moment onwards, Lueji begins to deconstruct the belief that 'o poder está concebido para os homens' (p. 37) [power is conceived for men], while admitting to herself that she will have to be 'mais esperta que eles' (p. 37) [smarter than they are].

Lueji's astuteness resides in knowing when to allow her opponents to fall into the trap of infantilizing her sex. Tchinguri reduces her to a child and can therefore never see the extent to which she is drawing on his own strategies. She beats her brother at his own game, by understanding more clearly who he is and which of his tactics to exploit, while he underestimates her, based solely on his preconceptions of gender.

Lueji's participation in the machinations of power challenges her destiny as a reproductive vassal. Her guile defines her as more cerebral than corporeal. Through her characterization, Pepetela gainsays the repeated relegation of the feminine to the realm of the bodily that predominated in the mythologies and ideologies of the MPLA movement. When Agostinho Neto spoke of creating conditions so 'that a woman shall not be afraid of having children, of educating her children',[20] and contrasted that aim with a position in which 'a man may feel that his future is secure, that he does not fear the future',[21] it set up, or rather reinforced, a gender binary in which the future was male and women were its womb.

In Pepetela's rendition of the Lueji myth, in contrast to the account Carvalho's *Etnographia e história tradicional dos povos da Lunda*, Lueji is barren. Pepetela's choice here is important. The one duty Lueji is incapable of fulfilling is biological motherhood. The child she passes off as her son, Yanvu, is borne by one of Lueji's relatives on her mother's side. Lueji's whole function as defined by the Tubungo, whose influence she gradually destroyed, was the production of an heir whose veins contained the blood of Kondi. The paradox is that, through Yanvu, tradition is ostentatiously restored through a male occupancy of Kondi's dynasty but secretly undermined as Yanvu is not biologically related to Kondi at all. The whole purpose of Lueji's transitional reign — the use of her uterus to guarantee her father's perpetuity — is publically performed as the *lukano* is transferred to Yanvu, but the reality is a mere performance. The integrity of tradition is left in tatters. Kondi's bloodline would have been better served with Tchinguri on the throne.

Despite the power she accumulates, Lueji's portrayal is ultimately tainted by failure. As the novel's narrator puts it, 'Lueji criou o Império e criou as condições da sua destruição. Só podia ser assim' (p. 483) [Lueji created the Empire and created the conditions for its destruction. It could be no other way]. The inevitability of her own fall, as she is reluctantly forced to hand over power to her 'son', leads to the narrator's final question, 'porquê culpá-la da sua humanidade?' (p. 483) [why blame her for her humanity?].

At the very moment of power transfer, Lueji's reign takes on a different dimension. Her rule becomes her own rather than a stop-gap between Kondi and his grandson. She becomes a queen in her own right: a woman who defied the patriarchal mandates of her father, and transformed the Lunda into an empire ruled by a leader who happened to be a woman. She did not provide a womb for future revolutionaries, but lead a revolution herself, in which she was able to take what she needed from the past to forge a very different reality in the world in which she lived.

While placing a woman in a position of power, and challenging post-independence Angola to countenance the same, *Lueji* delivers another stark message to 1990s Angola. The MPLA had been in power for fifteen years, against the backdrop of an increasingly brutal civil war. Post-1977, executive power had been consolidated in the hands of the presidency — a presidency no longer controlled by Agostinho Neto. Corruption was becoming an increasingly endemic problem, as

José Eduardo dos Santos developed an effective system of clientelism to solidify his grip on power — a power that was initially only meant to be a stop-gap. The novel suggests that political outcomes cannot necessarily be controlled. Movements — be they the Tubungo or the MPLA — are less able to control the direction of history than they like to think because power has a habit of taking on its own dynamics. The most potent message to emerge from the novel is that, although power needs to be kept in check, it will eventually escape those who think they possess it.

Lueji questions the rhetoric of tradition as a mechanism of privilege. It also questions the possibility of power being exercised differently in the hands of those who have not had access to it previously. Lueji — the stop-gap ruler — turns out to be just as ruthless as the alternative (Tchinguri), if not more so. She may be a woman, who deserves the chance to lead, but the greatest check on power is to ensure her reign comes to an end.

As Pepetela wrote *Lueji*, the greatest changes in the global order since the Second World War were taking place. With the collapse of the Berlin Wall in 1989, the tenets of the MPLA revolution were left bereft of their ideological base. Yet the movement was quickly able to reinvent itself, and retain power against the odds at the end of the Cold War. As Pepetela would go on to explore in some of his work in the next decade, that, in part, was down to understanding how power works, and being able to rupture rhetoric and ideology while providing a continuity in personnel.

Notes to Chapter 5

1. See Roland Barthes, *Mythologies* (Paris: Éditions du Seuil, 1957).
2. Henrique Augusto Dias de Carvalho, *Etnographia e história tradicional dos povos da Lunda* (Lisbon: Imprensa Nacional, 1890), pp. 60–112.
3. Valéria Maria Borges Teixeira, 'A ruptura com o discurso do colonizador em *Lueji (o nascimento dum império)*', in *Actas do IV Congresso Internacional da APLC-Relações Intraliterárias, Contextos Culturais e Estudos Pós-coloniais*, 3 vols (Évora: Universidade de Évora, 2001), I, 1–10.
4. From personal interview with author in 2002.
5. See Ana Paula Tavares, 'Contar Histórias', in *Lendo Angola*, ed. by Laura Cavalcante Padilha and Margarida Calafate Ribeiro (Porto: Afrontamento, 2008), pp. 39–50 (p. 42).
6. Manuel Pedro Pacavira, *Nzinga Mbandi* (Lisbon: Edições 70, c. 1979); José Eduardo Agualusa, *A Rainha Ginga e de como os africanos inventaram o mundo* (Lisbon: Quetzal, 2014).
7. Linda M. Heywood, *Njinga of Angola: Africa's Warrior Queen* (Cambridge, MA: Harvard University Press, 2017), quote available at <http://www.hup.harvard.edu/catalog.php?isbn=9780674971820> [accessed 27 March 2018].
8. Igor Cusack, 'Perfomance and the Mobilization of Identity in Pepetela's *Lueji. O Nascimento de um Império*', *Portuguese Studies*, 25.2 (2009), 169–81 (p. 174).
9. MPLA, *História de Angola* (Algiers: MPLA, 1965).
10. Interviewed by Aguinaldo Cristóvão, 'O escritor é um ditador no momento da escrita', União dos Escritores Angolanos website (2015) <http://www.ueangola.com/entrevistas/item/384-o-escritor-é-um-ditador-no-momento-da-escrita> [accessed 27 March 2018].
11. Pepetela gave a number of public lectures while visiting Rutgers University in 2002, in which he discussed the process of writing *Lueji*.
12. Phyllis Peres, *Transculturation and Resistance in Lusophone African Narrative* (Gainesville: University Press of Florida, 1997), p. 81.
13. Igor Cusack, p. 177.

14. Ibid., p. 179.
15. Ibid., p. 178.
16. Harold Scheub, 'Lueji Inherits her Father's Kingship', *A Dictionary of African Mythology* (Oxford: Oxford University Press, 2000), pp. 132–34.
17. Igor Cusack describes the various versions of the myth, and argues that Pepetela seems to follow the story as relayed by Duysters, a colonial administrator from Katanga, who was based in the Lunda court.
18. Eric Hobsbawm and Terence Ranger, *The Invention of Tradition* (Cambridge: Cambridge University Press, 1983).
19. Pepetela, *Lueji, o nascimento de um império* (Lisbon: Dom Quixote, 1990), p. 41. Subsequent page references given in the text.
20. A. Agostinho Neto, *Speeches* (Luanda: Department of Politico-Ideological Education, Propaganda and Information, 1980), pp. 47–48.
21. Ibid., p. 47.

CHAPTER 6

❖

The 1990s: Plus Ça Change

As the 1990s progressed, and the full extent of communism's global collapse became apparent, Pepetela began to write novels that dealt explicitly with disillusionment. In 1992, he published *A geração da utopia*. It tackled head-on the betrayal by those who had been at the forefront of the liberation movement. Fernando Arenas reads it as the first novel 'to offer a sustained, probing, heart-wrenching, as well as in-depth critique of the postcolonial national project as executed by the MPLA'.[1] In many ways, the novel continued more explicitly the critiques of why Marxist-Leninism was doomed to fail that were raised in *Mayombe*, and even in *Yaka*. As already discussed, both earlier novels had pointed out parallels between the revolution's shortcomings and colonial legacies. For example, the MPLA's use of 'autocrítica' is equated with the Catholic confessional in *Mayombe*, as an easy-to-manipulate exemption mechanism for the corrupt and unrepentant,[2] while Olívia's near-erotic fervour for Che Guevara in *Yaka* is linked to a prior passion for Jesus Christ, and is Pepetela's way of critiquing the cult of personalities.

The preoccupation with the same power relations masquerading under different ideological façades resurfaces throughout Pepetela's work. Anibal/Sábio, for example, in *A geração da utopia*, is a hero of the liberation struggle who condemns the post-independence government for assuming the role and methods vacated by the Church:

> O regime é como o Papa, nunca erra porque nunca errou e por isso nunca errará. Devemos ter confiança cega, Fé, nos dirigentes, nos Partidos, eles são como Deus. O curioso é que as pessoas não percebem que estes partidos ateus foram os que mais copiaram os ensinamentos da Igreja.[3]

> [The regime is like the pope, it never errs because it has never erred and thus it will never err. We must have blind confidence, Faith, in our leaders, our parties, they are like God. It's interesting that people don't realize that these atheist parties were the ones that most copied the Church's teachings.]

These are sanctioned continuities that stood in the pathway of the MPLA's aim of creating a truly revolutionary New Man. The difference by the time Pepetela writes *A geração da utopia* is that the dialectical structure present in earlier work is on the wane. The revolution's failings are less frequently juxtaposed with the positive agenda it furthers. There is no longer a synthesis projecting hope and belief in the ability of Angolans to bring something qualitatively different and paradigm-shifting into being. Instead, the crass mediocrity of the self-serving comes to the narrative foreground.

David Brookshaw argues that, in *A geração da utopia*, 'the ideal which sparked revolt against colonial rule is lost before that independence is accomplished'.[4] Equating one of the novel's protagonists, Vítor, with *Mayombe*'s political commissar, João, Brookshaw suggests that in the latter portrayal, João/Vítor becomes 'the representative of the links between the Party and the new, unbridled capitalistic opportunities that individuals can grasp under the protection of the state'.[5]

The way the post-communist market functioned to the benefit of socialist-era elites became one of Pepetela's primary concerns from the 1990s onwards. These elites, predominantly based in the nation's capital, are the target of his depictions in novels like *Jaime Bunda, agente secreto* (2001) and *O tímido e as mulheres* (2013). In them, Luanda society provides the backdrop to Pepetela's potent critique that repeatedly points to the corruption in which risk is socialized among the most vulnerable in society and profit privatized among those with links to the ruling party. The rapidity with which Angola morphed 'from Afro-Stalinism to Petro-diamond Capitalism', as the title of David Hodges's seminal book puts it, may have surprised some.[6] Prescience about the change, however, was always decipherable in Pepetela's work. What many did not foresee was a peace process in Angola that would quickly fail.

The fall of the Berlin Wall removed the Cold-War excuse for the continuation of the civil conflict. As a result, a range of international powers made a concerted effort to bring the conflict to an end. As part of that process, the year *A geração da utopia* was published (1992) saw the first multiparty elections in the history of Angola. They were mandated by the Bicesse peace accords signed the previous year. Up until that point, the conflict had provided convenient cover for MPLA incompetence and corruption. The UNITA alternative was cast as beyond the pale, led by an unstable and capricious autocrat, Jonas Savimbi, whose erratic behaviour contrasted with the seemingly mild, bland manner of the MPLA's José Eduardo dos Santos. Dos Santos would continue as Angola's president until 2017, when his chosen successor and former defence secretary, João Lourenço, took over as head of state, although dos Santos did not immediately relinquish his control of the party.

When dos Santos became president in 1979, he was initially a compromise, stop-gap candidate, acceptable to all factions within the MPLA because they foolishly assumed he would be a malleable puppet. At first, he continued the official line that cast the MPLA as a vanguard party through much of the 1980s. At the same time, the choices dos Santos was taking, including where to educate his children and how to structure Angola's oil economy, demonstrated a clear lack of ideological commitment to the tenets of the party well before the fall of the Berlin Wall.[7]

Dos Santos was born in Sambizanga, Luanda, in 1942. He became involved in the anti-colonial struggle in the late 1950s, fleeing in late 1961 to Leopoldville to evade a crackdown by the Portuguese security apparatus following an uprising against colonial rule. There, he coordinated the youth wing of the MPLA. In 1963, dos Santos moved with the help of a student grant to Baku, in the ex-Soviet Union, where he qualified in 1969 as a petroleum engineer. While a student, he became the leader of the Organization of Angolan Students in the USSR. He also married Tatiana Kukanova, a Soviet chess champion who was a student of geology, although it took them seven years to acquire the necessary permission to marry, an indication of the reluctance of Soviet authorities to foster inter-racial relationships.[8] Tatiana gave birth to Isabel José dos Santos in Baku in 1973, while José Eduardo dos Santos was away fighting in the independence struggle in the Cabinda enclave of Angola, alongside Pepetela. He chose the name Isabel in honour of his sister, with whom he had been very close in his childhood, and who had taken care of him while his mother was out working long hours.[9]

Dos Santos's daughter went on to become Africa's richest woman, and there are certainly echoes of her and her father's personalities satirically portrayed in *Predadores*, as I shall discuss in the next chapter. However, the level of the dos Santos's family enrichment at the expense of the Angolan state was not yet so grotesquely obvious, although the clues were there to be read in the 1990s. The nation, however, was more concerned with achieving peace, after nearly three decades of conflict — first against colonialism and then in a struggle that pitched Angolan against Angolan.

As Justin Pearce points out, 'UNITA and the MPLA both originated as anti-colonial movements, and echoes of anti-colonialism remained in the ideologies of both sides for decades after the Portuguese had left. With the real coloniser gone, the anti-colonial movements turned anti-colonialism against each other'.[10] The MPLA leadership saw UNITA as little more than a servant of South African racism, and an agent of Western imperialism. For UNITA, 'the MPLA was led by the mixed-race offspring of the erstwhile colonisers and had become the tool of the godless Cuban invaders'.[11]

By 1990, the MPLA had jettisoned the pretence of Marxist-Leninism and officially become a social democratic party. With the departure of the Cubans, a peace deal could be brokered that paved the way for the 1992 elections. When the MPLA appeared to be on course to win the elections, UNITA, previously assured by its allies in Washington of a democratic victory based on an erroneous assessment of Angola's demographics, refused to accept the result. A second phase of the civil war broke out, no longer underpinned by Cold War politics but clearly one of its lasting aftermaths. The war only ended in 2002 when the MPLA regime crushed UNITA militarily and assassinated Savimbi. Rarely, in post-independence sub-Saharan Africa, has a civil war resulted in such an outright victory for one side.

For over a decade following the fall of the Berlin Wall, post-communism in Angola continued to be characterized by violence and a state of exception that had initially been triggered by disputes and distrust between distant superpowers around the time of Angolan independence. The manner of the MPLA's eventual victory meant that the movement did not need to come to any accommodation with its opponents. Its leadership — and most particularly its president — was more powerful than it had ever been at any point since independence, including in the aftermath of 1977.

The regime embarked on a process of what Ricardo Soares de Oliveira terms 'illiberal peacebuilding',[12] in which MPLA elites consolidated their control in a way that flew in the face of the liberal norms underpinning the demands of Angolan civil society in the late 1990s. Peace would be presented not as 'a matter of reconciliation between adversaries' but rather as 'the work of the MPLA and more specifically of President dos Santos'.[13] After the final peace accord, dos Santos was praised as 'the architect of peace, a formulation the state media invoked repeatedly in the years that followed'.[14]

Pepetela had, to some extent, foreseen the behaviour that would increasingly characterize the MPLA elites as the civil war resumed and party apparatchiks took advantage of a state of exception and generalized violence to line their own pockets. He followed the disillusionment of *A geração da utopia* with a caustic novella, *O desejo de Kianda* (translated into English by Luís Mitras as *The Return of the Water Spirit*). The novella is set against the backdrop of the 1992 elections, and the subsequent return to civil war. Its narrative conceit is a series of collapsing buildings near Luanda's Kinaxixi Square. The buildings fall without injuring anyone but their former inhabitants are left without material possessions. Given the architectural high modernism of the socialist project for Luanda, it is easy to read the collapsing buildings as a metaphor for the crumbling ideological vision of the MPLA.

Laura Cavalcante Padilha points to the novella's 'desconstrução paródica'[15] [parodic deconstruction]. She reads it as an instance of Angolan post-modernism. In light of Frederic Jameson's equation of post-modernism with the logic of neo-liberalism,[16] the novella's aesthetics parallel the monumental change Angola appeared to undergo in the 1990s as the charade of free-market capitalism swept aside the logic of the planned economy, with the full and enthusiastic approval of the MPLA regime. The pace of change accelerated with the end of the civil war a decade later and the boom in oil prices that allowed for major advances in the regime's recast project for the nation. *O desejo de Kianda*'s importance lies, once again, in Pepetela's prescience. What he depicts in his extremely parodical characterizations of 1995 was, in retrospect, a vision of what was to come in spades over the coming decade.

The novella narrates the ideological shift of one of Pepetela's most colourful protagonists, Carmina. From an early age, she reveals a propensity to dominate those around her. The death of her father allows her to occupy his position in an essentially patriarchal set up at the age of twelve. Her control of her mother and siblings is an early sign of her ability to adapt circumstances to favour her acquisition of power. In the Luanda of her youth, that meant espousing the virtues of Marx. As the novel progresses, Carmina begins to use Marx to justify her application of the market economy. Challenged by her hapless husband, João Evangelista, about the corrupt selling of state assets, a process that 'descapitaliza o Estado, o património de todos'[17] [that'll make the State poorer, and we'll be the poorer for it[18]], Carmina declares:

> O mais velho Marx explicou há bué de tempo. Para se criar os empresários, alguém tem de perder capital a favor deles. E sempre é melhor ser o Estado, assim é menos sensível, do que expropriar ou roubar directamente os cidadãos. Não decidimos ir para a economia do mercado? Então, alguém tem de pagar, nesta vida não se multiplicam pães por milagre. (p. 24)

[that old Marx explained it all ages ago. To create a business class someone has to lose money to them. How's this class going to make money? And it's always better if it's the State that's losing the money, instead of expropriating or stealing directly from citizens. Didn't we decide to move forward towards a market economy? So someone's got to pay. In real life one can't multiply the fish and the loaves]. (p. 17)

By the end of the novel, Carmina's transition is complete, as she rapaciously becomes a member of that new post-Berlin Wall business class, and even contemplates trading arms for profit.

One of the consistent messages to emerge in Pepetela's work is that, with each ideological shift, the logic of previous paradigms reasserts itself. In Carmina's case, her success as a member of the emerging capitalist class rests on her prior connections with the socialist state, and her willingness to exploit the opportunities of apparent chaos, including the return to civil war. At the same time, she mimics the mores of the colonial era, obliging the ever-changing domestic servants in her house to bear just one name, Joana, thus avoiding the inconvenience of having to learn their actual names, and subordinating their individuality to a functionality within her power structure.

Portuguese colonial mistresses were apocryphally so demanding and discarding of their domestic help that they neither had the time nor the inclination to learn their phonologically difficult names, preferring, so the stereotype goes, to brand them all with one simple Christian name. In Carmina's case, the point is not the unpronounceability of her servants' names, but rather a signalling of the persistence of power structures in Angola that began in the colonial era, were not extinguished during official Marxist-Leninism, and have resurfaced in the crass discursive practice of neo-liberal capitalism. Even the name of the import-export company Carmina establishes to trade in arms and exploit the bargain-basement sell-off of state assets in the name of globalization, 'Ultramar', harks back to the colonial era, when Angola was the 'ultramar' [overseas] to a distant metropolis, a nostalgic association of which she is well aware and even hopes to exploit for profit.

For Grant Hamilton, the speed of Carmina's metamorphosis — representing the MPLA leadership's transformation into 'profit capitalists' — reveals 'the fact that political ideology is a less potent force than that expressed by a particular organization of power. After all, it is the will to reorganize power that explains both the anti-colonial struggle in Angola and the inevitability of the following civil war'.[19] He continues: 'ideology, it seems, will always fall casualty to the organization of power'.[20] For Hamilton, 'the organization of power determines the way in which people think and act'.[21] Power, as I have repeatedly argued, is always at the centre of Pepetela's critiques. *O desejo de Kianda*'s treatment of power is particularly salient because of the specificity of its time and place — Luanda in the 1990s — precisely the moment at which the structures of power change the rhetoric in play, but crucially not the players. *O desejo de Kianda* exposes the increasing rift between a small class that benefited from the unbridled capitalist opportunities they gained in the 1990s because of privileged connections with the formerly socialist state, and a burgeoning underclass. That underclass, as well as bearing the brunt of the return to civil war and the increasingly destabilizing effect it had on rural areas, was plunged into destitution because of the corrupt privatization of state assets.

The state no longer pretended to have plans that included the provision of basic needs for the masses. Instead, Angola had entered the era of the 'entrepreneur' or 'empresário', as Carmina styles herself, because 'capitalista' or 'agente económico' [economic agent] still bore the stigma of the rhetoric of socialism. When there is a move in the Angolan parliament, to which Carmina belongs, to prevent the people's representatives from holding other jobs on the side, Carmina's reaction is furious:

> Cambada de incapazes, querem ser políticos profissionais, viver do salário miserável de deputados? Cultivar a miséria como virtude, armados em franciscanos de meia tigela. Como se isso os elevasse aos olhos do povo. O povo respeita só os ricos e poderosos, ainda não perceberam? (p. 69)
>
> [A bunch of incompetent idiots who want to be professional politicians, and live off a miserable Member of Parliament's salary? Do these half-baked Franciscans want to nurture misery as though it's a virtue? As if this would make the people think better of them. The people only respect the rich and powerful. Haven't they got it yet?]. (p. 56)

Once again, Pepetela draws religious analogies. But his characters no longer act out altruistic virtue, cloaking a national revolution in the rhetoric Catholic self-sacrifice. Instead, agents of power, like Carmina, now feel they can dispense with pretence and be openly contemptuous of the people whom they once purported to serve.

So what, if anything, is left of the revolutionary spirit, in Pepetela's work from the 1990s? Did the fall of the Berlin Wall leave him without any hope that a progressive agenda could be pursued in Angola? Were we, as Francis Fukuyama hastily claimed, at the End of History?[22] Was Pepetela suggesting that, in the wake of communism's demise, neo-liberalism was the only game in town?

Pepetela has always written in the spirit of idealism, informed by the need to critique in order to perfect. When the revolutionary project seemed viable in the 1970s and early 1980s, his writing pointed to its shortcomings precisely because of his commitment to it. As the revolution receded to an ever more distant, utopian horizon, his work became more humorous. While *A geração da utopia* seems at times a little despondent and certainly expresses disillusionment with those charged with bringing about revolutionary change, *O desejo de Kianda* is the first of several of Pepetela's works in which satire and wit expose the vulnerabilities of the human condition. Against the backdrop of the reader's smirks, alternative possibilities to a neo-liberal globalization are explored, while the pusillanimous nature of the nation's leaders is parodied. In other word, Pepetela begins to use laughter to explore alternatives to an unpalatable status quo.

O desejo de Kianda makes clear that Angola's self-serving leadership — the vanguard Pepetela once defended — is primarily responsible for choosing a course of national inequality. Where, in *Lueji*, one of the lessons to be drawn is that power corrupts any leader, no matter their provenance or intentions, and therefore reigns must be limited, O desejo de Kianda posits an altogether more anarchistic line: if leaders cannot be trusted with power, dispense with the leaders.

The character of Honório, João's friend in the novel, exemplifies this position. He is caught in an act of minor corruption because corruption in the new Angola is the only way to survive. And yet, the system moves against him, and he is threatened with prison. As the narrator puts it, 'Pobre é tão pobre que nem roubar sabe, é logo apanhado' (p. 92) [The poor are so poor that even when they steal they are poor at it — they get caught in no time (p. 78)]. In other words, while corruption has become the only way to succeed, it is also the reserve of the rich and powerful. It is not a modus operandi the privileged are willing to share.

Prior to his fall from grace, Honório had always believed in the system:

> Honório sempre fora servidor exemplar, nos tempos em que havia sábados vermelhos, era o primeiro no trabalho voluntário. Primeiro membro da Organização de Defesa Popular da empresa, até mereceu um elogio por ter apanhado um ladrão a tentar levar mercadorias. Convertido à nova filosofia com as mudanças políticas, era um militante da democracia e da tolerância. Sempre fiel ao mesmo partido, o de Carmina. (p. 93)

> [Honório had always been an example to others. During those days when there were Red Saturdays, he would be the first to volunteer to work. He was the first to join the company's People's Defence Organization, and he had received praise for catching a thief who was trying to steal company goods. Converted to the new philosophy as a result of the political changes, he preached democracy and tolerance. Always faithful to the same political party, Carmina's]. (p. 78)

Despite this, he will lose everything: his wife, his home and all his belongings, and earn the contempt of Carmina and her party in the process. Angola in the 1990s no longer needs his belief or commitment. His class of idealists has become an irrelevance to the future. The only thing left for him is to join an increasingly angry mob, who initially revert to the language of the revolution, crying out against the 'cambada de burgueses, ladrões do povo, ainda havemos de vos fusilar' (p. 96) [band of middle-class prigs, robbers of the people, we'll have you shot by a firing squad yet (p. 81)].

Their anger intensifies as the population's relative and absolute poverty increases, and 'as pessoas importantes tinham carros de luxo, de vidros fumados, ninguém lhes via a cara, passavam por nós e talvez nem olhassem para não se incomodarem com o feio espectáculo da miséria' (p. 100) [important people had luxury cars with smoked glass. No one ever saw their faces. They drove past and perhaps they didn't even look so as not to have their consciences made uneasy by the spectacle of all that misery (pp. 84–85)].

Ultimately, the people's protest takes the form of nudity — a spectacle of abjection in which their nakedness is a metonym for their generalized condition. As Honório, who participates in the movement puts it, 'É a nova moda do Kinaxixi. E está a pegar. Os desalojados do Kinaxixi protestam contra o governo que não faz nada por eles, lançando o nu como traje nacional, o único que está de acordo com o nível de vida do povo. Já nem de tanga se pode andar, a tanga é um luxo para burguês' (pp. 110–11) [It's the new fashion in Kinaxixi. It's taking on. The homeless in Kinaxixi are protesting against a government that does nothing for them. Nakedness is our new national garb, the one that's in accordance with the standard of living of our people. We can't even walk around in a loincloth. A loincloth is a middle-class luxury (p. 94)]. The protestors' nakedness offends the false morality of Carmina and her social class, in a newly defined structure in which there are those who have everything, and those who are left with nothing, not even their underpants. The key aspect of the protestors' movement is that the naked are the ones who take on the act of defining the new class structure, and they will soon pass to a point where they will use nakedness as a social leveller. Like their colonized forebears, the Angolan population is oppressed by a class enabled by a corrupt state. As Grant Hamilton argues, 'the people's collective abandonment of the state', suggested by the actions of the naked protestors, 'is the only significant means by which they can take charge of the production of meaning'.[23]

What it means to be Angolan can no longer be the preserve of a discredited state. For Hamilton, 'in writing the truths of a nation, Pepetela shows that a truly revolutionary Angola — an Angola "yet-to-come" — can only be born from the practices of a people who feel the necessity to invent themselves in the process of a new and urgent struggle against the post-colonial state'.[24] Like the colonial state before it, the post-colonial state has become the source of oppression, and the practices of the MPLA learned too much from the elitism of the Estado Novo. The vanguard became a class of oppressors.

For the character of Honório, who refuses to accept any mantle of leadership of the essentially anarchistic naked protestors, nakedness is a social leveller. He warns 'vamos começar a despir as pessoas que passam nas ruas' (p. 111) [we're going to start taking off the clothes of the people who walk around in the streets (p. 95)]. For Honório, the spontaneous protests that take hold on Luanda's streets as the novella draws to a conclusion are a way of regaining a truly nationalist project — a collective sense of national self that was somehow lost to the former vanguard party with its imported theories and flawed methodologies. If restored, a collective spirit could change the nation's destiny for the better: 'Estamos a criar História. Chega de copiar fórmulas do estrangeiro, inventemos os nossos próprios métodos de luta' (p. 115) [We are creating history because we are inventing our own ways. It's time to stop copying our formulas from overseas. We have to invent our own methods for the struggle (p. 99)]. The agent of that history is no longer, in Pepetela, one formed from above, versed in European theories and adept at making perpetually deferred promises. If there is to be a revolution, it needs to be spontaneous and horizontal, not directed and vertical.

So, to return to an earlier question, is there any hope left in 1990s Angola for Pepetela? *O desejo de Kianda* suggests that there is still hope — but no longer in heroic forms. It no longer rises from *Mayombe*'s supermen or *Yaka*'s ideological commitment to the discredited theories of a European age. Nor does hope lie in the leadership of one person like Lueji. Hope is born as a collective and organic entity, in which the constituent parts, like Honório, are flawed and fragile. Together, they are strong because they reinforce a seemingly lost sense of justice and human decency. One of the most potent messages to emerge from *O desejo de Kianda* is that the collective can no longer put its trust in a national leadership.

Pepetela published *O desejo de Kianda* in 1995, three years after the efforts to end Angola's civil war floundered and the country was once more plagued by a vicious conflict. Its damning portrayal of the small-mindedness of the MPLA elites was still tempered by the spectre of a possible UNITA government. MPLA corruption was preferable to UNITA brutality, to Pepetela's urban mindset. However corrupt Carmina becomes, there is still a space for her redemption in the novel. She could conceivably join the naked protest. In the final pages of the novel, her home will be reduced to rubble too, bringing her down to the same level as Honório.

Ten years later, Pepetela published *Predadores*, a novel that takes up *O desejo de Kianda*'s critique of the MPLA's stewardship of the Angolan state. The difference in 2005 was that the civil war had been brought to a definitive end, and UNITA had been eviscerated as an effective political and military force. As a result, and as we shall see in the next chapter, there was no longer any restraint in Pepetela's portrayal of the MPLA leadership: they had become rotten to the core, and were beyond redemption.

Notes to Chapter 6

1. Fernando Arenas, *Lusophone Africa: Beyond Independence* (Minneapolis: Minnesota University Press, 2011), p. 168.
2. A similar equation is repeated in *O desejo de Kianda* (Lisbon: Dom Quixote, 1995), p. 23.
3. Pepetela, *A geração da utopia* (Lisbon: Dom Quixote, 1992), p. 231.
4. David Brookshaw, 'Narration and Nation-Building: The Angolan Novels of Pepetela', in *Fiction in the Portuguese-speaking World: Essays in Memory of Alexandre Pinheiro Torres*, ed. by Charles M. Kelley (Cardiff: University of Wales Press, 2000), pp. 107–16 (p. 111).
5. Ibid., p. 111.
6. David Hodges, *From Afro-Stalinism to Petro-diamond Capitalism* (Bloomington: Indiana University Press, 2001).
7. Isabel dos Santos was educated at Saint Paul's School in London. For more on the way in which President dos Santos set up an oil sector that bypassed the Angolan state, see Ricardo Soares de Oliveira, *Magnificent and Beggar Land: Angola since the Civil War* (London: Hurst, 2015).
8. Filipe S. Fernandes, *Isabel dos Santos: segredos e poder do dinheiro* (Alfragide: Casa das Letras, 2015), p. 29.
9. Ibid., p. 27.
10. Justin Pearce, *Political Identity and Conflict in Central Angola, 1975–2002* (Cambridge: Cambridge University Press, 2015), p. 13.
11. Ibid., p. 13.
12. Ricardo Soares de Oliveira, 'Illiberal Peacebuilding in Angola', *Journal of Modern African Studies*, 49.2 (June 2011), 287–314.
13. Justin Pearce, *Political Identity*, p. 165.
14. Ibid., p. 165.
15. Laura Cavalcante Padilha, *Novos pactos, outras ficções: ensaios sobre literaturas afro-luso-brasileiras* (Porto Alegre: EDIPUCRS, 2002), p. 327.
16. Frederic Jameson, *Postmodernism, or, the Cultural Logic of Late Capitalism* (Durham, NC: Duke University Press, 1991).
17. Pepetela, *O desejo de Kianda* (Lisbon: Dom Quixote, 1995), p. 24. Subsequent page references given in the text.
18. Pepetela, *Return of the Water Spirit*, trans. by Luís R. Mitras (Oxford: Heinemann, 2002), p. 17. Subsequent page references given in the text.

19. Grant Hamilton, 'Pepetela's Proposal: Desire and Anarchy in *The Return of the Water Spirit*', *African Identities*, 11.4 (2013), 343–52 (p. 345).
20. Ibid., p. 345.
21. Ibid.
22. Francis Fukuyama, *The End of History and the Last Man* (London: Hamish Hamilton, 1992).
23. Hamilton, p. 344.
24. Ibid.

CHAPTER 7

Failed Fathers, Phallic Futures and Commodified Children: The Dehumanization of Post-War Angola

In 2005, three years after the end of Angola's civil war, Pepetela felt 'a sense of obligation' to write *Predadores*.[1] The novel centres on the Caposso family, and particularly VC (the self-styled Vladimiro Caposso) who, like Alexandre Semedo from *Yaka* and Baltazar Van Dum from *A gloriosa família*, is characterized by mediocrity. As Fernando Arenas puts it, Vladimiro Caposso is 'an archetype of mediocrity, itself the product of systematic political opportunism'.[2]

The novel narrates the rise and fall of Vladimiro, in an anachronic series of chapters stretching from November 1974 — in the run-up to Angolan independence — until December 2004, shortly before the book's publication. As such, it covers the then lifespan of Angola as an independent nation, and reflects on the extent to which the promise of one of Africa's most resource-rich countries was squandered by a state-sanctioned pusillanimity incommensurate with the lofty ideals embodied in MPLA revolution-era rhetoric. The book begins in 1992, the year in which *O desejo de Kianda*'s action is also primarily set. *Predadores*'s first chapter, dated to September 1992, recounts Caposso's killing of his unfaithful lover, Maria Madalena. The episode represents a point in time when certain cadres in the MPLA realized they could act with impunity.

In the legislative elections of September 1992, the MPLA claimed 54% of the vote. The results of the presidential elections, though requiring a second round, strongly favoured the MPLA candidate and incumbent president, José Eduardo dos Santos. UNITA cried foul, and both sides quickly resumed a war footing. The tensions culminated in what became known as the Halloween Massacre of UNITA supporters around the country, as the MPLA unleashed the frustrations of violent elements among its supporters over three days at the end of October.

Several prominent members of the opposition were assassinated, including UNITA's then vice-president Jeremias Kalandula Chitunda, who had been sent to Luanda, supposedly to negotiate the terms of the second round of the presidential election. The country quickly slipped back into civil war. The resumption of

Angola's conflict no longer had the ideological cover of a Cold War proxy-dispute: it was now brazenly about exclusive control over the nation's resources. As Pepetela ably captures through Vladimiro Caposso's voting preferences, support for the MPLA was now firmly rooted in clientelism and had little to do with political commitment.

The opening scene of *Predadores* does not appear to be relevant to the subsequent narrative. In some ways, it reflects a narrative trope in Pepetela's 2001 parody of Luanda's self-importance *Jaime Bunda, agente secreto*, where a dead girl's body triggers the story and yet seems to be tangential to the plot. However, like the dead body in *Jaime Bunda*, Maria Madalena's death alongside her lover, some 'Toninho' or other, highlights the corruption at the heart of Luanda's society. Vladimiro murders Maria Madalena primarily because he knows he can.

Pepetela chooses to begin in the approximate chronological middle of the story, selecting a moment when Vladimiro's mediocre hubris is at its height. He will end the story with the Caposso clan's fortunes on the wane in 2004, a year in which Vladimiro contemplates another killing. This time his target is Bernardino Chipengula, the troublesome head of a human rights organization, DECTRA, which seeks to protect access to traditional grazing pastures against the owners, including Vladimiro, of corruptly privatized land. The contrast between the two incidents is stark. In the first, Vladimiro's murder of Maria Madalena is almost banal and inconsequential. He implicates UNITA in her homicide, showing himself adept at riding political currents. In the second incident, however, Chipengula is not murdered by Vladimiro; instead, the Capossos are forced to reach an agreement with the traditional cattle herders whose land they have appropriated. The agreement does not signal that equality and respect for traditional rights has suddenly flourished in Angola but, rather, that Vladimiro's usefulness within the power structure has run its course.

The novel astutely observes how mediocrity is co-opted by power and, in so doing, cancels out the image of a man capable of riding a political tide. That initial image of Vladimiro as astute gives way to a subtler portrait, in which he is merely a pawn (something that becomes increasingly apparent, despite his delusions of being a self-made man). Crucially, Pepetela never portrays unsavoury characters like Vladimiro as victims, and yet, he does show how expendable they are and, to a certain extent, how they are created by a structure whose logic dehumanizes.

In *Predadores*, Pepetela rails against that dehumanization. In some ways, it has been a recurrent concern of his narratives — to show how the weaknesses that make us human play into and nurture the power structures that create us, and how those same structures owe us no loyalty, and will ultimately discard us. His true heroes in his post-war narratives, characters like Nacib and Sebastião in *Predadores*, are flawed but never wholly submit to the logic of power — and that refusal to submit to power's logic is the source of their heroism.

Sebastião, who was once Vladimiro's friend and tried desperately to educate him in the Marxist ideology of the independence-era MPLA, ends up imprisoned for pointing out MPLA hypocrisy. Despite his incarceration and the party's attempts to intimidate him, he never gives up on the ideals that led him to support the MPLA in the first place. Sebastião's 2004 understanding of what communism meant and still means mirrors Pepetela's own evolution on the ideology and is worthy of full citation:

> Nunca fui [comunista], não sabia muito bem o que isso era no fundo. Julgava ser e julgava saber. Aliás, proclamava isso aos quatro ventos. Só mais tarde descobri, aquele comunismo que eu seguia, aquelas ideias generosas de todos iguais e ninguém acima do outro, não existia em parte nenhuma do mundo, era tudo uma tremenda mentira. No entanto, as generosas ideias de solidariedade para com os outros, não pretender explorar ninguém, lutar para que todos os angolanos tenham oportunidades semelhantes na vida independentemente do que foram os pais, essas ideias ainda são as minhas. Se isso é comunismo, tudo bem, assumo.[3]

> [I was never [a communist]. At heart, I didn't really know what that meant. I thought I was and I thought I knew. In fact, I shouted it out to the four corners of the globe. Only later did I realize that the communism I followed, those generous ideas of everyone's equal and no one's above anyone else, didn't exist anywhere in the world, it was all one big fat lie. Even so, generous ideas of solidarity with others, of not trying to take advantage of anyone, of fighting for equal opportunities for all Angolans regardless of who their parents were, these are still my ideas. If that's communism, ok, I come out as communist.]

The key characteristic that makes Sebastião one of Pepetela's few heroes is the evolution of his ethical compass. His is an understated heroism that tries to bring a shared humanity back into the national foreground. He never enriches himself despite being capable and articulate. He is one of the counterpoints that offer a glimmer of hope against the ominous closing line of the novel, articulated after Jonas Savimbi's death and the end of civil hostilities — 'Nunca mais?' (p. 380) [Never again?]. That interrogation implies the nation could plunge back into conflict. The threat is no longer premised on the clash of two self-serving groups of narcissists — the MPLA and UNITA — but rather by the ingrained inequality that has systematically been fostered in Angola, and which the novel graphically depicts.

Foremost in Pepetela's critique is the rampant capitalism whose rise is portrayed not as a meritocracy that selects and rewards the most gifted, but rather as a cancerous mechanism that proliferates in the absence of ethical constraints. Periodically, unrestrained capitalism sacrifices those it uses (such as Vladimiro Caposso) to ensure its continued unfettered growth. And as Pepetela depicts in *Predadores*, predatory capitalism metastasized in the immediate aftermath of the civil war.

The fundamental question Pepetela's portrayal of the rise of capitalism in Angola raises is one of agency. Are there subjectivities in a system of rampant capitalism, able to make decisions with responsibility for those decisions, or can every character ultimately be cast as a victim of their role in a macro-structure beyond their control? The answer resides in those counter-balancing characters to the Caposso family, like Sebastião and Nacib, who offer alternative visions for what Angola might become.

In particular, Nacib Germano de Castro contrasts with the Capossos. His first name points to a popular soap opera from the 1970s that captivated Angola and was based on the Brazilian author Jorge Amado's *Gabriela, Cravo e Canela*. Nacib wants to construct something in and for Angola. His love for Caposso's eldest daughter, Mireille, is doomed by her superficiality and serves as a marker that there can be no reconciliation between the Angola that the Capossos represent, and the society Nacib envisions. It is far from clear, at the end of the novel, which Angola stands the greater chance of survival. However, only Nacib's vision of the nation might avoid future conflict triggered by worse levels of inequality than those colonialism enacted. Like colonialism, the speculative and unproductive form of capitalism with which Caposso engages will, in Pepetela's mindset, eventually lead to a violent revolt.

Nacib is always interested in the practical implications of what he learns. He aims to marry theory and practice. Although his father is eager for him to follow in his footsteps as a carpenter, Nacib is more interested in metal. He owes his middle name, Germano, to another lusophone source beyond Angola, his Cape Verdean godfather, who helps him study engineering. He eventually wins a grant to do research in the USA. His dream is to invent an ecological car — a symbol of conserving resources in oil-rich Angola. In contrast to the self-serving Capossos, Nacib saves up to pay for restorative plastic surgery for his childhood friend Kasseke.

Kasseke was a street child who came to Luanda from Benguela after his father's death in a road accident. Nacib's family welcome him into their home, which Kasseke perceives as a palace, despite their poverty, as it contrasts to his life on the streets. Nacib and his family eventually discover that Kasseke has no penis. His father, in a drunken stupor, had insisted on taking Kasseke to Dombe, his ancestral home, to be circumcised. A horrific accident, caused by the drunken elder who was to perform the circumcision, led to the loss of Kasseke's genitals.

Kasseke's mutilation functions at a number of levels in the plot. It serves to question the rationale of pointless traditions with unintended and harmful consequences. It interrogates the role of fathers who selfishly take decisions against the interests of their children. It also functions as a phallic metaphor around which the identity of Kasseke — and by extension the innocent of Angola — is warped and in need of restoration and reconstruction. Something in the national conception of masculinity — something in the New Man — has gone awry and can only be fixed through a renewed solidarity and an altruistic spirit.

Kasseke represents Angolan innocence. In some ways, he inherits the mantle of Ngunga, the protagonist of Pepetela's early didactic novel, *As aventuras de Ngunga*. According to Ondjaki, the book remained one of the most widely read in Angola even three and a half decades after independence.[4] Pepetela initially wrote the novella as a language-learning exercise to 'redigir para si próprio, e eventualmente para os pioneiros e guerrilheiros da área em que se encontrava, um instrumento que em tradução literal o ajudasse a aprender a língua mbunda e àqueles o português'[5] [write for himself, and then for the pioneers and guerrillas in the area where he was, an instrument in which literal translation helped him to learn Mbundu, and them to learn Portuguese].

Costa Andrade (also known as Ndunduma)[6] points out that *Ngunga* quickly turned into something more ideologically than linguistically didactic. The child-protagonist, who becomes an MPLA stalwart during the struggle for independence, 'é irreal como homem, mas constitui a realidade psicológica de um todo [sic], a verdade íntima de cada militante que entende a Revolução como dimensão universal para a definição nacional da liberdade e da justiça e do homem novo'[7] [is unrealistic as a man, but constitutes the psychological reality of a whole, the intimate truth of each militant who understands the revolution in its universal dimension as the national definition of liberty and justice and the New Man].

Ngunga became the ideal against which the (doubtless male) soldiers were to judge themselves. Costa Andrade enjoins the readers of Pepetela's most didactic work, 'tentemos encontrá-lo real e vivo, concreto em cada um de nós'[8] [let's try and find him in flesh and blood, present in each one of us].

After four decades of conflict in Angola, the optimism, rural vibrancy and belief of Ngunga is superseded by the exploitation of Kasseke in a relentlessly predatory Luanda. The most irreproachable character in *Predadores* is never able to steal, even when he is in dire need on the streets. Kasseke is sacrificed at the altar of traditional customs that are not conscious of what they are doing. The drunken elder's lack of reflexivity, mixed with Kasseke's father's drunken intransigence, cost Kasseke the marker of his masculinity and identity.

Yet, Pepetela implies, Kasseke's masculinity can be restored, and not just via Brazilian plastic surgery, which intimates that Angola has something to learn from Portugal's former American colony. For the identity associated with Kasseke to be recuperated — for Angola to be Angola again, or at last — Nacib's hard work and commitment are required. The novel suggests that Angola's identity can be reformulated and restored through citizens like Nacib, who is not one of the predators of the book's title, but one of the reconstructors required to correct the corrupt and self-interested path down which the State has raced.

Kasseke's character finds a parallel in Simão Kipiangala, who lacks three of his four limbs. He drags himself around using his one arm, having been blown up by a landmine while conscripted in the Angolan army during the civil war. Saved by Cuban doctors, his attitude is reminiscent of the character of Jossias in Mia Couto's short story 'De como o velho Jossias foi salvo das águas',[9] who resents being saved from flooding only to be forgotten by society, or Vitório, in Zézé Gamboa's 2004 Angolan film, *O herói*, who returns from the civil war without a leg, and is sidelined by society that no longer has any use for him.

Kapiangala is a much more extreme example. He represents the residue of Angola's civil war. Sleeping in a tomb, he eats food left for dead relatives of the rich in the cemetery and begs on one of Angola's main thoroughfares for scraps from Luanda's mobile elite. Occasionally, he is swept away in official clean-up operations in which beggars are removed from Luanda and dumped on the city's outskirts, but he always returns, a tenacious residue uncomfortably reminding the city of the sacrifice others have made. Then, one of Caposso's sons, Iván, runs over what is left of Kapiangala. Thinking he was just a dog, Iván eliminates an uncomfortable residue that nem cão era para a maior parte dos que passavam ali. Para um cão olha-se, pode se pensar é um rafeiro cheio de sarna, mas vê-se, faz-se notar, ao passo que com ele as pessoas passavam pressentindo a presença e incomodados por ela, desviando logo a vista para o lado, fazendo esforço para não terem visto. (p. 166)

[wasn't even a dog for the majority of people who passed by. One looks at a dog, one might think it's a mongrel, and mangy, but it's seen, it's noticed, while with him people walked passed sensing his presence and made uncomfortable by it, immediately averted their gaze, making an effort to not have seen him.]

Significantly, Iván is not punished for Kapiangala's death. His father finds the whole episode a distracting irritation, but Caposso's influence is still strong in 1998 (when the accident occurs) and he overcomes his disdain for his son in order to pull some strings and orchestrate his release. Thus, both father and son are able to kill others with impunity, as members of a newly created Luanda elite for whom the lives of the marginalized are irrelevant and expendable.

For their part, Kapiangala and Kasseke represent things that are missing and haunt through their absence. Kapiangala, 'metade de homem' (p. 166) [half a man], is a constant unwelcome presence insinuating himself into the consciousness of those who 'apressados de acumular dinheiro estilando nos carros de última geração mais caros do mundo' [in a hurry to accumulate money, dripping from the latest generation of the world's most expensive cars] would rather forget that their wealth came by sacrificing others. Kasseke points back to a paternal failure — a father pointlessly sacrificing his son to a tradition that makes no sense.

Kasseke shows the dangers of subscribing thoughtlessly to traditions, and challenges — in his sheer innocence — the notion of patriarchal authority. In some ways, Kapiangala represents an expunged past: the recent memory of the civil war is too strong for those who came out of it better off to be willing to confront its legacies. They are, deep down, relieved not to have to confront Kapiangala on a daily basis from the comfort of their luxury cars. In contrast, Kasseke, through his friendship with Nacib, represents the possibilities of constructing a future — of refashioning an identity for Angola in which the folly of patriarchy and clientelism can be replaced by the solidarity of genuine friendship and hard work.

Compared with Pepetela's other novels, *Predadores* portrays fatherhood in the most damning fashion. Unlike Alexandre Semedo in *Yaka*, none of the fathers in *Predadores* realizes or cares that their actions and prejudices will have repercussions for future generations. Why did fathers become so pernicious in Pepetela's universe by 2005? Was his characterization of them an effort to challenge the lynchpin of patriarchy? Or, was he suggesting that, in the age of neo-liberal capitalism, by then firmly entrenched in Luanda, fathers were quite simply an irrelevance? Were fathers to blame for the less-than-pleasant conditions of rampant self-interest depicted in *Predadores*? As Angola transitioned from the Marxist New Man to the 'agente económico' (p. 231) [economic agent] Vladimiro claims to be, encouraged and able to operate beyond the traditional confines of familial obligation, does the novel suggest any responsibility resides with the nation's 'founding' fathers?

MPLA propaganda, unsurprisingly, often depicts Agostinho Neto as the nation's founding father but also casts President José Eduardo dos Santos as the 'arquitecto da paz e pai da nação'[10] [architect of peace and father of the nation]. The epithet formerly applied to dos Santos arises from the fact that the long-running civil war came to an end during his presidency. The latter plays on a stereotype of which Portugal's long-lasting dictator Salazar would have been proud.

Dos Santos assumed office in 1979, and became one of the world's most enduring political leaders. By 2004, he had ruled Angola for a quarter of a century, and showed no signs of intending to step down. With the defeat of UNITA and the adoption of the free market, the opportunities for the enrichment of his own family abounded. During his time as president and head of the nation's armed forces, he and his children amassed a fortune.

His eldest daughter, Isabel, was declared Africa's richest woman by Forbes in 2013,[11] and was a vehicle, not unlike the fictional Caposso's favourite daughter, Mireille, through which Angolan wealth was relocated abroad in the then first family's name. Despite MPLA assertions of patriotic fatherhood, President dos Santos's function as a father is, to the popular mind, now less associated with shepherding Angola, and more with overseeing that accumulation of family assets at the expense of the state. It is not difficult to see the parallels within *Predadores*, or to understand why fatherhood becomes such a suspect concept within the current ideological set-up prevalent in Angola.

In *Predadores*, fathers rarely provide a grounding on which their children can build. Instead, they are something to be despised, escaped or used, because what they teach is that familial relations are a utility. Even relatively 'good' fathers, like Sebastião's who secretly gets his son into law school enabling him to work for the dispossessed, bear some mark to be escaped. In the case of Sebastião, his father was a sepoy, compromised by his allegiance to the colonial regime. For his part, Nacib's father, Bernardo Domingos, is unable to conceive of a future beyond his own limited world of carpentry, and does little to encourage his son, who depends on his mother's interventions and godfather's goodwill to move beyond his father's restrictive universe.

The most defective paternal line is the Capossos. Vladimiro's own father had been a nurse. When Vladimiro was eight, his father had abandoned the boy's mother, claiming she was a witch. From then on, father and son never settled, as Vladimiro's father always seemed to be running away. He tried beating his son to instil in him an interest in his studies. Ultimately, it is not studying that changes Vladimiro's life, but his willingness to be co-opted by the dominant discourse and the power structure it envelops. In fact, even his name, Vladimiro, is a fabrication, brought into being to be in line with the prevalent Soviet MPLA ideology of the time.

Caposso is the worst of fathers. His four children, Djamila, Iván, Yúri and Mireille, are variously named in response to political fashions. They are judged, rather like Baltazar van Dum's children in *A gloriosa família*, in relation to their usefulness as a means to their father's ends. This is particularly the case of his most problematic son, Iván, who ran over the dismembered veteran Kapiangala. Yet,

Iván eventually appears to earn his father's respect because of his management of the family estate. This respect is short-lived, as Vladimiro insists that his son's prized calf be slaughtered, treating Iván, in a Freudian reversal, as competition to be defeated and an object to be instrumentalized, rather than a son to be encouraged.

Everything, according to Iván, is used by his father to 'mostrar que era o proprietário e senhor não só das coisas que conseguia mas também da mulher e dos filhos' (p. 282) [show how he was owner and lord not just of the things that he had gained but also of his wife and children]. In Caposso's world, nothing has any value beyond its ability to be owned. It is a world of pure exchange value — a neo-liberalism that breaks patriarchy not out of any commitment to social equity or gender justice but because, under its sign, even a father's relation with his children is commodifiable, and no longer a sacred lineage.

In *Predadores*'s world of commodified children, simulacrum reigns supreme. Everything about Caposso is fake. From his name, to the grotesque imitations of American ranches and Eiffel Towers that are incongruously replicated where he lives, Vladimiro can discern nothing in terms of quality. Even the abstract paintings adorning his office walls are only bought in order to copy the Medici of Florence, and as a means to fabricate social status as a patron of the arts, on the advice of his daughter who, like Isabel dos Santos, has a link to the art world.[12]

At a discursive level, Vladimiro is always capable of mouthing words and slogans without understanding or wishing to understand them, which is primarily the reason his then friend Sebastião was unwilling to vouch for his membership in the MPLA at independence. He embodies the vacuousness of the petty bourgeoisie, and its willingness to be co-opted by power.

Predadores is a product of the decade it was written. Angola had emerged from the civil war. Neo-liberal capitalism fused with extreme corruption was given free rein. The novel captures the moment of an erosion of a national sense of being, in a cut-throat world in which nothing is worth protecting, not even your children. Yet the portrayal is not completely negative: amid the fraudsters and the mediocrity, there are still those able to believe and construct. For Pepetela, Angola still has a future. It will be a future in which new familial structures are forged — in which the Kassekes are adopted by the Nacibs, and the Sebastiãos will remain true to the revolution. In keeping with the true tenets of Marx — an ideology whose spirit Pepetela never abandoned — the innate cruelty of capitalism will eventually prey on those it built up.

Predadores is a novel in which Pepetela's ethical turn becomes more pronounced. The morality of the revolution — guiding the nation's behaviour by way of a hierarchical structure that replicated the Catholic faith it sought to displace — had revealed itself to be flawed. The only hope for Angola rested on the choices of individuals rather than a vanguard imposition on the collective. *O desejo de Kianda* had demonstrated a loss of faith in the post-colonial state. *Predadores* continued that exploration and began to suggest that individual choices are the only way to reach new possibilities for solidarity beyond the party. Against the backdrop of mediocre leaders and the parasites they encourage and then discard, discerning individuals with reconstructive projects in the aftermath of so many decades of war are the future Pepetela intimates within the realm of the possible.

Part of Pepetela's ethical turn involved revisiting historical narratives. His Marxist-Hegelian belief in History wending its way towards progress had been challenged by the fall of the Berlin Wall and by Angola's experience of the MPLA. The theory learned in his youth as a sociologist had come unstuck at a collective level. He had always seen and exposed the flaws of the revolution, even before independence as *Mayombe* demonstrates. He had also questioned from his time at the Centre for Angolan Studies — and in writing *Lueji* — which strand from the discipline of history legitimately feeds into History as an evolving process. Recuperating marginalized voices from the past is the modern historian's ethical task. Giving a previously muted voice from history some say in History is one of his undertakings in *A gloriosa família*, to which we shall now turn our attention.

Notes to Chapter 7

1. Interview with Pepetela in *Speaking the Postcolonial Nation: Interviews with Writers from Angola and Mozambique*, ed. by Ana Mafalda Leite, Sheila Khan, Jessica Falconi and Kamila Krakowska (Oxford: Peter Lang, 2014), pp. 111–31 (p. 122).
2. Fernando Arenas, *Lusophone Africa: Beyond Independence* (Minneapolis: University of Minnesota Press, 2011), p. 195.
3. Pepetela, *Predadores* (Lisbon: Dom Quixote, 2005), p. 338. Subsequent page references given in the text.
4. Ondjaki, 'Let's Share the Dream: Stories for Children in Angola', *Bookbird*, 2 (2009), 46–52, (p. 47).
5. 'A propósito de *As aventuras de Ngunga* — Prefácio à primeira edição', in Francisco Fernando da Costa Andrade, *Literatura angolana: opiniões* (Lisbon: Edições 70, 1980), pp. 91–102 (p. 98).
6. Costa Andrade was the editor of the *Jornal de Angola* and strongly associated with Agostinho Neto's reaction to the 27 May uprising. He was accused of participating alongside Pepetela in the subsequent interrogations.
7. Costa Andrade, Op. Cit., p. 100.
8. Ibid.
9. Mia Couto, *Vozes anoitecidas* (Lisbon: Caminho, 1987), pp. 119–29.
10. MPLA, 'José Eduardo dos Santos, o modelo de angolano', 28 August 2012 <http://www.mpla.ao/mpla.6/artigos.14/jose-eduardo-dos-santos-o-modelo-de-angolano.a403.html> [accessed 27 March 2018].
11. Kerry A. Dolan, 'Daddy's Girl: How an African "Princess" Banked $3 Billion in a Country Living on $2 a Day', *Forbes*, 2 September 2013 <http://www.forbes.com/sites/kerryadolan/2013/08/14/how-isabel-dos-santos-took-the-short-route-to-become-africas-richest-woman/> [accessed 27 March 2018].
12. Isabel dos Santos married the Congolese art collector Sindika Dokolo, the son of a Danish mother, Hanne Kruse, and the founder of the Bank of Kinshasa, Augustin Dokolo.

CHAPTER 8

The Ethical Challenges of History

History has always fascinated Pepetela. From his years at the Centre for Angolan Studies, where he helped to write anti-colonial accounts of the nation's past, he has been concerned with interrogating who gets to speak in history's narratives. Much of his fiction has been fundamental in rewriting the Angolan national narrative as part of a collective project of recuperation, imbued with a sense of History in its Marxist inflection of Hegel. Indeed, History (with a capital) was once for Pepetela 'the process whereby the spirit discovers itself and its own conception'.[1] It was teleological, and part of a dialectic. As Marxist notions of History faltered in the 1990s, history lost its conceptual capitalization for Pepetela, becoming a far more reflexive discipline in which the positionality of the historian was paramount. At the same time, History as a moral exercise in collective progress became history as a set of ethical choices, left to its readers to decode. In other words, history acquired an author, with ideological biases and persuasive rhetoric to further a particular agenda. That switch is clear in *A gloriosa família*, which I shall discuss in this chapter.

History has always had authors, who have attempted to pass themselves off as mere observers. One of Portugal's first historians, Fernão Lopes is the master of what we might call ostensible objectivity — a voice that claims impartiality and is anything but impartial. In the fifteenth century, he deftly manipulated an ideological apparatus that furthered a cause while claiming the position of neutrality. He gave us gripping accounts of the machinations of the courts of Dom Pedro, Dom Fernando and Dom João I. His turns of phrase repeatedly seek to shore up the fiction of his disinterested observation of events. Part of his brilliance is his knack of transferring to his reader the responsibility of passing judgments, while claiming he only presents the facts.

An example of this occurs after he narrates Dom Pedro's revelation of his secret marriage to Inês de Castro. This marriage effectively legitimized Pedro's offspring by her as heirs to the throne of Portugal. Having heard the king's assertions, Fernão Lopes's narrator tells us 'aqueles que de chão e simpres entender eram' [those who were lowly and simple-minded] believed everything they heard. A second group, 'mais sotis de entender' [subtler in their understanding] thought the whole story 'ser muito contra razom' [very contrary to logic].[2] Having outlined their counter-arguments to the validity of the king's marriage, the narrator ostensibly leaves judgment to his reader, claiming it is not for him to 'determinar se foi assi ou nom' [to determine if it was like that or not] but rather to leave 'cárrego ao que isto ler que destas opiniões escolha qual quiser' (p. 77) [the onus on whoever reads this to choose from these opinions which he pleases].

The reader's choice is between agreeing with the fools who swallowed the king's version of events hook, line and sinker, or to align with the 'leterados e bem discretos' (p. 76) [educated and wise] who had their reasonable doubts. What is fascinating is the extent to which Fernão Lopes uses this tactic of ostensible objectivity as part of a grand strategy, as outlined by Helder Macedo, to legitimize João I's claim to the throne.[3] It is history used to convince you of a position rather than to relate a sequence of facts. It is history as narrative, dependent on an omniscient narrator who at key moments self-effaces to make sure his readers occupy the space of judgment, and come to the right, predetermined conclusions. The tactic reveals the very nature of history as a discipline — the biases fundamental to its voice that Hegel sought to obscure by assuring us that History was going somewhere, and Foucault sought to highlight by assuring us it was not.

Pepetela takes his cue from Fernão Lopes in his 1997 historical novel, *A gloriosa família*, a true landmark in Angolan literature. In it, Pepetela constructs another self-effacing narrator, whose ostensible objectivity constantly slips to reveal that the voice of historical narrators always passes judgment, even and especially when the responsibility for judgment is apparently transferred to readers. The reader's job when confronted with ostensible objectivity is to understand which judgments are passed.

To do this, we need to trace how those judgments evolved historically — performing a kind of archaeological scrutiny that unmasks how dominant discourse always develops in a contested space. It never spontaneously comes into being as a given that is only subsequently contested.

Given how history is fashioned, whether it lies in the realm of morals or ethics is one of the questions *A gloriosa família* raises. The answer for Pepetela is that history, with its subjective judgments, is always an ethical challenge, in which those who write, rewrite and read history are constantly confronted with their own compromised positionality. The only honest approach is to assume your judgments, and acknowledge that precisely because it is a figment of the past imagination, observation of historical events always changes the object of its study. Or as Helder Macedo puts it in one of his novels, 'o problema da História é a latência [...] o que fica de permeio entre o que foi e o que poderá ser'[4] [History's problem is its latency [...] what remains in between what was and what might be].

Where Pepetela's earlier works *Mayombe*, *Yaka*, and *A geração da utopia* relied on prominent historical backdrops, and *Lueji, o nascimento de um império* delved deep into the myths surrounding the Lunda queen, *A gloriosa família* is, most self-consciously, about the nature of history as a discipline and, as Inocência Mata deftly analyses, 'os limites da imparcialidade do discurso da História'[5] [the limits of impartiality of history's discourse].

The novel raises fundamental questions regarding whose voices are permissible in the histories we inherit, and the dynamic, ever-changing nature of History as a dialectic. Set in a six-and-a-half-year period between 1642 and 1648 during which the Dutch occupied Luanda, the novel is narrated by a nameless, mute slave who follows his owner, Baltazar van Dum, wherever he goes. The slave's voice, which always strives but ultimately fails to be an impartial observer, both enunciates from a position of alterity and takes centre stage as a voice of reason and judgment. As Margarida Calafate Ribeiro has argued, 'this slave [...] is mute and illiterate. As such, he does not have at his disposal the instruments required to tell his story. Yet precisely through this ontological silence, the subaltern's history emerges. In other words, the Other does have their own story to tell, and they are quite capable of telling it. It is just that the conditions of production and pronouncement they long endured led them to an apparent silence'.[6]

The nameless narrator comes into being through his 'ontological silence' and reveals, through his account, the partial nature of any history. As Ana Lucia Sá has highlighted, it is precisely in the narrator's slippages into critical judgment rather than mere description of the historical facts, that the slave gains subjectivity.[7] At the same time, that slippage highlights the ideological framework of any historical voice. History has always been most pernicious when it has failed to come to terms with its normative tendencies, and misunderstood that all narratives, and especially those tinged by a faith in History, imply subjective judgments. They are never about objective facts. As such, the telling of history veers between moral judgment and ethical act. As a normative tool of power, History plays the moral game of reinforcing the values of the power structure under which it operates. However, as the narrator of *A gloriosa família* will demonstrate, different stories can be told, under an ethical assertion of partiality, in which a conscious choice is made to intervene in History's dialectic — changing its course and discourse.

The Van Dum family in *A gloriosa família* is steeped in the slave trade. Its patriarch — a Catholic polyglot from southern Flanders — embodies the entrepreneurial class on whose adventurous spirit modern global capitalism thrived. As he plays his part in opening up the world to Western Europe and generating its material wealth through commerce, Baltazar van Dum exemplifies the darker side of the European narrative of modernity, namely coloniality. As Walter Mignolo highlights, coloniality — shorthand for the colonial matrix of power — 'is constitutive of modernity', operating as its clumsily hidden partner.[8] Pepetela's genius in *A gloriosa família* is to lay bare that hidden relationship with which the discipline of history — a discipline under the spectre of Hegel that initially denied Africa a voice — traditionally conspired.

Baltazar van Dum, the historical figure found in Cardonega's historical account of seventeenth-century Angola on whom Pepetela bases his novel, founded one of Luanda's great dynasties. His descendants provided nineteenth-century Luanda with 'teachers and soldiers, as well as politicians and merchants'.[9] In fact, the family name is still prevalent in Angolan politics, having provided one of the prime ministers in the post-independence era, and one of the most famous victims of the 27 May purges. The original Baltazar is thought to have been a Jewish refugee from Portugal who took a Dutch name, and helped his adopted nation infiltrate the Atlantic trading network, eventually settling in Angola.[10]

The novel operates on two narrative planes: the macro and the micro. At the macro level, it shows the European global power struggle as it played out in Angola — with military and political personalities struggling to further their own interests and ideologies. At this level, the principal message of *A gloriosa família* seems to be that trade favours peace. A good trading relationship between the Dutch and the Portuguese is the best way to avoid unnecessary conflict and is mutually beneficial. Baltazar van Dum embodies this spirit, claiming 'ser um homem de paz e que esta alimentava melhor os negócios que a guerra'[11] [to be a man of peace and that this nurtured business better than war]. His assertion that 'o comércio é a melhor maneira de unir as pessoas e os interesses e de evitar guerras que só trazem desgraças' (p. 272) [business is the best way to bring people and interests together and to avoid wars that only bring misfortune] was a creed popularly followed by free-trade third-way politicians in the 1990s, precisely when Pepetela produced the novel.

What it overlooks — the coloniality behind the modernity — is the cost of that peace, which Baltazar alludes to unwittingly when he says, 'pretender vender escravos aos holandeses é comércio, não é política' (p. 272) [trying to sell slaves to the Dutch is business, not politics]. That is, for Pepetela, the crux of the issue — the false logic of a skewed syllogism relentlessly if subtly critiqued in *A gloriosa família*, in which slaves are trade, and slaves are not politics, therefore trade is not politics.

The era when Pepetela wrote the novel was dominated by a seeming global consensus, certainly within the Eurocentric universe, which sought to depoliticize global trade as a global good. It followed the discrediting of alternatives signalled by the fall of the Berlin Wall, and pre-dated the rhetoric of terrorist threats and axes of evil. Pepetela undermines that consensus by pointing to the obscene backbone on which trade and the politics of modernity were built, namely slavery. The text most often refers to slaves as mere 'peças' [pieces] in keeping with the vocabulary of the slave-trade era that needed to deny the humanity of the 'objects' it shipped around the world as merchandise.

Pepetela does not directly critique the slave trade in *A gloriosa família*. There is very little direct referencing to the actions of the slave traders as slavers in the novel. Instead, the critique is born at the micro-level, by giving the potential 'peças' names or, in the case of the nameless narrator, a voice. At this micro-level, within the Van Dum household, we witness the workings of coloniality rather than the narrative of modernity. There, coloniality is not presented as a crushing force of enslaving evil, but as a continuously contested logic of gradually amassed power.

Occupying a hybrid position between the pure capitalism of the Dutch who colonized Angola through the West India Company and the Portuguese who 'apenas pretendem escravizar todo o povo' (p. 93) [just try to enslave a whole people], Baltazar generally sees his relatives, like Caposso in *Predadores*, in terms of their usefulness in furthering his business ends. They, in turn, represent a wide range of opinions and attitudes that do not all concur with the particularities of coloniality but nevertheless never challenge its overarching logic.

In many ways, the Van Dunem clan represents the gamut of liberal democracy, with a range of attitudes and quirks but no fundamental critique of the underlying, exploitative, economic structure. Even Baltazar, reversing his initial disapproval of his son Ambrósio's choice of partner Angélica Ricos Olhos, goes through the façade of wanting 'a opinião de toda a gente da família' [all the family's opinion] since 'não vou decidir nada sozinho' (p. 350) [I am not going to decide anything alone]. He claims he does not want to be designated 'um tirano' (p. 351) [a tyrant]. It is a face-saving use of 'democracy' to reach his predetermined conclusions — the cover for achieving what he wants without admitting what he wants.

Only through the subjective, judging eyes of the slave does the voice of alterity challenge the status quo. Unlike the clumsy Portuguese — who sacrificed the papers detailing Luanda's early history on abandoning the city as the Dutch arrived, and then burned all the documentation the Dutch had left as 'escrituras dos demoníacos hereges calvinistas' (p. 401) [the scriptures of the devilish Calvinist heretics] — the slave has a sense of History (as a teleological process). He is meticulous in his conveyance of the facts he has overheard and witnessed. He is always careful to trace any information to which he has not had first-hand access. Even as the 'mute' voice, steeped in ostensible objectivity, the narrator retains a characteristic the philosopher and historian R. G. Collingwood deemed fundamental to the best historians: imagination.[12]

Collingwood's theories of historical imagination were born in resistance to positivist approaches to knowledge that took hold at the end of the nineteenth and beginning of the twentieth century.[13] He argued that the events historians study had an 'outside' observable aspect, such as specific troop movements, and an 'inside' which can only be described 'in terms of thought' covering elements like a general's motivations for ordering such a manoeuvre. Because all events in the remit of history (as a discipline) took place in the past, there is no way to observe them, so the only possible recourse if one is to see the patterns that the documentation and sources leave is to imagine them. Ever careful to maintain the distinction between fanciful flights of the imagination that would correspond to fiction and a historical imagination that has to be grounded in documentary sources, Collingwood nevertheless understood the need for a creative faculty in the historical mind.

For Marcia Shore, historical imagination has an ethical component, because of our compromised positionalities as products of the histories that our privilege helps us to write: 'understanding the past is inextricably bound up with guilt: writing history requires an imaginative leap into a time and a place where one was not, an exercise insisting upon a simultaneous violation of and identification with the other'.[14] Who one identifies with in historical accounts is at the heart of our ethical choice. For Pepetela, in *A gloriosa família*, the mute slave is our only source of information. The choice is made by the author to force identification with a voice traditionally excluded by history.

The nameless slave narrator in *A gloriosa família* exemplifies historical imagination, as he fills in the gaps in his account, conjecturing the moments he has not witnessed. He also highlights the power of collating knowledge in the historical process — being able to determine what to select in order to frame the narrative. Pepetela could also be considered a practitioner of historical imagination — filling in gaps left by European-authored accounts of Angola's history, while striving to give voice to those marginalized by those dominant historical discourses.

The slave narrator only shows irritation with his master Van Dum on two occasions. The first is when he learns that his master has withheld knowledge from him, having somehow managed, in the slave's absence, to meet with Domingos Fernandes. Fernandes relates the feelings of the Portuguese in Massangano, where the colonial capital was transferred following the Dutch invasion of Luanda. The narrator, whose only task is to follow Baltazar van Dum wherever he goes, feels the 'fel da traição' (p. 118) [bile of betrayal]. It pains him that he is not privy to all the facts as he constructs his micro-history of the Van Dum clan.

The other occasion is at the end of the novel, when we learn why the slave is writing his history. Coincidentally, the incident involves Domingo Fernandes again, who discreetly asks Baltazar about 'este seu escravo mulato' (p. 393) [this mulato slave of yours]. Surely Baltazar should fear that the slave, who overhears all his conversations, might 'revelar algum segredo' (p. 393) [reveal some secret]? Baltazar's reaction is to laugh raucously, in a response that reveals the level of contempt based on ignorance he has for the slaves around him. Dismissing him as 'mudo' [mute] and 'anafabelto' [illiterate], incapable of understanding much, and certainly nothing beyond a few phrases in his native Kimbundu, the slave-trading patriarch equates the narrator to 'um túmulo' (p. 393) [a grave].[15]

The slave's reaction is to assert 'se tão pouco valor me atribuía, então também não merecia o meu esforço de lhe fazer compreender o contrário, morresse com a sua ideia' (p. 393) [if he attributes so little value to me, then he really isn't worth disabusing, let him die with his idea]. It will not be Baltazar's consciousness that the slave changes, but his place in history as he goes on to explain: 'uma desforra para tanto desprezo seria contar toda a sua estória, um dia' (p. 393) [vengeance for such contempt will be telling all his story, one day]. The slave's revenge, then, is the book we read, or rather, the judgment of history its ostensible objectivity imposes on us as readers — as we are able to view Baltazar as a very human character, with foibles, skills and prejudices, as well as coming to terms with his horrendous place in the development of the slave trade.

The narrator allows us to see in Balatazar van Dum the embodiment of what Hannah Arendt in the context of the Eichmann trial termed the 'banality of evil' — the ordinariness of individuals who perpetrate sociopathic acts.[16] In everything he does, Baltazar acts as both an agent and product of the trading system to which he subscribes. Most importantly, and like several of Pepetela's later protagonists such as Vladimiro Caposso in *Predadores* and Jaime Bunda, Baltazar is distinctively mediocre. Heroes are consigned to Pepetela's utopian narratives. History — at its worst — is, for Pepetela, constituted by the most painfully mundane and banal characters.

A gloriosa família is replete with historical figures from the era of Dutch occupation. There is a role for António de Oliveira Cadornega, whose *História geral das guerras angolanas* is one of the foundational texts of Angolan history. It is from this text that Baltazar van Dum 'Flamengo de Nação, mas de animo Portuguez' (p. 9) [Flemish by nationality, but Portuguese in spirit] is introduced to the reader, in the opening epigraph of *A gloriosa família*, as someone whose 'cabeça' [head] was 'mui arriscada' (p. 9) [very risky]. Risk-taking, we will learn through the novel, is the lifeblood of Baltazar — the quintessential capitalist, who sees opportunities and seizes them whenever he can.

The opening line of the novel contrasts with Cadornega's depiction: 'O meu dono, Baltazar Van Dum, só sentiu os calções mijados cá fora, depois de ter sido despedido pelo director Nieulant. Mijado mas aliviado, com a cabeça ainda em cima dos ombros' (p. 11) [My owner, Baltazar van Dum, only felt his wet pants outside, after being dismissed by Diretor Nieulant. Wet but relieved, with his head still on top of his shoulders]. From the first moments of the slave's narration, it becomes clear the history we are going to read is an alternate view: one that can see the vulnerabilities of the agents traditional histories heroicize. How we decodify those heroes, and how we locate the voices excluded from the narrative all together, is one of the concerns of the novel.

Joan Scott's observation that 'subsequent history is written as if [...] normative positions were the product of social consensus rather than of conflict'[17] is precisely the practice that Pepetela seeks to contest. He shows how the arrival of modernity, or more appropriately, coloniality in Angola was always a complex mishmash of contested voices, exemplified through the enormous diversity characterized in the Van Dum clan.

As ever, in Pepetela, it is never a case of black and white. Even the narrator slave, whom we might expect to be African, turns out to be the mestizo son of a Napolitano priest, initially enslaved by Queen Jinga. Likewise, Baltazar's wife, one of the greatest enforcers of hierarchies, is a black woman of aristocratic stock and is concerned with 'improving' the race by a process of whitening. At every turn, Pepetela strives to reveal the racial and ideological complexity of the slave trade as the bedrock of capitalist development.

Cadornega is characterized in the novel as a note-taking soldier, smitten with Van Dum's licentious daughter Matilde. He explains how history, as a narrative, must always be decoded, and how victors control its dominant discourse. Asked by Ambrósio, Baltazar's well-read son, how he will portray Sottomayor, one of the less popular Portuguese governors to be installed in Angola, Cadornega asserts: 'chega a ser uma questão moral. Se escrevo sobre as grandezas de Portugal, como posso contar as coisas mesquinhas? Não, essas ficam no tinteiro, pois não interessam para a história' (p. 269) [that's a moral question. If I write about Portugal's greatness, how can I relate small-minded things? No, those remain in the inkwell, since they are not relevant to history]. Cadornega continues: 'será necessário interpretar a crónica. Personagem que não aparece revestida de grandes encómios é porque não prestava mesmo para nada e só o pudor do escritor salvaguarda a sua memória' (p. 269) [it might be necessary to interpret the chronicle. A character who does not appear regaled in panegyrics is thus because he really wasn't worth anything and only the writer's reserve saved his memory].

The 'moral question' of history is thus transferred over to those who read it. They must be equipped to interpret the discipline's omissions and hyperboles properly, and constantly rewrite the story as they read it. In other words, history as a field enters the realm of ethics — of choices made rather than customs received. The writer of history may well be constrained by the dominant ideological framework of his or her time, a framework into which she or he feeds as a narrative is written. However, for the very humanized character of Cadornega, history is a novel that requires us to read between the lines, if we are to understand it. As we read between the lines, the gaps are often more important than what is present. A case in point is the epigraphs.

The novel contains twelve chapters, ten of which are preceded by epigraphs. The first chapter is immediately preceded by a citation extracted from Cadornega's already cited text, which essentially functions as both an epigraph for the book and for its opening chapter. The epigraphs in the remaining chapters are drawn from a variety of European and Angolan historical and archival sources, pertaining to some aspect of the Dutch occupation of Angola. The one exception is the tenth chapter, which begins without an epigraph. Why? What is it about this point in the novel that makes an epigraph inappropriate when the rest of the book's structure demands an epigraph begin each chapter?

The answer lies in what surrounds the chapter's beginning and how we interpret the function of epigraphs. Roberto Vecchi has argued that an epigraph turns what is denoted into what is connoted.[18] It is an insinuation silently yet prominently directing our attention before we enter each chapter, colouring our vision of what will follow. In the case of *A gloriosa família*, the epigraphs add to an ideological framework that grounds the story in fragments from historical texts. It assists the slave-narrator's pretentions to ostensible objectivity by foregrounding documentary sources as 'impartial' evidence behind the narrative we read. In some ways, each chapter functions as a commentary on the fragment that introduces it. Yet, Chapter 10 begins with a gap. There is no fragment available, calling our attention to some malfunction in the narrative. Something in its premises is remiss.

Immediately preceding Chapter 10, we witness one of the strongest interventions of an unusually and obviously opinionated narrator. His mask of ostensible objectivity — supported in the historical technique of documentary citation — slips. This is because of his anger and passion. The narrator is in love with Catarina, one of Baltazar's semi-legitimate offspring who occupies the status of both dear sibling and reviled servant (at least on the part of Dona Inocência, who despises her partially recognized step-daughter). Earlier in the narrative, a young slave, Thor, had been executed on Baltazar's orders because he had been conducting an affair with Rosário, one of the patriarch's daughters. Thor was a smart, well-liked slave, who had shown his worth in the capitalist structure by helping to control the other slaves. Yet, he overstepped the gender-specific honour code that allows Baltazar and his sons to sleep with any slave they wish, but prevents his daughters from enjoying the same 'rights'. It is a specifically racialized class prohibition that Baltazar enforces because one of his other daughters, Matilde, is able, despite her father's disapproval, to sleep with any white man she wishes.

Rosário's problem is to have misunderstood which boundaries cannot be crossed, as she proactively seeks sexual comfort from the black slave Thor. The result is Thor's clumsy decapitation, despite Rosário's pleas and those of her brother, Hermenegildo, who even suggests marriage as a solution. During the affair between Rosário and Thor, the slave-narrator reveals how he achieves sexual gratification from his voyeurism, as he secretly witnesses their encounters. Subsequently, Catarina — the object of his secret adoration — is seduced by Redinckove — one of the directors of the West India Company. She loses her virginity to Redinckove in Chapter 9, immediately preceding the missing epigraph. Once again, the narrator witnesses a sexual act, which takes place in the same room where Rosário had sex with Thor. This time, the narrator's voyeurism is tempered with rage and mourning: 'Me encostei à parede, como antes, engolindo soluços e rancores, para ouvir os gemidos da minha amada conhecendo homem pela primeira vez. O meu orgasmo foi acompanhado de lágrimas e luto no coração' (p. 316) [I leant against the wall, like before, swallowing my sobs and rage, to listen to the moans of my beloved, knowing a man for the first time. My orgasm was accompanied by tears and mourning in my heart].

There is no suggestion that the slave-narrator would ever have had a relationship with Catarina, who operates as muse for him, elevated to a pedestal of pure innocence he feels only he knows. As Catarina succumbs to carnal knowledge, the two acts of the narrator's voyeurism fuse in his mind, demanding the reader draw analogies. As the chapter ends, the narrator curses Redinckove, in a powerfully subjective intervention, in which he wishes for the Dutchman's death, and deems such a death to be justified. In contrast, he asserts, Thor's death was totally unjust.

As readers, we witness a collapse in the narrator's impartiality. We are called upon to question his judgment. After all, Catarina was a very willing partner. There is no suggestion of a rape by the Dutchman. Instead, the vitriol is a result of the narrator's subjective emotions, no longer controlled under the façade of ostensible objectivity. As the next chapter begins, without the crutch of historical impartiality feigned in an epigraph from a documentary source, we as readers are left to contemplate what its lack signifies. The missing epigraph draws attention to the role of citation in the ideological framework of history, lulling us into accepting the truth of a narrative. The historian's claim to objectivity is always as shallow as Fernão Lopes's assertion that his readers should decide the validity of Dom Pedro's claims to have married Inês de Castro.

The façade breaks for the slave-narrator of *A gloriosa família* precisely because of his irrational, highly emotional attachment to Catarina. Once the façade is broken, the narrator's pretence at impartiality gives way to a sense that historians can and do intervene in the events they observe. Up until this point, the narrator has repeatedly asserted that his role means he cannot comment on or change the course of events. His commitment to the discipline of history more than his status as a slave prevents him from taking actions.

Once that impartiality is revealed to be untenable for the narrator — as it is for anyone who writes history — the narrator's attitude changes, culminating in his greatest intervention in the text, when he helps the slave Dolores escape with her son Gustavo from the clutches of Dona Inocência, the child's grandmother. As he retells the event, the narrator claims, 'Não entreguei o Gustavo, juro que não, apenas não fiz muita força nas mãos que o seguravam. Dolores pegou nele e puxou. As minhas mãos cederam' (p. 371) [I didn't hand over Gustavo, I swear I didn't, I just didn't hold on very tightly to him. Dolores grabbed him and pulled. My hands gave way]. He later confesses, 'ninguém soube do meu delito' (p. 372) [no one knew of my offence], and rejoices in the freedom the slave and her child consequently enjoy.

The narrator thus foregrounds his intentional intervention while retaining the veneer of not having directly impacted the history he relates. After the missing epigraph, the story becomes less about the 'questão moral' [moral question] that the character of Cadornega linked to history, with its controlled choices, and more about the ethical positions of those who write (and read) the narrative. In other words, it is no longer so much a question of working out what customs and mores allow for which stories to be told, but rather understanding the fraught position of the historian as story-teller, and the power that the individual's choices has on subsequent events.

Pepetela's move away from a subtle questioning of inherited morality to an encouragement of ethical choices parallels the seeming loss of a collective project within the MPLA. The New Man gave way to the 'empresário' [entrepreneur]; the pioneer to the street child. The individual rather than the common good appeared to be the new currency of the State. With the end of the civil conflict in 2002, the MPLA's transition was complete.

The publication of Pepetela's pair of Jaime Bunda novels fell on either side of the end of the civil war. As José Ornelas points out, through them, Pepetela introduced detective fiction to Angola, using the genre 'to illustrate the collapse of the nation and denounce its rampant corruption from a different angle, especially from the perspective of an insider whose character, behavior, and actions lend themselves to portrayals of Angola through parody, pastiche and irony'.[19] At its heart, detective fiction is about the search for truths. One of the truths Bunda reveals is, for Sharae Deckard, a 'neoliberal turpitude' configured through the 'corporal tumescence' of the protagonist's body.[20] In other words, Angola's overweight response to James Bond embodies the self-indulgent excess of the nation's elites in the early years of the new millennium.

The character of Jaime Bunda is, in fact, the only protagonist to make a lead appearance in more than one of Pepetela's novels. In the next chapter, I shall discuss the implications of Pepetela's repetition, and ask if there are differences between the two works that may be related to the end of the civil war that the novels' respective publication dates encase.

Notes to Chapter 8

1. Georg W. F. Hegel, *Lectures on the Philosophy of World History*, trans. by H. B. Nisbet (Cambridge: Cambridge University Press, 1975), p. 62.
2. Fernão Lopes, *Crónicas*, ed. by Maria Ema Tarracha Ferreira (Lisbon: Verbo, 2005), p. 76. Subsequent page references given in the text.

3. See Helder Macedo, 'Fernão Lopes, A Sétima Idade e os princípios de Avis', in Helder Macedo and Fernando Gil, *Viagens do olhar: retrospecção, visão e profecia no renascimento português* (Porto: Campo das Letras, 1998), pp. 143–73.
4. Helder Macedo, *Tão longo amor tão curta a vida* (Bacarena: Presença, 2013), p. 48.
5. Inocência Mata, *Ficção e história na literatura angolana: o caso de Pepetela*, preface by Pepetela, postface by Laura Padilha (Luanda: Mayamba, 2010), p. 127.
6. Margarida Calafate Ribeiro, 'Literary Voices of Luanda and Maputo: A Struggle for the City', *Journal of Lusophone Studies*, 1.1 (2016), 88–106 (p. 104).
7. Ana Lúcia Sá, 'Vozes na narrativa da história de Angola', *The Scientific Journal of Humanistic Studies*, 1.1 (2009), 35–41 (p. 36).
8. Walter D. Mignolo, *The Darker Side of Western Modernity* (Durham, NC: Duke University Press, 2011), p. 39.
9. David Birmingham, *A Short History of Angola* (London: Hurst, 2015), p. 23.
10. Ibid., pp. 23–24.
11. Pepetela, *A gloriosa família* (Lisbon: Dom Quixote, 1997), p. 254. Subsequent page references given in the text.
12. R. G. Collingwood, *The Idea of History: Revised edition with Lectures, 1926–1928*, ed. by Jan van Der Dussen (Oxford: Clarendon Press, 1994), p. 245.
13. See Lynn Speer Lemisko, 'The Historical Imagination: Collingwood in the Classroom', *Canadian Social Studies*, 38.2 (Winter 2004) <https://canadian-social-studies-journal.educ.ualberta.ca/content/articles-2000–2010#ARhistorical_imagination_collingwood202> [accessed 27 March 2018].
14. Marcia Shore, *The Taste of Ashes: The Afterlife of Totalitarianism in Eastern Europe* quoted in Norman Davies, 'The Deep Stains of Dictatorship', *New York Review of Books*, LX.8, 9 May 2013, p. 51.
15. In Portuguese, the word can also connote a trustworthy person.
16. Hannah Arendt, *Eichmann in Jerusalem: A Report on the Banality of Evil* (New York: Viking, 1963).
17. Joan W. Scott, 'Gender: A Useful Category of Historical Analysis', *The American Historical Review*, 91.5 (December 1986), 1053–75 (p. 1068).
18. Roberto Vecchi discussed this at a meeting of the Post-colonial Cities Project held at Coimbra University in July 2015.
19. José Ornelas, 'Pepetela', in *Dictionary of Literary Biography, Volume 367: African Lusophone Writers*, ed. by Monica Rector and Richard Vernon (Detroit, MI: Gale, 2012), pp. 131–48 (p. 142).
20. Sharae Deckard, 'Deformed Narrators: Postcolonial Genre and Peripheral Modernity in Mabanckou and Pepetela', in *Locating Postcolonial Narrative Genres*, ed. by Walter Göbel and Saskia Schabio (New York: Routledge, 2012), pp. 95–107 (p. 101).

CHAPTER 9

The Ethics of Forgiveness

The narrator of Helder Macedo's fictionalized memoir, *Parts of Africa*, declares in the penultimate chapter of his literary voyage through twentieth-century Portuguese colonial and post-colonial history:

> There are things that benefit from being said more than once. However, they must be said differently. In fact, everything is said more than once, but either with a lot of effort or without noticing it, you say them differently.[1]

For an author like Pepetela, with over half a century of writing under his belt and multiple ground-breaking novels published to date, the question arises: is he saying the same thing more than once and, if so, does he manage to say it differently?

In an interview in 2013 with Luís Ricardo Duarte, Pepetela asserted, 'procuro não escrever sempre o mesmo livro'[2] [I try not always to write the same book]. Given the unique circumstances under which he was writing, from a privileged political position as the Angolan nation came into being, it is not surprising that much critical reception about his work, particularly in the late twentieth century, focused on the role of history and nationhood as his primary literary concerns. These concerns were dictated by the circumstances of Angola's independence in 1975: there was a need to 'nationalize' Angolan history quickly — to extract it from a narrative based purely on Portugal and its overthrown dictatorial regime.

The struggle for independence formed a key component of the MPLA narrative. The party's role in the gaining of independence granted it a degree of leeway, particularly among progressive intellectuals, who were often prepared to give the movement and its leadership the benefit of the doubt, and either did not notice or chose to remain silent about some of the excesses of Agostinho Neto's regime, as I discussed in Chapter 3.

Pepetela was once closely allied with the power structures of the regime. He witnessed the MPLA move away from the concerns he held dear, yet the triggers for his writing have remained remarkably constant from his early work onwards. As he asserted in 1997, 'a minha ideologia não mudou. Eu continuo a ser uma pessoa que pensa primeiro no povo, e depois no resto'[3] [my ideology has not changed. I continue to be someone who thinks first and foremost of the people, and only then of the rest].

In most of what he has written, social justice and the intricate machinations of power — including its formative effects on subjectivities — are never far from the surface. The difference in Pepetela's later work is, therefore, often a question of the narrative structure. However, something does alter profoundly in *Jaime Bunda e a morte do americano*, a novel with which Pepetela claims to be unhappy.

This is rather strange because it is the second novel in a series of two in which the author presents a bumbling Angolan parody of James Bond — with a quixotic passion for living out what he has read in other literary texts. He uses Jaime Bunda as a means to offer another prescient analysis of the direction in which Angolan society was moving after the turn of the millennium. It is as if Pepetela wanted to use apparent iteration to say something different, precisely because he was, for the first time, consciously and explicitly using the same cast of characters in novels in quick succession, with a similar narrative structure and a repetition in one of the narrative voices. So, rather than saying something 'more than once', while obeying Macedo's injunction that it 'must be said differently', 'either with a lot of effort or without noticing it', Pepetela is saying something new in the same way. That is a very post-modern trick.

As Stephen Henighan points out, for Pepetela 'the hegemony of globalized postmodern discourse obscures memory and national history. [His] approach to Angolan reality in the Jaime Bunda novels is guided by a dissatisfied awareness of the prevalence of post-modern phenomena in shaping contemporary life'.[4] Henighan also points out that the Angolan author responds by using the literary tropes of post-modernism — pastiche and citation — as a 'counterattack' to what politically post-modern discourse represents: as embodied for Henighan in Francis Fukuyama's thesis of the End of History. Fukuyama published his influential *The End of History and the Last Man* following the fall of the Berlin Wall, arguing that liberal democracy was now the only governing game in town, and that humankind's political systems had evolved to a global end point in which Western-style democracies would increasingly prevail as the paradigm.[5] For Fukuyama in the 1990s, the age of competing ideologies was over. His work has been read as a direct challenge to Marxist History's progressive trajectory.

Henighan's terminology, accusing Pepetela's anti-post-modern tactics of being 'drenched in postmodern thinking' (p. 139), is a provocative and valid critique. He asserts that post-modern hegemony 'necessitates a change in Pepetela's presentation of the Creole Luanda elite' (p. 139), the depiction of which has been a staple of the author's literary project. Luanda's Creole elite was the intellectual and political backbone of the MPLA since its foundation. The question, then, arises: does Pepetela's stooping to such anti-post-modern post-modern tactics imbricated in an end-of-ideology ideology offer any political solution to the nation's state of affairs in the noughties? In other words, is Pepetela using the tropes of post-modernism to challenge the underlying assumptions of post-modern thought?

And, comparing the two Jaime Bunda novels, what is that new thing that is said 'in the same way'? What novelty, if any, emerges in the repetition? For the first time, Pepetela suggests that an accommodation needs to be made with the worst excesses of human nature, with its overpowering self-interest. That flawed nature has been at the heart of the revolution's failure. A desire for justice — the prevalent leitmotif of Pepetela's work — must, he suggests, be tempered by pragmatism. Furthermore, an intrinsic part of that accommodation draws on a cynical — or rather post-modern — reinterpretation of the Christian concept of forgiveness.

Throughout his writing, Pepetela has been adept at pointing to the parallels between how religious — particularly Catholic — thought and secular power function in tandem and in sequence. As I have already discussed at various points, in *Yaka*, for example, Olívia's passion for Christ is replaced by a crush on Che Guevara. In *Mayombe*, the practice of Marxist 'autocrítica' is traced to an Angolan mindset rooted in the Catholic confessional. Pepetela brings up the Catholic dynamic behind 'autocrítica' again in O *desejo de Kianda*, as well as notions of divine wrath being deployed for secular means. The same novella portrays a competition between different creeds in terms of market forces.[6]

Pepetela's comparisons with religions are never favourable. For him, religious thought is a defective legacy that the Church bestows on the praxis of the Angolan nation. While not as marked, Pepetela's critique extends beyond the Catholic faith. His materialist mindset is one of the primary characteristics of his writing, even when he draws on Angolan foundational myths, such as in *Lueji, o nascimento de um império*, in which he lays bare the hypocrisy of sacred sites being strategically deployed in the exercise of power by the eponymous empress.

One of Pepetela's concerns is to expose the agents of power benefitting from the disciplining authority of belief systems. Catholicism, in particular, bears a colonial vestige so strong that rarely is a true believer to be believed, and if they do believe, that belief goes hand-in-hand, in Pepetela, with the potential for manipulation at the hands of the unscrupulous. In an interview in which he was asked to comment on the post-colonial in contemporary Angolan fiction, Pepetela quickly skewed his answer towards a commentary on the colonial residues of the Catholic Church:

> I think the work of most writers has escaped this latest fashion of trying to defend concepts related to colonialism or colonization. Sometimes it is not that easy for certain specific people, those who are heavily influenced by the Catholic religion — as you know, Catholicism and colonialism arrived here at the same time. But even they have some notion of the country as being independent and trying to think for itself, despite all the influences.[7]

Clearly, in Pepetela's hierarchy, Catholicism does not rank highly, but it appears that, forty years after independence, Catholics are resigned to the existence of the nation. Some would argue they are now at the heart of it.

Particularly in the early years following independence, the relationship between the Church and the Angolan state was chequered. As outlined by the persecuted Angolan journalist, Rafael Marques de Morais, 'the relationship between state power and religion has been marked by political intolerance, ambivalence and co-optation, sometimes in turn and sometimes simultaneously'.[8] A key moment for the Church occurred in 1992, when President dos Santos abandoned his Marxist atheism, married in the Catholic rite, and baptized his children.[9] There is a barely concealed reference to dos Santos seeing the Catholic light in *Jaime Bunda e a morte do americano*, when the narrator, commenting on temporal power's insecurities when it comes to the possibility of a life judged after death, asserts that secular authority 'treme todo perante os poderes divinos. Para comprovar esse temor, basta lembrar a quantidade de casamentos religiosos e baptizados que se seguiram ao fim do regime de partido único' (p. 236) [shivers before divine powers. To prove this fear, you just need to remember the number of religious weddings and baptisms that followed the end of the one-party state regime].

A cynic might link dos Santos's Catholic reconversion to the first multiparty elections that occurred the year of his religious marriage. Despite over a decade and a half of being an atheist state, clearly an important proportion of the potential electorate still harboured Catholic sympathies in the 1990s. Around half of Angolans nationals profess Catholicism, and most importantly, Luanda's Creole elites were generally educated in Catholicism even if they took a detour via Marxism before reaching the 'End of History'.

By 2009, President dos Santos received Pope Benedict in Luanda, in one of the scholar-pontiff's few trips outside Europe when he came pay tribute to Africa's first Catholic convert, who was baptized in Angola in 1491.[10] In 2014, Pope Francis held an audience with President dos Santos and his wife in the Vatican in which they discussed what were termed 'the good relations between the Holy See and the Republic of Angola'.[11] This is a far cry from the days under Agostinho Neto when there was a Mao-like attempt to separate the Angolan Catholic Church from the Vatican and the government closed down the Catholic broadcaster, Rádio Ecclésia.[12] While parts of the Church within Angola remain critical of the discrepancy in wealth distribution characteristic of the post-conflict nation, it enjoys a much more comfortable position within Angola's elites today than at any point since independence, and the MPLA is generally considered to be a Catholic-sympathizing party in Angola. Catholic discourse on forgiveness found a willing partner in the immediate aftermath of the Civil War, which ended in 2002.

Pepetela published his Jaime Bunda novels in 2001 and 2003 respectively. He wrote the novels during a phase in his life when he claims he was trying to rediscover pleasure in writing, a pleasure he had lost. The first book in the Jaime Bunda series, he thought, worked. 'The second one wasn't as successful. The second one was a bit contrived. But it was going in the same direction that *Berkeley*, [and] *O quase fim do mundo* went: [namely] freedom'.[13] For a writer who has often felt compelled to write on topics of national importance at particular junctures in his nation's history — his 2005 *Predadores* is an explicit example of this, a book written out of a 'sense of obligation'[14] — the notion that there should be pleasure in the writing of his novels and that he strives for the rather elusive concept of freedom through them is revealing. The place of utopia — that unattainable strategic necessity occupying so much of his early work — evolves into the concept of freedom as something to which he aspires as he writes, increasingly in a Kantian reversal describing Angola as it is, instead of as it should be. What emerges is not a realist writer, but a writer in search of different variants of a truth, ever conscious that no single version exists.

The fact that he tried his hand at detective fiction at this point in his literary trajectory — and rendered it as pastiche and parody — speaks volumes. Mia Couto produced a Mozambican version of detective fiction with *A varanda do frangipani*, published in 1996, in the aftermath of his county's civil war.[15] In different ways, both Couto and Pepetela play with unreliable narrators, and both appear to turn to the genre as conflict gives way to an uneasy peace. The genre — detective fiction — embodies a search for truth and justice. In the case of Jaime Bunda, the parody aspect of the detective format reveals the enterprise of truth location to be comical and justice to be impossible. Truths may be revealed but justice will not be served by those epiphanies.

Given the realization that there is no justice in the revolutionary sense in twenty-first-century Angola, with its increasing discrepancy between abject poverty and billionaires, Pepetela reaches the conclusion that something needs to change for the nation to move forward in any sense. In his second Jaime Bunda novel, the only way forward, it seems, is for a parody version of forgiveness, in which it is not so much that warring factions come together, but that those with power have their dubious slates wiped clean in return for establishing a new national ethics.

Jaime Bunda e a morte do americano (2003) offers a vision of the world of policing mediated through a series of misquoted detective novels and impressions from films. It follows *Jaime Bunda, Agente Secreto* (2001), in which the young nepotistically connected Jaime had cut his teeth on police work and accidently uncovered an international counterfeit money operation, while officially attempting to solve the mystery of a dead girl. In the sequel the anti-hero has matured, and is sent to solve the mystery of who, if anyone, killed an impotent American engineer in Benguela. The American ambassador to Luanda makes thinly veiled threats against Angola: a perpetrator must be caught because, as the USA makes clear, a verdict of suicide is not an acceptable option.

Pepetela resurrects the format of the detective novel to write a powerful reflection on the new twists and turns of the global imperial order. He uses parody to focus on the absurdity of the seriousness with which a new version of global Empire began to take itself as it emerged in the aftermath of 9/11 and initiated President Bush's global war on terror. In the novel, the fictional American president, Dean Mumford, a phonetic pastiche of Donald Rumsfeld, affectionately known in Angola as Dino Mefode [Dino Fucksme], leads a trigger-happy super-power in an era when designating one's opponents as terrorists became, as I shall discuss in the next chapter, a licence to obliterate.

Within this parodical tone, which deflates many of the pretences of Angolan internal power structures too, there is always a serious edge. We are no longer in the carnivalesque era of Bakhtin's polyglottic discourses, capable of undermining master narratives by a temporary but essentially irrevocable suspension of their sanctity.[16] Nor does this parody mimic the new master narrative menacingly à la Bhabha, for the narrative itself is born of the post-modern age of unreal mimetic image exchange.[17] Instead, the parody ends up paradoxically bringing humanity back to the fore.

The plot is replete with the human touches of men and women — their loves and jealousies — and in keeping with the dialogic technique Pepetela has mastered since *Mayombe*, the narrator's omniscience yields the narrative to the thoughts of individual characters in the plot, with one noticeable exception — the FBI agent, the lesbian Shirley, sent to investigate the death of her compatriot. Her thoughts are never revealed, although Jaime Bunda constantly tries to surmise what they are.

The tale begins with the rhetorical question, as to why, when other nations existed that were ideal 'para um americano morrer de morte matado' (p. 9) [for an American to die a killed death], like Afghanistan, Iran or Somalia, was peaceful Benguela chosen? Against all probabilities, Angola's second city and birthplace of Pepetela is the place where a gringo engineer is found with a bullet in his head, 'para grande preocupação dos governantes [...] e perante a indiferença da maioria da população' (p. 9) [to the great consternation of the powers that be [...] and the general indifference of the majority of the population], an indifference tempered by private glee on the part of a small section of the society who 'guardava ainda na memória os ressentimentos pelo apoio descarado que o governo dos Estados Unidos sempre brindara ao detestável regime do *apartheid* na vizinha África do Sul, embora ninguém mais tivesse coragem de em viva voz chamar os bois pelos nomes e o imperialismo pelo imperialismo, preferindo hoje blandiciosas globalizações mais pós-modernistas' (p. 9) [still retained in their memories resentment about the shameless support the US government always provided to the detestable *apartheid* regime in neighbouring South Africa, even if no one any longer had the courage to call a spade a spade or imperialism imperialism out loud, preferring today the most post-modern and bland globalizations]. So ends the first page of the novel. The reader is in little doubt that the abuse of language — the change and exchange of discourses be they on terror or democracy — will come into play.

Pepetela claims that the humour present in *Jaime Bunda* helped him to overcome writer's block — the hours he spent in front of a computer screen with others thinking he was churning out serious prose.[18] As he ages, he claims, it has become more difficult to write, presumably for fear of repetition:

> I find all types of excuses not to write. I spend a lot of time in front of the computer, but I am not writing. No one knows about this. I don't write. They think I am writing, but I am not. It has become more difficult. Yes, the humour in *Jaime Bunda* helped me to recover a bit.[19]

The first Jaime Bunda novel, *Jaime Bunda, agente secreto*, had multiple narrators, one of whom was dismissed in exasperation by the author. The second, *Jaime Bunda e a morte do americano*, sees a return of that recalcitrant narratorial voice. The voice becomes a much more salient and ironic critic of the narrative process — positioning itself as self-mocking.

The dates the novels were published are particularly relevant as they fall either side of the year (2002) rebel UNITA leader, Jonas Savimbi, was assassinated by government forces, bringing a definitive end to the armed conflict. The novels also fell between two trips by Pepetela to the US, where he toured several universities and took up a writing residency at Berkeley. In fact, he was due to set off to the USA for a tour of East coast tertiary institutions the day that Savimbi was assassinated, and although he claimed he was not able to reach Luanda airport because of inclement weather, a suspicion remains that the delay was not unrelated to the outbreak of general jubilation in the Angolan capital on news of Savimbi's death. He did eventually arrive in New Jersey, a few days late, and subsequently produced his first novel that explicitly targets US mores, followed later by another humorous critique of the absurdities and excesses of the Bush-era discourse on terrorism, *O terrorista de Berkeley, Califórnia*, which I shall discuss in the next chapter.

Asked about the effect of the end of the civil war on Angola's literary production, Pepetela replied: 'Perhaps it is too early to know that. Perhaps things have not been published about it. But there can be no doubt that it will leave its mark. It's a milestone. We can certainly say that. We can't see it very clearly now, but it is. But it will have repercussions in literature'.[20] I would argue that to understand fully *Jaime Bunda e a morte do americano*, we need to read it as the first post-conflict novel in Angola and recognize that, as such, it initiates a new literary era.

Angola's civil war ended in such a way that the MPLA victory was absolute. Rarely in the history of post-independence Africa has that been the case: in most civil conflicts, an accommodation between the warring factions has been necessary to bring an end to hostilities. In Angola, the MPLA eventually crushed UNITA and was subsequently able to define completely the terms of the peace. In the early years of independence, when the MPLA hold on power had often been precarious, it had relied on the cultural hegemony of its Creole elites to advance the perception beyond Angola's borders that it was on the side of the people. Pepetela, as I have discussed, was integral to that process.

As the MPLA moved further away from its founding principles, only the threat of a UNITA government muted Pepetela's critique of what had become of the movement of which he was once a fully fledged member. In an interview in 1995, he admitted that the 'espectro da UNITA' [the spectre of UNITA] obliged Angola's urban society to align with the MPLA, but that 'é preciso surgirem outras forças, até para o MPLA se modificar'[21] [other forces are needed, so that the MPLA can reform]. With the disappearance of the UNITA spectre in 2002, the MPLA's fuller responsibility for the state of the nation came into clearer focus. With no credible alternative, and the undisguised rise of the party's elites, Pepetela became more concerned with how, within the limiting parameters of MPLA hegemony, positive change could be possible.

In *Jaime Bunda e a morte do americano*, he posits the possibility of popular forgiveness of the elites as a means of national survival. Complete disengagement with the state is, despite the suggestion made in *O desejo de Kianda*, no longer a pragmatic option. As in *Mayombe*, the concept of forgiveness is once again tied in with a Marxist understanding of how capitalism and power operate. But it is no longer linked to the morality of the convent or to a critique of 'autocrítica'. Now it is offered as the only viable solution — post-'End of History' — for a nation depicted as corrupt and malfunctioning.

In floating forgiveness as the only solution for MPLA corruption in the post-conflict nation (rather than as a symptom of colonial heritage), the second *Jaime Bunda* novel represents a radical departure. In a sense, Pepetela accepts some of the premises of Fukuyama's argument, but reverts to an adapted Marxist analysis to suggest how History can carry on. He does this in *Jaime Bunda e a morte do americano* through the voice of a poet, an authorial alter-ego, Julião Domingos de Sousa, the 'vate de Benguela' (p. 248) [bard of Benguela]. Julião Domingos de Sousa is introduced at the beginning of the novel, on the second page of the text. Even though he appears to play a secondary role, part of his importance *qua* alter-ego resides in his suggestion of a national policy of PGL or 'Perdão Geral aos Ladrões' [General Pardon for Thieves] as the only way to move Angola forward.

Hailing from the same city as Pepetela, Julião Domingos de Sousa is one of the author's stereotypical commentators from the sidelines. He is an anti-American poet, possibly with Cape Verdean blood flowing through his veins (a heritage he denies), and he writes one poem twice a year. Noted for his hairstyle from the 1950s and his 'estilo de galã antiquado, género Robert Taylor' (p. 103) [antiquated gallant style, sort of Robert Taylor], everything about him is a little dated. The comparison with one of Hollywood's heart-throbs from the 1940s represents an oxymoron between style and substance. He mirrors the dated styles of a culture he purports to detest.

A leader of a 'grupinho de esquerdistas saudosistas' (p. 10) [a small band of nostalgic left-wingers], Domingos de Sousa declares on hearing of the death of the American engineer that is the trigger for the novel's investigation: 'um gringo a menos, sempre melhora a qualidade do ar' (p. 10) [one gringo less always improves the air quality]. In fact, he goes on to ask for the name of the national hero, who 'ajudara o engenheiro a transpor as pesadas e irreversíveis portas de Caronte, palavras atribuídas pelo inefável poeta ao Inferno de Dante, livro que, se não manuseava com assiduidade, pelo menos regularmente citava' (p. 10) [helped the engineer pass through the heavy, one-way gates of Charon, words attributed by the ineffable poet to Dante's Inferno, a book that, if he didn't leaf through assiduously, at least he regularly cited].

The texture of Julião Domingos de Sousa's hair points to mestizo blood, one of the hallmarks of the MPLA Creole elite. In part, he represents the part of that elite which became disillusioned with where the revolutionary movement ended up, but that could offer nothing other than sarcastic criticism as material benefits accrued to them, as well as to the MPLA leadership. A lazy facileness characterizes Domingos de Sousa, who makes superficial readings of Dante, from whom he plucks random quotes without reading the poet attentively, and who expends very little effort in writing his own poetry. His parasitical approach to Dante is part of the novel's postmodern thrust in which anything can be used to support anything — and those who once had convictions now only have comments and discursive emptiness.

Another of the characters in the novel is a citation from one of Pepetela's earlier short stories in which the role of American relativism is key. The rather incompetent Benguela police officer, Rosas, is a residue from a prior era when he worked for the colonial authorities. He is now deployed with the approval of the Americans to beat a confession out of an innocent man. He shares his name with a Benguela-based policeman from 'Agarra que é polícia!' published in Pepetela's 2011 collection

Crónicas com Fundo de Guerra but written in 1994 before the Jaime Bunda novels.

The short story is about how American moral relativity — witnessed in a Hollywood film in which not all the cops were good cops — helped Pepetela to understand there was something awry with his childhood Manichaean mindset, and that there must be something wrong with colonial culture for him to acquire that mindset:

> Vi o tal filme americano e perguntei-me: o Rosas ou o Silva [local police officers] seriam também capazes de perseguir e maltratar um inocente só porque era negro, ou para lhe extorquir dinheiro? Foi uma pergunta que durante algum tempo me perseguiu, até me informar de mais coisas e acabar por perder a inocência virginal. Nessa altura respondi à pergunta pela afirmativa, claro que eram capazes disso e de muito mais, eram polícias do fascismo.[22]

> [I saw the American film in question and I wondered, could Rosas or Silva [local police officers] be capable of persecuting or mistreating an innocent man just because he was black or to shake him down? It was a question that stayed with me for quite some time, until I found out about more things and ended up losing my virginal innocence. That's when I answered yes, of course they were capable of this and much more, they were fascism's police.]

He develops his chronicle by pointing out that no ten- or twelve-year-old in Angola today is so naïve as to believe in the integrity of the police force. Everyone knows they are corrupt, as they are the world over, be they 'milícias dos países que se dizem socialistas' (p. 74) [militias from so-called socialist countries] or FBI agents. After exemplifying their systemic corruption, Pepetela comes to the crux of the story — the nostalgic admission that is characteristic of so many of his chronicles, and distinguishes their concept of History from how it operates in his earlier novels:

> Se não acabo por ter saudades do Rosas e do Silva, figuras protagonistas de um tempo que ninguém quer que volte, tenho pelo menos saudades da minha ingenuidade perdida que me fazia acreditar na integridade policial, que ao menos era uma referência (p. 74).

> [If I don't end up being nostalgic for Rosas and Silva, leading figures from a time which no one wants to return, I'm at the very least nostalgic for my lost innocence that made me believe in police integrity, and gave me some kind of benchmark.]

The nostalgia is not a desire for the colonial order, but rather for the simplicity associated with an as-yet unshaken belief in right and wrong. The underlying point is not that colonialism gave you right and wrong, even if the wrong way round. Even at its most offensive and vile, colonialism was never simply a case of black and white.

Pepetela's nostalgia in the short story is for the dream of utopia lost in *A geração da utopia*, a new world that did not happen as it was supposed to after independence. More importantly, it is a nostalgia for circumstances untainted by the relativism inherent in American films that took the child Artur Pestana's virginal innocence away when Angola was still a colony of Portugal. Those were the conditions of possibility for that utopian space to be imagined. Rather than utopia being the end point of History, since History proved to be flawed by the post-independence politics of the Angolan state, the utopian moment is very concretely located in the innocence of Pepetela's childhood.

But the world as it is, is one of relativism — not absolutes and utopia. And relativism in Pepetela's literary universe is often linked to the post-modern world of American cultural hegemony with which the author seeks to come to terms in a novel whose title promises the death of an American. *Jaime Bunda e a morte do americano* is a novel with two possible endings.

In the first, an epilogue signed by Pepetela and dated to Luanda in February 2003, the consumption-ridden Júlio Fininho — a Robin-Hood-style railroad thief, falsely accused of murdering the American engineer, and the physical antithesis of Jaime Bunda — may or may not survive. For his part, the American probably committed suicide because he could not deal with being impotent. The possibility of a 'happy-ending' in keeping with American taste is dangled before the reader.

In the second ending — followed by an author's note dated in Berkeley in April 2003 — Júlio Fininho is declared innocent but dies before he can be released from prison, a victim of heavy-handed policing, tuberculosis and bad luck. In this alternative ending, the American was murdered by another American in a warped love triangle. Both endings highlight a defective state of affairs in Angola, in which cycles of domination and corruption spiral unchecked and no matter what truth is discovered, there seems to be an impunity for those with power to exercise as ruthlessly or banally as they see fit. Justice is never served.

So what, then, does Pepetela offer as a way of breaking this cycle of History — or in keeping with Stephen Henighan's reading of the novel — to counter Fukuyama's *End of History*, with the moral relativity that work implied? The key comes in the pages immediately preceding the two alternative endings, in which the peripheral Domingos de Sousa re-emerges to argue for his PGL — or General Pardon of Thieves. His logic is as follows. Socialism in Angola collectivized everything, removing vigilance over personal property, so that the elites could easily take advantage, privatizing what they had grouped together and buying collective assets at bargain-basement prices. There is nothing particularly groundbreaking in the Benguelan poet's assessment of his nation's socio-economic process. It is also a logic affirmed by Carmina in *O desejo de Kianda*.[23]

The problem as Domingos de Sousa sees it is that having stolen all the nation's assets, the elites moved them abroad, and the nation desperately needs the money back in order to build a modern economy. His solution is strategically to pardon them — to legitimize prior thieves and make them the guardians of a new ethics, so that future larceny will not be tolerated by those who have already stolen the most. Society as a whole will benefit from a new bourgeois mentality that criminalizes theft to protect property. In this new order, justice must cede to a resentful form of strategic forgiveness in which what is required is a new social pact through which the predatory classes of Angola are turned into the new bourgeoisie.

Domingos de Sousa admits that the fate of poets is to be unheard until society catches up with them, so he expects his plan to fall on deaf ears. Since Pepetela felt obliged to write *Predadores* two years later — a novel that catalogues the continued and increasing impunity of the MPLA elites as they pillaged national assets — it seems that the political formulas proffered by poets take more than a few years to sink in.

Clearly, *Jaime Bunda e a morte do americano* marked a sea change in Pepetela's thinking — a change that had an evolutionary path and coincided with the consolidation of MPLA hegemony as the civil war definitively ended. In subsequent novels, like his 2013 *O tímido e as mulheres* and his 2009 attempt at a love story, *O planalto e a estepe*, he reverts to Helder Macedo's injunction to say the same thing more than once but differently, as novel plots are now used to suggest that pragmatism is the only antidote to the disillusionment of betrayed utopian vision. It took the death of an American for him to reach this very American conclusion.

American hegemony would be an increasing topic of interest for Pepetela in the noughties. As I shall discuss in the next chapter, the backdrop of George W. Bush's War on Terror informed the characterizations of both *Jaime Bunda e a morte do americano* and the subsequent novella, *O terrorista de Berkeley, Califórnia*. In both works, America assumes the mantle of an adolescent empire, still coming to grips with what its power means.

Notes to Chapter 9

1. Helder Macedo, *Parts of Africa*, trans. by Phillip Rothwell (Dartmouth: LAABST, 2015), p. 187.
2. 'Pepetela: crónica de uma Angola em mudança', interview with Luís Ricardo Duarte in *Jornal de Letras, Artes e Ideias*, 30 October 2013, pp. 8–9 (p. 8).
3. Pepetela interviewed by Roberto Castro, 'A dura luta para escrever', *Jornal da USP*, 30 June 1997, p. 12.
4. Stephen Henighan, '"Um James Bond Subdesenvolvido": The Ideological Work of the Angolan Detective in Pepetela's Jaime Bunda Novels', *Portuguese Studies*, 22.1 (2006), 135–52 (p. 138). Subsequent page references given in the text.
5. Francis Fukuyama, *The End of History and the Last Man* (London: Hamish Hamilton, 1992).
6. See *O Desejo de Kianda*, p. 23, pp. 39–40 and pp. 44–45.
7. Ana Mafalda Leite et al., *Speaking the Postcolonial Nation*, p. 131.
8. Rafael Marques de Morais, 'Religion and the State in Angola', *Maka Angola*, 27 April 2014 <https://www.makaangola.org/2014/04/religion-and-the-state-in-angola/> [accessed 27 March 2018].
9. Ibid.
10. No byline, 'Pope takes African pilgrimage to Angola', *Philstar Global*, 20 March 2009 <http://www.philstar.com/breaking-news/450000/pope-takes-african-pilgrimage-angola> [accessed 27 March 2018].
11. Junno Arocho Esteves, 'Pope Francis Meets with President of Angola', *Zenit*, 2 May 2014 <http://www.zenit.org/en/articles/pope-francis-meets-with-president-of-angola> [accessed 27 March 2018].
12. Marques de Morais, op. cit.
13. Leite, *Speaking the Postcolonial Nation*, p. 121.
14. Ibid., p. 122.
15. Mia Couto, *A varanda do frangipani* (Lisbon: Caminho, 1996).
16. M. M. Bakhtin, *Problems of Dostoevsky's Poetics*, trans. by Caryl Emerson (Manchester: Manchester University Press, 1984).

17. Homi Bhabha, 'Of Mimicry and Man: The Ambivalence of Colonial Discourse', *October*, 28 (Spring 1984), 125–33.
18. Leite, p. 121.
19. Ibid.
20. Ibid., p. 114.
21. Interview with Rodrigues da Silva, 'Da utopia à amargura', *Jornal de Letras, Artes e Ideias*, 29 March 1995, pp. 14–16 (p. 14).
22. Pepetela, *Crónicas com fundo de guerra* (Lisbon: Nelson de Matos, 2011), p. 72.
23. *Desejo*, p. 24.

CHAPTER 10

❖

The American Bogeyman: Empire and the Terror Cell

If, as I argued in the last chapter, the second Jaime Bunda novel can be read as a sequel whose similarity to the first is deceptive — representing a definitive break rather than a continuity, through Pepetela's treatment of the role of elite forgiveness — *Jaime Bunda e a morte do americano* does present us with another kind of replication: that of empire. The novel portrays Angola in 2003, and suggests the 1974 revolutionary rupture that forced a colonial discontinuity (with the demise of the Portuguese empire) did not prevent an imperial reiteration (under the guise of American-backed neo-liberal globalization).

In his early anti-colonial writing, novels like *Mayombe* and the novella *As aventuras de Ngunga*, Pepetela was always careful to make clear that the independence struggle was not against a people (namely the Portuguese), but against a system. Imperialism was, for Pepetela, not the essence of the Portuguese nation but a systemic practice underwriting a pernicious variant of capitalism. This was an important distinction, one made repeatedly by Amílcar Cabral, and certainly endorsed by Agostinho Neto, whose wife was Portuguese and whose convictions were Marxist.

In the context of the Portuguese New State, which failed to educate the majority of its population to any significant degree and used repression to limit the aspirations and freedoms of its own people, it was not a difficult argument to sustain, even if emotively many of those fighting for their freedom in Africa saw their enemy embodied in the Portuguese colonizer. The rapidity with which Angola under the MPLA normalized diplomatic relations with post-dictatorship Portugal is a testament to that underlying understanding. Diplomatic relations were formally established between Portugal and Angola at the end of 1976. By 2011, Angola under dos Santos was loaning the Portuguese government funds, in a post-colonial twist, to help it to deal with its sovereign debt crisis.[1]

The MPLA's attitudes towards the United States were always far more ambivalent. The USA only recognized the MPLA as the legitimate government of Angola in 1993, appointing its first ambassador to Luanda in 1994 nearly two decades after independence.[2] The Cuban presence on Angolan soil had been the sticking point for many years. At the same time, American companies were heavily involved in the extraction of Angolan oil, even at the height of the Cold War.

American culture, particularly its film industry, was highly influential on

Angola's Creole elites, including Pepetela, even in the colonial era, as we saw in relation to his short story 'Agarra que é polícia!' discussed in the last chapter. With the end of the Cold War, the pervasiveness of that culture, and its associations with a globalized marketplace, became a fundamental issue for Pepetela. America had become the new Empire. Unlike the Portuguese Empire before it, American economic interests effectively used culture as part of an arsenal of expansion. Its people were suffused in that culture. As a result, unlike the Portuguese soldiers forced into a colonial conflict by a regime they did not support, Americans — not just their economic system — became a legitimate target of Pepetela's critique. Portuguese culture (particularly in its literature) had provided the Creole elites with a grammar to challenge the imperialism of the New State. In contrast, American culture was now part of the imperial problem.

In this chapter, I shall discuss how Pepetela depicts America as the latest version of an imperial order in *Jaime Bunda e a morte do americano*, before turning our attention to *O terrorista de Berkeley, Califórnia*, a novella that portrays the inner workings of that empire and the small-mindedness of a people restricted by the discourse of terror that predominated in the aftermath of 9/11.

Jaime Bunda e a morte do americano was written in the run up to the Second Gulf War. At the time, Angola had the misfortune to be one of Africa's representatives on the UN Security Council as the US administration lobbied to gain the endorsement of that international body for its invasion of Iraq, under the rubric of its War on Terror. In February and March 2003, there was a renewed 'Scramble for Africa',[3] as France and Britain dispatched prominent ministers to Cameroon, Guinea and Angola, in an effort to persuade the African members of the so-called 'middle-six' on the Security Council, who had yet to decide which way to vote on a resolution authorizing the use of force against Iraq. Britain's minister, Valerie Amos, visited Luanda twice in two weeks — a record by most accounts — reinforcing phone calls from then US Vice President Dick Cheney and George W. Bush to President dos Santos. Dos Santos was promised US help for post-civil war reconstruction and given a conditional assurance that the US would abstain from criticism of his government should its moves to open democracy stall.[4]

Angola's government was placed in an awkward position, dependent as it was on both French and American oil companies for the continued exploration of its offshore reserves. The two NATO powers articulated opposing positions. Angolan oil at the time accounted for a sixth of US oil imports and, as the US ambassador to Luanda vociferously asserted in early March 2003, Washington spent a very conditional $100 million a year on development projects in Angola. Yet, despite the potentially grave consequences of failing to back the American administration's position, there was overwhelming disapproval, at least among the chattering classes of Luanda's press, for endorsing any recourse to violence until all other means had been exhausted. As an editorial in the *Jornal de Angola* put it: 'Angola is all too familiar with the social and economic horrors that follow in the wake of war, for these reasons alone she owes it to herself to support a peaceful resolution'.[5]

We will never know how Angola would have voted had Bush not decided to go to war without UN authorization. Doubtless, dos Santos's government was relieved not to have to play its hand. The whole debacle demonstrated the extent to which the USA, post-Cold War, was seen to be dictating the agenda in Angola. As a result, words uttered in Washington resonated with a colonial charge in Luanda. *Jaime Bunda e a morte do americano* was written against that backdrop. For all the humour that adorns his narrative, Pepetela is damning of what he casts as the American inheritors of the colonial order in Angola, their repetition of the colonial paradigm, and their ability to use lightly words that kill.

As we have repeatedly seen, Pepetela is no stranger to critiquing the processes of power. The way Marxist-Leninism came to be practised in Angola left much to be desired, with theory rarely corresponding to practice. Like the system it replaced, the MPLA government created elites — men who were more equal in a system rhetorically grounded in a naïve, or worse still, deceptive notion of equality for all.

Pepetela has never made much secret of his dislike of José Eduardo dos Santos — a man he considers to be little more than an opportunist. In that optic, dos Santos's ideological gymnastics, from card-carrying communist to a paladin of the free-enterprise culture, always happened at just the right moment to permit the survival of Angola's elite, and rarely benefited society at large. With the realization of Angola's immense oil wealth, it ceased to be a poor nation, and became one of the world's biggest exporters of the fuel. Yet, as is so often the case, only a small proportion of this newly realized wealth finds its way into social programmes or reaches disadvantaged sectors of society. As the discrepancy between massive national wealth and massive poverty becomes more stark, so too does the exercise of surplus repression.

The concept of surplus repression is explored by Herbert Marcuse in his *Eros and Civilization*.[6] Investigating Freud's psychology through a philosophical lens, Marcuse argues, drawing on *Civilization and its Discontents*,[7] that in an era when resources are scarce, repression of the individual is essential to the survival of society. This repression becomes surplus once society has more than enough to sustain its population comfortably but chooses to distribute resources inequitably. The individual must be surplussly repressed in order to permit that status quo. While Marcuse's solution — a kind of uninhibited sexual revolution — is fanciful and dated, his critique of the system's exercise of power over the individual is still useful. The idea of surplus repression found a new configuration in dos Santos's Angola, where inequalities grew unchecked because of a systematic use of a discourse of fear or, post-millennium, one of terror.

Fear in post-independence Angola had emerged in the repercussions of the events of May 1977, and the repressive state apparatus Neto's reaction enabled. Fear also emerged as a result of the long-running civil war, particularly at moments when cities felt under threat. Following the death of Jonas Savimbi, fear of civil strife subsided, but fear as a debilitating force re-emerges in Pepetela's 2003 text in response to the words and actions of the new empire.

The threatening rhetoric of the Bush administration in the aftermath of 9/11, which many intellectuals in Africa saw as the new imperial centre flexing its muscles,[8] posed a new kind of existential threat — one explored by Pepetela in

Jaime Bunda e a morte do americano. Pepetela draws parallels between imperial orders, historic and contemporary, to once again demonstrate how the different external hues and soubriquets of power constantly reconfigure and conceal essentially similar structures.

When, in *Jaime Bunda e a morte do americano*, the American ambassador interrupts the Angolan foreign minister's frolics on the beach, demanding that immediate action is taken to determine the cause of death of his compatriot, he makes clear the terminology which will be employed at the earliest juncture if the world's only remaining superpower does not get its way: 'Se não esclarece rápido, pode pensar-se que foi deliberadamente um atentado a um cidadão americano. Terrorismo. Sabe-se lá as consequências disso...'[9] [If this isn't cleared up quickly, it could be thought that this was a deliberate attack on an American citizen. Terrorism. Who knows the consequences of that]. The foreign minister is all too painfully aware of the possible consequences.

A word that was used against the MPLA by the Portuguese colonizers, and then against the MPLA government by *apartheid*-era South Africa was, in the past, deemed risible. Suddenly it is not: 'Os senhores chamam terrorista a alguém ou a algum país e logo enviam uma bomba atómica' (p. 18) [Those gentlemen call someone or some country a terrorist, and next thing they drop an atomic bomb]. The verbalization of that fear, which according to the minister is not an exaggeration, but rather an anticipation, is, in effect, a call on the American ambassador to temper his language, and to realize the absurdity and, yet at the same time, extreme danger of repeating a shibboleth that can kill.

In the context of Angola in 2003, it is no longer a joke to be called a terrorist: it is a potential death sentence, for it is no longer a relative term interchangeable with freedom fighter but rather an absolute as defined by 'o americano' [the American], and justified through his culture.

According to novel's narrator, the greatest contribution of America to global culture is hamburgers and ketchup, which Angola's now-deemed-to-be hackneyed die-hard left term 'má alimentação' (p. 11) [poor nutrition]. The ironic tone used by Pepetela in relating how the USA was suddenly 'reciclado à categoria de amigo' (p. 11) [recycled into the friend category] and all terminology used to propagate the previous socialist order suddenly rendered inadmissible, is in fact a jibe at the transfer of one form of totalitarianism into yet another. From colonialism to scientific socialism to the free-market, there is a steady progression into what Marcuse terms the totally administered society,[10] where choices are never choices and language as part of the cultural mechanism of Empire becomes completely detached from political content.

At the same time, language in such a context always serves a very clearly defined and oppressive political end. That, for Pepetela, was always the danger of over-embracing the 'blandiciosas globalizações mais pós-modernistas' (p. 9) [most post-modern, ingratiating globalizations]: language lost its meaning, and cultural empire transferred from high art into popular Hollywood films. The loss of language's fixed meaning, implied by post-modernism, becomes one of the subtlest forms of surplus repression, because, for Pepetela, it denies the possibility of articulating a meaningful alternative. The subject becomes enslaved to a facile, empty culture. The only permissible release is through the violent outburst of a narrative of terror.

Hollywood films and American television shows are what inform Jaime Bunda of the world around him. His uncritical appreciation of American culture initially leads him not to be able to grasp why the list of anti-American suspects drawn up to assist the investigation was the size of a telephone directory:

> Como podiam detestar tanto quem fazia aqueles fabulosos filmes de acção e escrevia os melhores livros policiais? Ó gentinha ignorante, rancorosa e invejosa. Então não eram os americanos os melhores amigos do mundo, sempre prontos a defender a democracia, mesmo que às custas de uns quantos bombardeamentos selectivos? (p. 155)

> [How could they so detest those that made such fabulous action films and wrote the best detective stories? Such ignorant, resentful and jealous little people. Weren't the Americans the best friends in the world, ever ready to defend democracy, even at the cost of a few selective bombardments.]

Under the influence of too many episodes of *CSI — Crime Scene Investigation*, Bunda is a firm believer in Americans' ability to solve any mystery through cutting-edge analysis of the victim's body, an analysis that extends, in his mind, to knowledge of the victim's tarot cards and sexual orientation. Yet, as the novel evolves, Jaime will progressively enter the real world, leaving behind the 'preocupações marquetísticas pós-modernas' (p. 51) [post-modern marketing concerns] that even lead Angolan journalists to change their names in order to become trendier. Bunda will come to realize that the man falsely but conveniently charged with the murder he is investigating is, first and foremost, a human being, not a discursive trope.

Before he can return to the reality of humanity — a trajectory repeatedly advocated by the Marcuse and the Frankfurt School as they critiqued the global rise of American consumerism in the 1950s and 1960s[11] — Jaime Bunda lives in the fantasy world created by his parallel universe of Hollywood films and detective novels. He revels in the discourse of fear that he can project because of his attachment to the intelligence services (the SIG). People tremble when they realize he works for the SIG. That power trip replicates the discourse of terror which is one of smoke and mirrors, where the source of fear is always in neurotic abstraction.

In the case of the Bunker — as the presidential residence is termed in the novel — it both houses and symbolizes a presidency far removed from the people it claims to represent, transforming the physically secluded president into a phantom. No one knows where it is, so, by perverse panoptic logic, it must be everywhere, and that nowhere-thus-everywhere produces a convenient source of fear for surplus repression. The presidency is a Wizard of Oz, now taking its cue in the logic of terror from its newly established American friends.

When Bunda learns that the USA will be sending an FBI agent (poorly disguised as an embassy official) to monitor the progress of the investigation, he is elated at the chance to work alongside the best. His fantasy is to be the sidekick partner of an inspirational Yankee policeman — for a man it must surely be.

However, the new Empire, as Pepetela depicts it, is more post-modern than patriarchal, and will therefore appropriate any difference into its structure, so it should be no surprise that Shirley is the agent sent. Not only is she an attractive mestizo, who infatuates all the Angolan policemen around her, but she is also a lesbian who will spend much of her time in Benguela in seductive moves on one of the city's beauty queens. Like every good non-white American, so Pepetela would have us believe, Shirley claims solidarity with black Angolans who see in her nothing but a new agent of repression.

Like her nation's ambassador, Shirley is determined to bring everything back to work. Time is of the essence in her stressed-out culture. Her nervousness is infectious. It jars with the stereotypical Angolan lack of time-consciousness. At every available opportunity, Shirley re-orientates any discussion onto the discourse of terror, warning of an Angolan holocaust should her government feel Angolan authorities were less than whole-hearted in their commitment to countering what the Americans deem to be a terror threat to the free world.

In *Jaime Bunda e a morte do americano*, there are various hypotheses surrounding the American's death. The one initially preferred by the Angolan government is suicide. But suicide is not an acceptable explanation to Shirley; at least, not at the beginning of the story. In scarcely concealed allusions to George W. Bush's speeches following 9/11, someone has to pay, and the price exacted must be high. As the Angolan foreign minister notes, one American life is worth more to the Empire than the thousands of Angolans who died in the Angolan civil conflict, propagated with American help. As colonial history shows, this has long been the case. When an opponent's humanity is obliterated discursively, it does not matter if they are guilty of anything at all — they pay the price for ceasing to be human. This is one of Pepetela's central criticisms of how US foreign policy operated in the early twenty-first century.

Pepetela aims to re-humanize where Bush spoke of Axes of Evil. For the Angolan author, the unsophisticated use of binary language by the Americans to describe human behaviour causes many more problems than it ever solves. At the same time, that binary simplification is itself a by-product of years of post-modern consumerism leaving an ideological void that Marcuse and the Frankfurt School warned in the mid-twentieth century might lead to totalitarianism and violence. By 2001, when the Twin Towers fell, there was already a space created for ideological certainty, and Manichean worldviews. Pepetela makes the link clear in *Jaime Bunda e a morte do americano* by repeatedly condemning both American-inspired post-modernism *and* the ideological certainties of the Bush era. The two extremes in the American cultural wars feed into each other and, for Pepetela, the rest of the world suffers the consequences.

In the twisting threads of *Jaime Bunda e a morte do americano*'s subplots, a heroic train robber, nicknamed Robin dos Comboios [Robin Trains] for his exclusive targeting of rich passengers, finds himself in prison, suspected of the murder by all but Jaime Bunda, who knows he is innocent. His real name is Júlio Fininho. He has fallen in love with Maria Antónia, a hardworking prostitute who uses her profession to pay for her younger sister's education so that she can escape the poverty and dysfunctional structure of their family. As a teenager, Maria Antónia was sexually abused by her stepfather, but kept quiet on the advice of a priest, who offered the Christian 'conselho de resignação' (p. 71) [counsel of resignation], another instance of Pepetela's potent barbs against the legacies of the Catholic Church in Angola.

As fate had it, at the time of his first encounter with Maria Antónia, Júlio Fininho was going out with the spiteful Josefina. Josefina decided to enlist the aid of an old woman to place a curse on the man she claimed to love, shackling him to her for the rest of his life. Unfortunately, as we discover towards the end of the novel, a plane thundered past at the precise moment that Josefina uttered the vital indirect pronoun. The old woman who was placing the curse on Júlio Fininho merely heard she was supposed to imprison him for the rest of his life, rather than imprisoning him to Josefina. Whatever the underlying cause of Júlio Fininho's arrest, the police reached him because Maria Antónia was the last person to be seen with the dead American, in her professional capacity, and as luck and the dictates of a good detective novel demand, she had left a piece of jewellery behind at the scene of the crime or suicide.

When the police went to talk to her, they found Júlio Fininho in her house, looking suspicious, because he thought they had come to arrest him for the train robberies. He makes a convenient scapegoat for the American's death, particularly when it becomes apparent, through the testimony of Maria Antónia, that the deceased was, despite all her professional efforts, impotent. Maria Antónia described the American as 'uma criança de 30 anos' (p. 150) [a thirty-year-old child], blaming his mother for his sexual dysfunction. The dead American operates metonymically for his culture and nation — an adolescent superpower that wreaks unintended havoc because he feels powerless. Shirley sees in Júlio Fininho a more convenient explanation for the American's death, avoiding the emasculation of one of her all-powerful, yet immature, nationals.

In her War on Terror, Shirley is tacitly prepared to sanction the use of torture, as idiotic police officers beat the innocent but now dehumanized Júlio Fininho to extract a confession from him. Angolan politicians in Luanda, particularly in the Bunker, are keen to close the case in a way that pleases their new allies in Washington, and put pressure on the all-too-human Jaime Bunda to stop asking awkward questions and return to the capital, now that someone has been found to take the blame. Bunda's stubbornness is the source of his heroism: he will not let go of his doubts for the sake of political expediency, and where politicians cower he is naively fearless. As a result, he uncovers the possibility that another American may have been responsible for the death in a vindictive feud that dates back to their college days.

This is where Pepetela introduces structurally the most damning and post-colonially charged indictment of the political and imperial situation in the Angola of 2003. The American's death mirrors a case that occurred fifty years earlier, when the nation was a discontented colony of the Portuguese, and the colonized of the era were discursively relegated to something below humanity. The so-called 'boas relações' [good relations] now enjoyed with Washington are, according to the die-hard 'más-línguas de esquerda' [slanderers on the left], 'apenas relações de vassalagem para com o Império emergente' (p. 59) [merely relations of vassalage with the emerging empire]. The mimetic nature of the plot — a repetition of an incident in the 1950s in which a Portuguese engineer died in the same circumstances and with similar consequences for an innocent scapegoat — renders the novel a pungent commentary on the iterative nature of the new imperial order. The referencing by the American ambassador to 'a primeira de uma série de operações terroristas tendo como alvo os interesses americanos na região' (p. 143) [the first of a string of terrorist operations targeting American interests in the region] is little more than the inheritance or, more precisely, the translation of a discourse favoured by Salazar which cast his anticolonial opponents as terrorists, in a discursive simplification that allowed for lives to be sacrificed in lands far away.

As the old left in the novel discusses the similarities between the 2003 mystery and the death of the Portuguese engineer five decades earlier, one of their number comments on the most obvious of the many coincidences between the two cases: 'Há cinquenta anos o morto tinha vindo há pouco tempo da potência colonizadora. Agora o falecido vem da nova potência colonizadora, do Império' (p. 110) [Fifty years ago, the dead guy had recently arrived from the colonizing power. Today, the deceased comes from the new colonizing power, the Empire].

A key difference between the two empires that Pepetela highlights is that humanity is no longer necessarily coded by race. In a post-modern appropriation, a black lesbian (or mestiza depending on who is looking at her) can become the agent of the Empire, and reserves her greatest bile for those who question the Empire to which she belongs. Commenting on a newspaper article that compares the deaths of the Portuguese engineer with the American's, Shirley is uncompromising in her reduction of those who dare to make such comparisons to 'terroristas' [terrorists] who 'alimentarem o ódio à América' (p. 211) [nurture hatred against America]. Her words echo President Bush's speeches before Congress, in which he put the world on notice of his intention to annihilate through military force those he deemed to hate American freedom.

Shirley concludes 'há frases assassinas' (p. 212) [there are killer phrases] referring to the comparison between Portuguese and American colonialism. Her fury reveals an uncomfortable truth. Words and phrases do kill, but not those uttered by the has-been left of Angola, that tiny minority of 'dez comunistas' [ten communists] who actually existed there after independence (p. 212). Rather, the words that kill are those that reduce and dehumanize anyone who will not be co-opted into the tantrum-throwing logic of the new imperial system. For Pepetela, one of the greatest threats posed by an immature, confusingly impotent America at the turn of the century was the sloppy use of language. After years of the post-modern cultural logic of capitalism, in which reality and referent did not have to correspond, the big guns and nuclear bombs of the Empire were a small rhetorical slip away from the reduction of all opponents to terrorists. Pepetela would continue his analysis of the power of discourse to kill in the context of Bush-era American hegemony in a novella that transferred that analysis over to the cultural centre of the empire: California. His novella, *O terrorista de Berkeley, Califórnia*, was sufficiently potent in its analysis of the discourses of fear that it was subsequently deemed to represent a threat by sections of the MPLA elites.

In June 2015, seventeen young Angolans were arrested and charged with planning to 'alterar a ordem pública e segurança pública'[12] [offend public order and security]. According to Amnesty International, who quickly began a campaign for their release, their 'crime' was to have taken part in political meetings that discussed dissatisfaction with the then thirty-six-year rule of José Eduardo dos Santos. The group included a university professor, a hip-hop artist with a degree in electrical engineering from Plymouth University, and a nineteen-year-old who was named after Nito Alves,[13] and who had first been arrested by the regime at the age of fifteen for protesting against autocracy. Only one of these prisoners of conscience was born before dos Santos took power, a thirty-seven-year-old self-employed mechanic from Lunda-Norte.[14]

The treatment of these young campaigners for political rights sparked an outcry across the Portuguese-speaking world, with international pressure mounting on the regime for their unconditional release, and an effective social media campaign highlighting every twist and turn in the saga. They were eventually convicted on what most human rights observers deemed to be spurious charges. The Angolan government had begun to claim they were plotting an attempt on the life of the president, and called for the harshest possible punishment as an example to all would-be 'malfeitores' [criminals]. Following their conviction and various sentences of between a couple of months and eight and a half years, the Angolan Supreme Court eventually granted all but one of the prisoners parole in June 2016.[15] With a faltering economy as the result of a collapse in oil prices, and an increase in dissent, particularly among the young who saw ever more limited prospects for their future, the MPLA leadership had reverted to heavy-handed repression and a 1977-style climate of fear to maintain its grip on power.

One of the strangest aspects of the MPLA persecution of the seventeen activists was the list of books they were banned from reading while in detention. While they were awaiting trial and kept in unhygienic conditions and solitary confinement in Calomboloca Prison, in tactics reminiscent of the obtuseness of the New State's playbook, the activists were prevented from reading Hannah Arendt's *The Origins of Totalitarianism* — with its obvious and relevant overtones for post-civil war Angola — and, more strangely, Pepetela's *O terrorista de Berkeley, Califórnia*.[16] This is the first of a trio of Pepetela novels that are not set in Angola. It critiques in a very humorous tone the absurd excesses of George W. Bush's War on Terror. It is full of astute observations of American culture, and critiques the belligerent and at times irrational logic that took hold of American political discourse in the aftermath of the 9/11 attacks. Why, then, ban this particular work by Pepetela? What is so offensive or dangerous about it that political prisoners in 2015 Angola could not be trusted to read it?

If it could, the MPLA probably would have liked to ban the book Pepetela had published immediately prior to *O terrorista*, namely *Predadores*, with its thinly veiled attacks on the dos Santos regime. Many of the stories linking Pepetela unfavourably to the events of 1977 surfaced around 2005, perhaps leading Pepetela to turn his acerbic focus away from Angola for a time. This denationalization of Pepetela's narratorial gaze began with *O terrorista*. However, the issues the novella raises — of a discourse of fear overcoming a collective common sense, and allowing the petty-minded to settle their own scores — was as applicable in Angola in 2015 as it was in the USA in 2007. Systemic paranoia and a sloppy use of language became the tools of power, with very real and violent consequences for those it oppressed.

Pepetela wrote most of *O terrorista* while he was writer-in-residence at the University of California, Berkeley, in 2005. It depicts what the author sees as the irrationality of American society and the fragmentation and alienation characterizing its human relations. Angola is never mentioned in the text. There is no Angolan character lost in the new imperial centre. All the characters are Americans, with the exception of a Professor of Bantu from Francophone Africa who is rebuked for closing the door of his office while with a student, without realizing the cultural prohibition on so doing. Like the America Pepetela observes, the characters come from a multiplicity of ethnic backgrounds. Some, like the illegal-Mexican-immigrant-cum-American-anti-terrorist-agent, Juan Martinez, were born outside the nation's frontiers. They all share American nationality, and some emotional investment in what it means to be American.

Despite the absence of any Angolans in the story, the narrative's epistemology, through which the reader accesses America, is utterly suffused with Pepetela's experience of Angola. Everything is related by the third-person narrator through the sensitivities of an Angolan Creole, who has known what it is like to endure direct colonialism and has fought for independence. The internal violence of imperialism is recognized in the logic of contemporary American society, and mirrored back for a Portuguese-language readership with its own colonial legacies. At the same time, the novella is replete with an irony Pepetela asserts is the principal characteristic of the Angolan way of seeing the world.[17]

O terrorista de Berkeley, Califórnia centres on the alienation of a star-student of Maths and Computer Science at the University of California, Berkeley. Larry, who is initially reluctant to leave his native Chicago, and who is effectively pushed out of his maternal nest, never looks back once he arrives on the West Coast campus. His gaucheness prevents him from taking any lead in relationships, so the beautiful Iranian American, Soraya, seduces him in order to get things started. When he finds her in bed with another woman, his reaction is to create a series of email fantasy friends, with whom he shares his disillusionment with the world. The language he uses in his emails alerts the San Francisco anti-terrorist unit, under the leadership of Steve Watson. They begin a heavy surveillance of all internet activity in the university. The surveillance is so intense that Larry, and his fellow Computer-Studies genius, Nabokov, become aware that a government agency is infiltrating their system.

After an initial panic, Larry determines to play a game of cat-and-mouse with the government agents, feeding their desire to find terrorists and terrorist plots wherever they look, and also to find them incarnated in the bodies of stereotypes. He expands his ring of email fantasy friends to include an Islamist martyr-in-waiting, code-named Jennifer, who is ready for instructions to be a suicide-bomber under the Golden Gate Bridge. To Larry, the whole episode is a game — a game he eventually sets aside to resume his doctoral studies. To the anti-terrorist operatives, who together form a string of caricatures of some of the most troubling aspects of post-millennial American society, the game is a way of life. It always involves defeating someone, preferably through annihilation.

The novel ends with the death of Larry, who by a series of coincidences is identified as being a member of the non-existent terrorist cell. He falls prey to the trigger-happy swat squad, hyped-up to believe that the person they have been sent to arrest may blow himself and them up in an instant. All that is left at the end of the tale is an official story of an imminent, yet thwarted, terror plot which has at its centre an innocuous and alienated youth, Larry, and the disbelief of all who knew him that he could have had any involvement in such activities. The only person who believes the official narrative is Soraya, his once girlfriend, turned lesbian, whose ultra-Americanism deflects any questions about her heritage as a woman of Iranian descent.

Pepetela uses the tale to relate the Angolan intelligentsia's view of American society, with all the prejudices that implies. His portrait is driven by the concerns of the global South faced with a superpower that, during the presidency of George W. Bush, overtly rejected bounds to its dominance. At the same time, Pepetela attempts to show how America internally fails to function as a coherent society. He points to the inherent contradictions of a nation immersed in post-modern culture in order to account for its systemic irrationality, violence and paranoia. In showing the collapse of relations at the individual level, he attempts to explain its devastating actions as a collective.

Pepetela portrays America as a nation of the lonely, in which families are fragmented and friends are easily betrayed. The prevalent mantra of the nation under Bush — as a victim of terror under imminent threat — is cast by Pepetela as a spectral presence, with nothing but vivid imaginations and ethereal fantasies to back it up. Steve Watson is the first character to appear, and the first thing we learn about him is that he is 'o chefe do grupo especial de combate ao terrorismo para a região de San Francisco'[18] [head of a task force to combat terrorism in the San Francisco region]. It is a carefully crafted initial phrase that reflects the most ingrained prejudice *against* America held by many intellectuals from the global South in the noughties, namely, that America was defined by its obsession with terrorism. To be a gringo meant, for a Southern epistemology, to have a libidinal investment in tracking down and destroying the terrorist spectres of the USA's own creation. For Pepetela, the terrorist from Berkeley is precisely and literally one of those: nothing but a figment of the imagination of a lonely youth whose cyber creation feeds into the fantasies of all the other fragmented parts of American society. For Larry, his actions are nothing but a game.

In the America Pepetela portrays, nearly everything is a game, but a rather vicious game — the result of 'os jovens a serem educados desde novos a lutarem sozinhos pela vida, enfrentando competição feroz' (p. 36) [young people being taught from an early age to fight for their lives, by themselves, against fierce competition]. It is a game in which hostages are not taken, and responsibility is never acknowledged. The whole structure, as Pepetela sees it, is constituted by people denying their true motivations to others and to themselves.

Juan Martinez, one of the anti-terror agents, exemplifies this well. He has a history of betrayal and grudges borne that the system uses to its advantage. He had left behind the reality of El Dorado for the American Dream, and cut a deal with the immigration authorities after being caught without permission in the USA, a deal that involved betraying a cousin he had disliked since a childhood dispute. Over the course of time, Martinez becomes a law-enforcement official for the country in which he was once an illegal immigrant. Pepetela's description of his career trajectory includes the fact that 'recentemente fora transferido para um organismo novo de combate ao terrorismo, porque precisavam de alguém falando espanhol e de comprovada lealdade na traição ao conterrâneos do Terceiro Mundo' (p. 9) [he had recently been transferred to the new anti-terror cell, because they needed someone who spoke Spanish with proven loyalty in the betrayal of fellow Third Worlders].

The America Pepetela critiques feeds off betrayal. Loyalty must be proved negatively, by destroying what you are and where you come from. It is part of the process of self-alienation that dominates nearly all the characterizations. Even seemingly sympathetic portrayals, such as Tom, the closest thing to a friend for Larry, are riddled with a sense of not belonging anywhere. Tom is an African-American who lives on the streets of San Francisco, apparently rejected by or rejecting his family. In many ways, he is the obscene underside of Pepetela's portrayal of Shirley, the black lesbian FBI officer in *Jaime Bunda e a morte do americano*. Where she represents the hyper-identity of alterity raised up as an example of the success of the American Dream, Tom represents a residue of racist legacies and capitalist exclusion. To the Angolan mindset of the narratorial voices in both novels, neither position makes sense. Shirley is seen for what she is — an agent of empire who has nothing in common with black Africans despite her claims to a shared heritage based on race. Tom is to be pitied, not for his rejection of the false values of corporate America, but rather because of the severing of his family ties.

The increased need for family ties, even reconstructed family ties, is an increasing concern in post-conflict Angolan culture, as we witness in Zézé Gamboa's 2004 film, *O herói*. Its denouement is the recreation of a family unit out of the shattered fragments of the Angolan civil war. Everything in the film points to fragmentation — from the loss of the hero's leg to the loss of the child Manu's family and the collapse of the capital's infrastructure under the pressures of an influx of dejected, wounded and demoralized refugees from the ravaged countryside. But as Fernando Arenas argues, the point of the film is to counteract that fragmentation, and to survive the Angolan situation by refashioning a societal solidarity.[19]

In the American setting of Pepetela's novella, Larry seems to wish to adopt Tom as his father, in order to forge a familial tie out of the fragments of society — one of the email pseudonyms he assumes is Tomson. But where Gamboa portrays an Angola in which the fantasy of a renewed familial linkage is given the chance of a positive outcome, Pepetela's America shows that the fantasy can only remain a fantasy. The fantasy drives itself. It is not an impulse towards change but rather a repetitive drive towards more fragmentation and alienation. The fragmentation of subjectivities in American society, as Pepetela portrays it, is too profound to allow for a truly affective linkage to be re-established. All Pepetela leaves Larry is the possibility of masturbating over the thought of Jennifer, another of his fantasized email friends, cast as the Islamic terrorist who fills in all the gaps that the reality of Soraya — the real Iranian American — cannot.

Pepetela uses the trope of cyber miscommunication to reflect on a society in which the various fragments are no longer able to liaise with each other. The sad University professor, Nancy, owns a German pointer dog, whose barking she is not able to understand. According to the narrator, the dog makes up for her lack of a loving husband or child. In the frustrated head of the anti-terrorist unit, Steve, we see a vindictive and lonely man who uses the opportunity presented by the 'terror threat' to settle scores by throwing his weight around with the Chancellor of Berkeley. As an undergraduate applicant, Steve had been rejected by the university because of his poor academic record, a grudge he bore viscerally for years, rather like his underling Juan, who betrayed his cousin in adulthood because of a fight in childhood.

Pepetela projects the image of an American society of petty jealousies and frustrations, where no one says what they are thinking and resentment runs strong. In it, prejudices may not be verbalized but they surface systemically. So, it is not appropriate for Steve to voice his homophobic, anti-Semitic or racist sentiments without censure, and yet, when one of the fantasy terror suspects is declared to be African-American because of a turn of phrase used in one of Larry's emails, there is widespread relief among the anti-terror unit, since there are so few black students on the campus from whom to choose.

Pepetela's point is that censoring individual prejudices does not resolve issues of systemic racism. More generally, he condemns the society he portrays as lying to itself. In part, he sees this self-deception as the root of individual loneliness and detachment. More importantly, as an Angolan observer, he links the collective failure of individuals to connect with each other to the catastrophic and paranoid behaviour of the superpower abroad.

The Angolan narrator of *O terrorista de Berkeley, Califórnia* seems to be suggesting that America needs to be truer to its unconscious drives. The nation should work out what its fears and resentments are. From an Angolan perspective, the most pervasive fear is an inability to sustain social ties because of the competitive way that American society is structured. If America's true sentiments could be identified, then sudden outbursts of paranoid violence against imagined opponents would become less likely.

The most telling moment in the novella in this regard occurs shortly before Larry plunges wholeheartedly into his cyber-fantasy, creating the conditions for his own demise. He is sitting, depressed, in the park, when suddenly he notices a young girl:

> Loira, melancólica na sua brincadeira solitária. Essa melancolia chamou-lhe a atenção, outro ser solitário. Não era difícil identificar-se com a menina, que tinha de inventar brincadeiras, como ele sempre fizera. Mas a mãe, ou quem lá era, viu-o a olhar para a criança. Levantou-se quase em fúria, fechou o livro, avançou para a menina e puxou-a por um braço para a rua, olhando de vez em quando para trás. Era óbvio, tinha pressentido nele um pedófilo ou coisa ainda pior a estudar a filha. Que raio de povo era o seu, que podia confundir assim os sentimentos, ele apenas descobrindo uma identificação com a melancolia da garota e a mãe lhe adivinhando as piores intenções? (pp. 46–47)
>
> [Blonde, melancholy in her solitary game. Her melancholy caught his attention. She was another loner. It wasn't difficult for him to identify with the girl, who had to invent her own games, as he'd always done. But her mother, or whoever she was, saw him looking at the child. She got up, almost in a rage, shut her book, went towards the girl and hauled her out onto the street by the arm, every now and then looking behind her. Obviously, she had sensed he was a paedophile or worse, studying her daughter. How wretched were his people, that they could confuse feelings like that, he was just uncovering an identification with the lass's melancholy and her mother was divining the worst of intentions in him?]

This passage, which occurs around the middle of the novella, is a clear example of the turn-of-the-millennium prejudices of Angolan epistemology being superimposed on an American space. The question that Larry raises is really a question that disoriented Marxist-trained Angolan Creoles ask of an America they instinctively deplore. How can you have all become so alienated from each other and most of all from your children? How, Pepetela's character wants to know, can identification with another be viewed so easily with such suspicion?

The way children are reared in the USA is a cause of repeated concern for the novella's narrator. As Pepetela depicts it, more than anything else, American childrearing is a symptom of a capitalist order that thrives on alienation and an ethos of the survival of the fittest. Such instilled competition, devoid of any human solidarity and personal connection can, the narrator implies, only end in disaster, as the novella does, with a death that makes sense to no one, but which the system must justify in its own warped logic.

Pepetela's novella marks a new direction in his own, and in Lusophone African, writing. It signals a desire to understand from within what made the global superpower in the noughties seem so violent to the outside world. A sociologist by training, Pepetela deploys the psychological mindset of Creole Angola to penetrate the deepest motivations of a culture he comes to pity. One of the strongest messages to emerge from the text is that the price paid to be the hegemonic culture is as high, psychologically, in the global North as it is, materially, in the global South.

The message of *O terrorista de Berkeley, Califórnia* became dated and more abstract with the rise of Barack Obama, and the sense that American foreign policy underwent a change in tone, if not always in substance. Read a decade later, the novella was deprived of its immediate context and the backdrop of anger felt against the Bush administration and by extension the USA by Lusophone Africa's intelligentsia, among many others. In 2015, *O terrorista de Berkeley, Califórnia* went beyond being a tale of American paranoia, and became a treatise on the paranoia of any capitalist power structure. It may well have been on those grounds that the authorities at Calomboloca Prison sought to block access to the Pepetela's text by the political activists they arbitrarily detained.

Pepetela's portrayal of America in the noughties was far from complimentary. Given the USA's foreign policy, he channelled the outrage shared by many around the world against the heavy-handedness of President Bush's reaction to 9/11. However, Pepetela's novels that deal with the America of the time also shamelessly over-essentialize a very complex people, equally capable of electing Barack Obama and Donald Trump, and of producing Joseph McCarthy and Martin Luther King.

While both *Jaime Bunda e a morte do americano* and *O terrorista de Berkeley, Califórnia* are superlative examples of astute humour, deployed to puncture the imperialism of a recharged American industrial-military complex in twenty-first-century overreach, they are also novels with narrative voices that dismiss any validity to the politics of identity. For Pepetela, identity politics are the post-modern correlate of capitalism. They go hand-in-hand with American imperialism.

However, there is an element of Creole male privilege undergirding Pepetela's narrative positions. He plays into the facile trope of 'political correctness gone mad' in his lampoons of the requirement that professors' doors remain open during meetings with students, or as he chooses the gaze of the essentially privileged man (Larry) confronted by the anxiety of a mother who whisks her daughter away from a stranger for fear of paedophilia. There is also a fetishistic element in his portrayal of the lesbianism of Shirley from *Jaime Bunda e a morte do americano* and Soraya from *O terrorista de Berkeley, Califórnia*. Both women represent American identity politics in the worst light, and are portrayed as shamelessly self-serving. Likewise, in his stereotypical depiction of Latino feuds embodied in Juan Martinez, Pepetela suggests that solidarity based on ethnicity or gender or sexual orientation is but an American post-modern illusion.

In essence, his wholesale reduction to the absurd of the multiple positionalities intersecting in the make-up of modern America is part of a career-long belief that the only truly valid category of analysis is that of class. That same belief led him repeatedly to portray women's bodies as rapeable, often complicit, material, serving a higher metaphoric class-based narrative of resistance. It also led him to overlook the racial overtones of 27 May. America was an easy and necessary target to parody in the first decade of the twenty-first century. As the century has progressed, Pepetela's anti-American parodies began to reveal more about his limitations as a Marxist New Man than about the ever-elusive pendular essence of the USA.

The year after publishing *O terrorista de Berkeley, Califórnia*, Pepetela released another work that eschewed Angola in all but narratorial epistemology. *O quase fim do mundo* (2008) marked Pepetela's venture into science fiction as a means of commenting on the limits of Western discourse, as I shall discuss in the next chapter.

Notes to Chapter 10

1. See Claire Gatinois, 'Portugal Indebted to Angola after Economic Reversal of Fortune', *The Guardian*, 3 June 2014 <https://www.theguardian.com/world/2014/jun/03/portugal-economy-bailout-angola-invests> [accessed 27 March 2018].
2. US Department of State, Office of the Historian, 'A Guide to the United States' History of Recognition, Diplomatic, and Consular Relations, by Country, since 1776: Angola' <https://history.state.gov/countries/angola> [accessed 27 March 2018].
3. Ewen MacAskill, John Henley and Rory Carroll, 'Scramble for Africa as Britain and France Go Head to Head for Key Votes', *The Guardian*, 11 March 2003 <https://www.theguardian.com/world/2003/mar/11/iraq.foreignpolicy> [accessed 27 March 2018].
4. See Rory Carroll, Duncan Campbell, Jo Tuckman and Rory McCarthy, 'The British Do the Diplomacy and the Americans Write the Cheques', *The Guardian*, 28 February 2003 <https://www.theguardian.com/world/2003/feb/28/iraq.unitednations> [accessed 27 March 2018].
5. Quoted in *The Guardian*, 10 March 2003, 'The Editor press review' <https://www.theguardian.com/world/2003/mar/12/usa.iraq2> [accessed 12 December 2017].
6. Herbert Marcuse, *Eros and Civilization: A Philosophical Inquiry into Freud* (New York: Vintage, 1961).
7. Sigmund Freud, *Civilization and its Discontents*, trans. by Joan Riviere (New York: Jonathan Cape and Harrison Smith, 1931).
8. In 2003 Mia Couto wrote a famous open letter to President Bush that articulated many of the concerns of Lusophone Africa's intelligentsia. The text of the letter was reprinted as 'Carta ao Presidente Bush' in Mia Couto, *Pensatempos* (Caminho 2005), pp. 33–39.
9. Pepetela, *Jaime Bunda e a morte do americano* (Lisbon: Dom Quixote, 2003), p. 10. Subsequent page references given in the text.
10. See the multiple arguments expounded in Herbert Marcuse, *One Dimensional Man: Studies in the Ideology of Advanced Industrial Society* (London: Routledge, 1964).
11. As well as Marcuse, Theodor Adorno explored the relationship between mass culture and capitalist enslavement, in addition to the violent export of that culture that became an increasing concern for Pepetela. See, in particular, Theodor W. Adorno, *The Culture Industry: Select Essays on Mass Culture* (New York: Routledge, 1991).
12. Anistia Internacional Brasil, 'AÇÃO URGENTE: Jovens ativistas presos arbitrariamente em Angola', 3 July 2015 <https://anistia.org.br/entre-em-acao/carta/acao-urgente-6/> [accessed 27 March 2018].
13. As discussed in Chapter 3, Nito Alves served in Agostinho Neto's government and was accused of leading a coup attempt.
14. Carlos Santos, 'Quem são os ativistas presos desde 20 de junho e as acusadas que não estão detidas', *Esquerdanet*, 21 October 2015 <http://www.esquerda.net/dossier/quem-sao-os-ativistas-presos-desde-20-de-junho-e-acusadas-que-nao-estao-detidas/39200> [accessed 27 March 2018].
15. Joana Gorjão Henriques, 'Activistas angolanos libertados da prisão', *Público*, 29 June 2016 <https://www.publico.pt/2016/06/29/mundo/noticia/jornal-angolano-diz-que-17-activistas-vao-aguardar-decisao-em-casa-1736689> [accessed 27 March 2018].
16. *Rede Angola*, 'Presos políticos proibidos de ler Pepetela', 14 July 2015 <http://www.redeangola.info/presos-politicos-proibidos-de-lerem-pepetela/> [accessed 27 March 2018].
17. Quoted in Luís Ricardo Duarte, 'Pepetela: crónica de uma Angola em mudança', *Jornal de Letras, Artes e Ideias*, 1124 (October 2013), p. 9.
18. Pepetela, *O terrorista de Berkeley, Califórnia* (Lisbon: Dom Quixote, 2007), p. 7. Subsequent page references given in the text.
19. Fernando Arenas, *Lusophone Africa: Beyond Independence* (Minneapolis: University of Minnesota Press, 2011), p. 150.

CHAPTER 11

Denationalized Dialogism and the Primordial Thing, or Reconciling beyond the Law of Capitalism

One of the most common literary techniques in Pepetela's literary output is dialogic characterization. In *Mayombe*, the dialogic technique was blatant, as a multiplicity of characters controlled the narrative, laying bare the tensions and inconsistencies of the struggle for independence. As Pepetela became a more accomplished writer, this dialogism remained, but in subtler forms, such as in *Lueji, o nascimento de um império*, a novel in which past and future fuse in a multiplicity of voices that all reflect on the corrupting processes of power across ages, genders, and classes.

In this chapter, I will focus on *O quase fim do mundo* (2008), a novel that demonstrates once again the author's commitment to narrative dialogism, as well as his constant probing of the machinations and mechanisms of power. As is often the case in Pepetela's writing, each character embodies an ideological position. The plot is designed to allow discourse to compete against discourse, as a means of teasing out the flaws and challenges of all the ideologies which have staked a claim to Angola, and more generally Africa, over its history as a political entity.

O quase fim do mundo was written after free-market, predatory capitalism was well established among Angola's elites. The novel imagines what would happen if the law of that capitalism were removed, positing that the discourse of scientific socialism (under which Angola laboured in the years following independence) was totally imbricated into the capitalism it opposed.

As was increasingly the case in the late noughties, Pepetela replaced Angola as the principal setting for his plot. As I discussed in the last chapter, in *O terrorista de Berkeley, Califórnia* (2007) Angola is only present in the epistemology of the narration, in a peculiar reconfiguration of the reader's gaze that thwarts the Orientalist tendencies of modern colonialisms by telling a story of American insanity through the appropriating voice of an Angolan third-person narrator. In *O planalto e a estepe* (2009) — Pepetela's story of two star-crossed lovers — most of the action takes place beyond Angola's borders in various parts of the communist world.

In *O quase fim do mundo*, the plot takes place primarily in Calpe, an imagined point in Africa at the centre of a triangulation between the sources of the Nile, the Zambezi and the Congo rivers, with a narrative sojourn in Europe. Calpe appears in several of Pepetela's texts, including *Parábola do cágado velho* and *O cão e os caluandas*. José Ornelas argues that Calpe in Pepetela represents 'the symbolic and utopian space where all dreams converge'.[1]

The Calpe of *O quase fim do mundo* is, in part, the stereotypical embodiment of Conrad's Dark Continent, where life persists among a very small group after the mysterious annihilation of all other living beings. Each of the survivors represents an ideology, from religious fundamentalism and scientific positivism to women's liberation and African 'traditions'. The contrived plot conspires to land them all together in a situation in which the dominance of the law of capitalism — both symbolic and judicial — has been suspended.

As a result, each ideology enacted through a character must interact unmediated by the symbolic frontiers that customarily govern our interactions in a global economy. It is Pepetela's greatest attempt to date to bring the primary discourses of Modernity into raw dialogue, and to oblige them to answer for the ways they have operated in colonial, post-colonial and post-globalization-era Africa, without being mere by-products or servants of Modernity's most prevalent ideology, capitalism.

The novel raises a set of issues around the meaning of frontiers in a world based on the paradoxical law of free-flowing capital and rigorously enforced borders. Pepetela speculates about how a variety of ideological positions predominantly from the realm of cultural politics (such as the discourses of religious fundamentalism, African traditionalism, feminism and race) interact when the dominant paradigm of global capitalism, which he sees as having successfully co-opted them all, is suddenly removed from the equation. How might these discourses from the realm of cultural politics negotiate with each other once they no longer bow before the capitalist law of appropriation? And what alliances would they make?

The narrative begins with the apparent near complete disappearance of all sentient matter. Simba Ukolo, a Western-educated doctor, gets out of his car to urinate, glimpses a flash, and returns to the centre of Calpe to realize that every creature, from the simplest microbe to the most intelligent species, seems to have vanished. Over time, other people who have avoided whatever the 'Thing' was that obliterated life also begin to appear. A cast of characters assembles to include Geny, a religious fanatic who is a member of the cult of the Paladins of the Sacred Crown; Joseph Kiboro, a thief by profession and a communist by inclination; Janet Kinsley, an American doctoral researcher more at home with gorillas than with the rest of humanity; Jan Dippenaar, a South African Boer with a mysterious past; Jude, a sensual sixteen-year-old who wants to be treated like an adult; Julius, an engineer who has erased his Masai heritage by living in a city; Riek, an Ethiopian shaman; and Ísis, a Somali academic.

The plot traces their interactions, and centres on discovering what the Thing was that led to humanity's near oblivion. Fortunately, Jan Dippenaar is a pilot, albeit with a flying trauma in his past. He is able to teach some of the others to fly, and thus facilitates a trip to Europe where they stumble across the cause of the demise of life. A perniciously racist sect — the same sect to which Geny unwittingly belongs — has conspired to 'cleanse' the world of impure races, by wiping out every living being with the exception of a select few of 'pure' white DNA, while themselves remaining hidden in a protected bunker in the Austrian Alps. However, the plan goes wrong, and the sect members are all eliminated alongside the rest of humanity. Furthermore, because of their disdain for Africa, they did not fully cover the continent with their annihilation beam, leading to the anomaly of a handful of survivors remaining in the middle of the continent whose people they most despise.

From his very first literary endeavours, Pepetela has always been intelligently critical of the shortcomings of power structures, even when he supported the ideologies behind them. As a writer, Pepetela had foreseen the MPLA's failure to live up to its promises. When he left the Angolan government, and dedicated more of his time to writing, he continued to document, through his fiction, the failures of the revolution to deliver on the ideals it had promised. His work witnessed the nation's transition into one of the most kleptocratic and inequitable embodiments of capitalism in Africa. His increasing trend to locate his narratives outside Angola signposts a realization of the extent to which national frontiers — even those gained at the expense of revolutionary blood and the anticolonial struggle — have become blurred in the globalized flow of market forces.

With *O quase fim do mundo*, Pepetela does not abnegate his interest in the Angolan polity. Instead, he foregrounds the extent to which power structures are generalized, and what applies in Calpe applies in Angola, or in many other previously colonized African countries. This does not mean that Pepetela homogenizes the post-colonial experience. Rather, he draws attention to a steady pattern in the functioning of power structures in the contemporary world and, with his 2008 novel, aims to interrogate what would happen if competing discourses of power were free to engage with one another in a primordial setting in which the future of the world literally depended on the outcome of their debates. To achieve this result, Pepetela fashions a circumstance that results in the collapse of all law, and he signals this collapse of the law — an occurrence that ruptures all the symbolic relations between competing subjectivities — as the "Thing" [a Coisa].

The Thing, or 'das Ding' or 'La Chose', occupied much of the French psychoanalyst Lacan's interest at the turn of the 1960s. He used the term to designate, among other things, a lost object that 'must be continually refound'.[2] It is impossible to attain, and as such, a constant object of desire. In the context of the Thing, Lacan interprets Freud's Pleasure Principle as the law that maintains each person at a distance from what they most desire, obliging us to circle the Thing, without ever being able to reach it. Until he transmuted many of the underpinning attributes of the Thing into his later 'objet petit a', the Thing occupied for Lacan the psychic space Freud assigned to the incest taboo — as something that is intensely desired but simultaneously absolutely prohibited. To achieve the Thing is to be destroyed — to have bypassed the Pleasure Principle's limit. It also would mark entry into a territory where there is no law.[3]

Pepetela's Thing has something of the Lacanian about it, in that its occurrence smashes all symbolic relations while simultaneously forcing them together. It annihilates almost everything, and the remnants of subjectivity that remain by accident are lawless. Pepetela's interest is to see what happens in such a situation, as the law seeks to reassert itself after all its symbolic strength has been sapped. The provenance of Pepetela's Thing is a mixture of science (the Gamma Alfa Ray that zaps the whole world is the creation of American defence contractors) and religious extremism (the Paladin sect triggers the technology's effect on the world) — two discourses with pretensions to be totalizing. The remnants of their discourses are represented in the novel by Simba (the medical, positivist doctor) and Geny (the only remaining member of the Paladin sect and the self-declared guardian of moral standards). It is no coincidence that the pair is the first to meet in the narrative, and never reach a mutual understanding. Each is suspicious of the other's motives, and in true Pepetela fashion, hypocritical and flawed within the parameters of the discourses they both represent.

Simba comes across Geny as they both rob banks. His medical materialism is confronted with her religious fundamentalism. She constantly exhibits the psychotic traits of her utter conviction, and yet both indulge in something they know to be prohibited by the disappeared law. For the greatest law of capitalism is that the banking system and those who own it are the only ones with the right to rob. The greatest proof that capitalist law has been suspended is the impunity with which they remove currency from the vaults. At the same time, Simba and Geny's theft of sacks full of money demonstrates the residual strength of the suspended law. The irony of their larceny — an irony that repeats itself as other characters appear in the novel — is that what they steal has no meaning. As they stuff their bags with paper currency, they remain captives of the financial fetishes of a previous (reigning) order. The currency has, post-Thing, assumed its status as a worthless paper marker only granted value by the residues of a fetishistic fantasy for a pair whose own discourses always officially disavowed the overriding value of capital exchange.

The narrator describes how Simba first resists the temptation to riffle through police files he comes across, as he still feels the threat of a law lingering even though there is no one there to restrain his formerly illegal curiosity. Yet, when the opportunity presents itself to walk into a deserted bank and remove its money, he no longer resists, a clear indication of the extent to which money fetishism has informed his prior existence despite his claims to the contrary. Likewise, Geny's high ideals and moral standing are betrayed by her instinct to indulge her fetish even in a new world where it is obvious that money is not worth the paper it is printed on, and is devoid of all value, both intrinsic or imagined. Its only worth is as a residual fantasy of a symbolic order that once gave it supreme meaning.

Significantly, the first character to realize the meaninglessness of money in the new world is Joseph Kiboro, the thief whose profession disappears with the law's demise. In fact, as someone who always acted outside the law, he is the character most able to adapt to the new circumstances. In a twist of fate, he — the guardian of the Proudhonian ideal that all property is theft — will end up in Europe as the adoptive father of another man's child, and, alongside his Somali partner, may become the founder of a New Europe populated entirely with African blood.

Kiboro's former profession is the underside of the law of capital flows. For all the talk of unfettered movement of capital and the rhetorical conflation of democracy and entrepreneurial opportunity for everyone within a global capitalist paradigm, the free market has never been about a generic removal of frontiers. Rather, from its colonial incarnation to its more recent neo-colonial practice, it has always rigorously enforced frontiers of exclusion, centripetally absorbing wealth and resources and concomitantly fomenting and exaggerating gross disparities between classes and regions.

As a Marxist kleptomaniac, Kiboro only ever robbed the rich from his first act of thievery as a six-year-old with no way to pay for the trappings of his education. His pilfering was always simultaneously an ideological statement against the sanctioned larceny of a society which internalized the profoundly bourgeois, European and colonial notion that exclusive ownership is a moral right, signalling a nation's progress into Modernity and away from 'primitive' concepts of collective stewardship.

There is another side to Kiboro's pacifist socialism and commitment to the redistribution of wealth: the extent to which he, too, has internalized the trappings flaunted by the capitalism against which he strove in his profession. In a typical Pepetela twist that prevents the complete deification of any single characterization, Kiboro takes advantage of the law's absence to indulge his desire to drive the most expensive vehicles available in the showrooms that the survivors plunder, regardless of their usefulness or reliability. For him, the car's price tag signifies its importance and value. This obsession reveals how much Kiboro is a product of capitalism and remains true to its law. It is not so much that he worked against the capitalist classes in his pre-Thing life, but rather that he aspired to be a capitalist. His profession (as a thief) was a symptom, revealing the true nature of the capitalist system as a project of colossal theft.

In some ways, Pepetela targets in Kiboro those who espoused socialism in Africa's transition to independence, and rapidly acquired a taste for the luxurious baggage of power, becoming more ardent supporters of the free market than their colonial masters had ever been. Their commitment to redistribute wealth became a commitment to sell off the nation's resources for their own personal gain. They were, psychologically, the greatest captives of capitalism's law, for they were created by that very law. Pepetela's point is that the socialists-turned-freemarketeers cannot exist without that law. His other point is that one of the greatest flaws of the African liberation movements was to depend so utterly on a European ideological posture created by the system against which they struggled.

The MPLA revolution in Angola (like its FRELIMO counterpart in Mozambique) sought to create Marxist New Men — scientific socialists who would be free from a mentality of either colonial enslavement or racial denigration. New Men would also be liberated from what the new regimes deemed to be the unsavoury superstitions of traditional Africa. These New Men were always males who claimed a near monopoly on the political arena of the newly born nations.

Throughout his work, Pepetela has been concerned with how women have been enmeshed in the discourses of post-revolutionary power, and how they have never fared as well as men, or been granted the same ground on which to operate as political agents. His depiction of Ondina, in *Mayombe*, a woman who acts on her desire and whose body becomes the target of appropriation by a range of different discourses, raised the opprobrium of Agostinho Neto as I discussed in Chapter 2. Pepetela repeated his depiction of women in positions of political strength in *Lueji, o nascimento de um império* (see Chapter 5) and less attractively in *O desejo de Kianda* (see Chapter 6). In the former, the narration focuses in part on the Lunda Queen, Lueji, whose Machiavellian spirit enables her to create a centralized empire. In the latter, Carmina is an MPLA party apparatchik whose rhetoric changes from a vacant Marxism to crude capitalism.

In *O quase fim do mundo*, Pepetela foregrounds the challenges that feminism poses to religious, traditional and (scientific) socialist discourses in Africa, as well as the challenges it faces in its own terms. The problematics of feminism beyond the confines of a Western, middle-class white, Anglo-Saxon academy have been extensively debated.[4] One of the greatest grounds of contention for feminism beyond the Western and Anglo-Saxon world is the role of motherhood.[5] The notion of motherhood as a positive sacrifice-for-another and intrinsic role for women, which infuses the culture of many non-Western societies, was, in certain earlier and radical strains of feminism, deemed to curtail the potential self-realization of women.[6]

In the African context, the political conflation of Africa itself with motherhood, over-utilized in the lusophone African context as part of the imagery of the independence struggles, has complicated the issue further.[7] A sleight of hand took place, post-independence, in which motherhood was designated an act of national service. The attitudes of Agostinho Neto, in Angola, and Samora Machel, in Mozambique, who nominally spoke in favour of equality of the sexes, were profoundly informed by the dogma that women's rights were a distraction from the real politics of the class struggle against colonialism and capitalism's oppression of the masses. With his suspension of capitalism's law in *O quase fim do mundo*, Pepetela interrogates what happens to feminism's various positions if it is no longer deemed politically subservient to an economic structure, or is seen as a 'cultural' issue that can wait for the success of the class struggle before any attention is paid to it.

Pepetela presents four principal female positions in his novel. The first is represented by Geny, who espouses a discourse of feminine abjection, grounded in extreme religious psychosis. The narrative gives her little credence, presenting her as the most pitiable of characters. Her delusions are not altered by the discovery that the sect to which she belongs is responsible for the near annihilation of humanity. Rather, she narcissistically sees the opportunity to rise up the ranks of her church, becoming one of its apostles in the absence of any male members. She sees her calling as the rapid conversion of as many survivors as possible to her psychotic belief system.

The second female position is occupied by Ísis, the Somali beauty, who is often confused with a mestizo, and whose father left their homeland to prevent his daughter being circumcised. Thanks to her father's progressiveness, she escapes a practice that denies female pleasure, and receives a high level of formal education. In the post-Thing world, she will be the first to become pregnant, inseminated by the shaman, Riek, whose appeal is precisely that he reminds her of her father. Most importantly, both her father and Riek are *African* men concerned with realizing the hopes and aspirations of women.

The third female characterization is Janet Kinsley, the white American and Berkeley doctoral candidate. Both her name and her research project (the sexual practices of gorillas) are haunted by Alfred Kinsey, one of the twentieth-century's greatest researchers of sexuality. He was, in part, responsible for breaking in the West many of the sexual taboos surrounding sexual orientation and pleasure. Janet, too, will become pregnant in the plot, pairing up with Julius, whose African phallus is so big it does not fit completely inside his American partner. The stereotyping is completed in the pairing by Janet's desire repeatedly to call Julius her gorilla. Having studied the simian's sexual practices, her primary fantasy is to be loved by a gorilla, a desire she transfers onto her relationship with Julius.

Finally, the fourth female characterization is Jude, the adolescent who is desperate to seduce Simba. She learns quickly whatever she is taught, from driving to flying. She is headstrong. At the same time, she is the only female prepared to accept Simba's declaration that the primary duty of women in the new order is to be reproductive vassals guaranteeing the future of humanity. Simba's assertion becomes the focus of a debate between discourses on the role of woman in Africa is today, and, more pointedly, whether feminism is a luxury that only developed societies can afford. His contention, as a scientist, is that women's biology assigns them a 'natural' role as mothers in the new world order in which they find themselves.

Neither Ísis nor Janet is prepared to countenance the role of perpetual reproducers. They hold firmly to the belief that a woman's rights to control her own fertility and to self-realization are inalienable. No matter how dire the situation, neither is prepared to give them up. Pepetela's deployment of this debate reminds us of arguments rehearsed at the time of the independence struggles, when women were expected to put on hold their aspirations for equal rights in the name of a greater struggle. Marxist-Leninism trumped all, and the woman's greatest national service, alongside policing her husband into an essentially Westernized family unit, was to produce and rear New Men for the revolution.

Simba, the Westernized scientist, is the greatest advocate of this policy of obliged reproduction. Pointedly, the representative of African tradition, Riek, the fertility shaman, is the character most in tune with female desire, and most capable of letting Ísis, the carrier of his own child, follow her own path. Ísis wants to see the world. She wants to visit where one of the first women heads of state, the female Pharaoh Hatshepsut, once ruled. She wants to see the sights of Europe. Ultimately, she will remain in Europe, with Kiboro, when the rest of the group returns to Africa. There, she will give birth to the shaman's child, who will be raised by her and Kiboro, the thief with leftist leanings and the obscene underside of the suspended capitalist model. Simba and Kiboro are closer to Geny's and Jude's positions on the role of women in society. Geny abnegates the equality of the sexes. Jude is happy to be used as a womb, as many times as necessary and possible. Simba, particularly, becomes obsessed with the need to reproduce for the sake of humanity.

Yet, both men find most attractive Ísis, and her ideological position is furthest from theirs. Once again, Pepetela uses the woman's body, like Ondina in *Mayombe*, as a conflict zone. However, the case of Ísis differs from Ondina. The moral charge associated with Ísis's claim to be the mistress of her own body and her own destiny has changed from the times when Pepetela fashioned Ondina. While Ondina ended up used by three men, and was blamed for it both in the text and by Agostinho Neto, Ísis literally rides the desire of the men near her. As the sexual atmosphere around her becomes increasingly tense, with most of the men competing for her attention, her narrative voice claims she was 'a ter prazer com o desejo deles'[8] [having pleasure in their desire].

Ísis's desire feeds off the men's desire, and has nothing to do with a duty to procreate but rather with the irrational promise of jouissance, which the text makes clear is hers to seize. She chooses to make love with Riek, the one man none of the others envisages as being a rival for her affection. An alliance is thus formed between her feminism and his African tradition — an alliance that counters the rationalist discourses of science and socialism, as well as the rhetoric of female abjection present in Geny's religious position.

Even in Geny's position, the power to decide may rest with a woman. Geny may make choices that the other characters abhor as self-abjecting, but she is making choices for herself. The result is that the discourse that remains intransigently least sympathetic to women's rights once capitalism's law is in abeyance is the scientific socialism that always claimed a sympathy towards female emancipation, even if as a tangential benefit of the revolution and progress of the masses. At the same time, African traditions, often disparaged as oppressive to women in the rhetoric of scientific socialism, are embodied in the man, Riek, who is most attuned to what a woman wants. It is no coincidence that one of Ísis's primary desires is, then, to see the place in the world where a woman ruled first — a place located in Africa.

Pepetela's message in *O quase fim do mundo* gives pause for thought. For Pepetela, in the absence of the symbolic mediator of Modernity — capitalism — the discourse revealed to be most caught up in the tenets of its law is a socialism born of it. The materialist coordinates of science, claimed by the socialist experiments of lusophone Africa as underpinning their ideology, also remain tied up discursively in that same law. Pepetela seems to be calling for new alignments, new commitments and new debates between ideologies that capitalism deemed utterly antagonistic and incapable of dialogue. In his (near) ending of the old world, the African way, Pepetela dreams of a new world where ideological positions come back into real dialogue, no longer constrained or silenced by the enforced frontiers and fictitious flows of global capital.

The one discourse without much of a place in this renewed dialogue is that of the scientific socialist — the rhetoric of the revolution that failed to deliver. Five years later, Pepetela would return to a sympathetic characterization of that discourse, in

O tímido e as mulheres. However, as I shall discuss in the next chapter, he suggests that even in their self-sacrifice, the proponents of that discourse always seem to do more harm than good.

Notes to Chapter 11

1. José Ornelas, 'Pepetela', in *Dictionary of Literary Biography, Volume 367: African Lusophone Writers*, ed. by Monica Rector and Richard Vernon (Detroit, MI: Gale, 2012), pp. 131–48 (p. 140).
2. Dylan Evans, *An Introductory Dictionary of Lacanian Psychoanalysis* (New York: Brunner-Routledge, 1997), p. 205.
3. Ibid., pp. 204–05.
4. See, for example, the essays in *Third World Women and the Politics of Feminism*, ed. by Chandra Talpade Mohanty, Ann Russo and Lourdes Torres (Bloomington: Indiana University Press, 1991); and Alice Walker, *In Search of our Mother's Gardens: Womanist Prose* (San Diego, CA: Harcourt Brace Jovanovich, 1983).
5. See the essays in *The Politics of (M)Othering: Womanhood, Identity and Resistance in African Literature*, ed. by Obioma Nnaemeka (New York: Routledge, 1997) for work referencing motherhood in the debate around feminism as a politics with concerns well beyond the sphere of white, middle-class women.
6. See, for example, Betty Friedan, *The Feminine Mystique* (New York: Norton, 1963). The Bolivian feminist, Domitila Barrios de la Chungara famously challenged Friedan and other American feminists at the UN conference on women, held in Mexico City in 1975, to address the very different issues faced by women and mothers of her class and ethnicity. See *The Essential Feminist Reader*, ed. by Estelle B. Freedman (New York: The Modern Library, 2007), p. 346.
7. See Hilary Owen's groundbreaking *Mother Africa, Father Marx: Women's Writing of Mozambique, 1948–2002* (Lewisburg, PA: Bucknell University Press, 2007) for an analysis of how the rhetoric of Africa-as-Matrix-for-another and paternal political authority inform and are contested by twentieth-century women's writing in Mozambique.
8. Pepetela, *O quase fim do mundo* (Lisbon: Dom Quixote, 2008), p. 231. Subsequent page references given in the text.

CHAPTER 12

The Bourgeoisie, the City and the Loner

In an article published in the *New York Times* in 1985, James Brooke argued that the Soviet Union's 'most orthodox ally in Africa' was marching to 'a different drummer on the subject of writers and writing'.[1] He pointed out that, despite the ravages of the civil war, twelve invasion attempts by apartheid-era South Africa, and a national illiteracy rate of 80%, by the mid-1980s, literature had become 'Angola's richest art form'.[2] Government support for Angolan writers under Neto meant that, over the course of his regime, the total annual printing of new books by national authors soared from 1,500 copies in 1976 to 500,000 by 1979. Brooke linked the boom in Angolan literature to Neto's injunction to Angola's writers to go beyond Soviet prescriptions for literature.

In a speech before the Angolan Writers' Union in 1979, Neto urged his fellow authors not to 'fall into fixed patterns or stereotypes like those of the socialist-realist theorists'.[3] For Neto, 'imported themes and forms'[4] were not appropriate in Angolan literature, even, or especially, when they emanated from the Soviet Union. Russell Hamilton recalls the 'collective sigh of relief' among Angola's writers when, amidst 'that atmosphere of revolutionary fervor', they were given licence by Neto to veer away from socialist realism.[5]

In fact, imported 'themes and forms' suffused Angolan literature, which was influenced culturally by Brazilian and Portuguese writers, and by the cosmopolitan outlook of the Casa dos Estudantes do Império. Neto was calling for a national literature that did not follow Soviet dictates, and, instead, assumed a broader progressive humanism. His concerns were the mirror image of those expressed in Alfredo Margarido's critique of Negritude in one of the Casa's publications in the 1960s.[6]

Margarido saw Negritude, at best, as a way of not fully comprehending the implications of class structure. At worst, through crass notions of phenotype, it positively obfuscated class oppression as the corollary of slavery. After independence, Neto, whose own poetry had passed through a phase of Negritude,[7] saw adherence to socialist realism as clouding a more sophisticated panorama of Angolan culture. At heart, both Neto and Margarido called for an appreciation of the nuances of the role of aesthetics in the revolution. In other words, culture could and should traverse the territory of complication in a way that politics did not.

Neto urged Angola's writers to 'go beyond class' and to 'understand the people just as they are defined'.[8] Significantly, this included a role for the representation of the bourgeoisie. 'To caricature the petty bourgeoisie, or to describe it, is as valid as exalting the peasant or the worker'.[9] The speech in which Neto asked writers to move beyond class, or rather, in which he gave them licence to represent the petty bourgeoisie, was proffered shortly after the events of 27 May, in November 1977. One result of those events was the assertion of the primacy of those from a historically bourgeois background within the MPLA.

As Ali Mazrui has pointed out, the most revolutionary classes in Angola (alongside those from Tanzania, Guinea and Zimbabwe) 'were the best advantaged'.[10] For Mazrui, 'Westernized Third World bourgeois intellectuals were the most likely to produce the dream of socialist transformation'.[11] In contrast to the conventional Marxist model, in which 'the least advantaged social class in the most advantaged society (the proletariat in the West)' drive the revolution, parts of Africa, and Angola in particular, gave rise to a situation in which 'the best advantaged social group in the least advantaged societies (the Westernized bourgeois intelligentsia in Third World countries)'[12] provided the leading cadres for the revolutionary party. This meant that culturally those determining the direction of the MPLA (particularly post-1977) were very distant from the vast majority of the population they claimed to represent.

Ildeberto Teixeira was a proxy for the Angolan attorney general in Lubango in the 1970s. In his memoirs, he recalls Lopo do Nascimento, Agostinho Neto's prime minister, talking about the need 'to get in step with the working class' and to 'crack the teeth of the petite bourgeoisie'. At the same time, 'the teeth of the leadership were becoming every bit sharper and they were learning quickly how to chew on the privileges of the bourgeoisie'.[13]

According to Teixeira, revolutionary rhetoric was used to cloak privilege, particularly under Neto. Lúcio Lara, Neto's deputy, may have used the term 'bourgeois theories' to dismiss Teixeira's concerns about the separation of powers in independent Angola,[14] but the foundations for the definitive rise of the national bourgeoisie were put in place in the 1970s. Neto's heirs and supporters (including Pepetela) may not like who gained most privilege after their hero's death, but the conditions of possibility for a new system of class privilege were firmly established under his leadership, particularly in the aftermath of 1977.

During the 2017 election campaign that marked the end of José Eduardo dos Santos's presidency, Neto's daughter, the MPLA parliamentarian Irene Neto decried a 'burguesia nacional escolhida a dedo e não por mérito próprio, com a delapidação do erário público para a acumulação primitiva de capital de alguns eleitos em detrimento da maioria' [national bourgeoisie picked by hand rather than for its merit, with the squandering of the public treasury for the primitive accumulation of capital by a select few to the detriment of the majority].[15] This, she felt, was the greatest betrayal after the death of her father. She accused the National Assembly of being 'esvaziada, passiva e subalternizada' [gutted, passive and subalternized] under the 'imperial' presidency of dos Santos.[16]

The journalist Nuno Ribeiro shares similar concerns, describing José Eduardo dos Santos as the father of 'uma burguesia nacional herdeira do triunfo militar, que distribui o poder económico aos vencedores' [a national bourgeoisie that is the successor to a military triumph, which distributes economic power to the victors].[17] The critique is not so much of a bourgeoisie per se — most of those left in the MPLA accepted its role after the 27 May purges — but rather of its mediocrity and clientelism and, as a result, its failure as a class to hold power to account. Rather like the parliament Irene Neto condemned, it had become a class that was 'gutted, passive and subalternized' under its presidential 'father'.

What binds Angola's bourgeoisie together as a social class? What are its defining characteristics? Pepetela, whose interest in class dynamics dates back at least as far as his time in the Casa dos Estudantes do Império, turned his attention to Angola's contemporary bourgeoisie in his 2013 *O tímido e as mulheres* and then again in his 2016 *Se o passado não tivesse asas*. It is, for him, a critical class from which eventual opposition to the excesses of the Angolan elites portrayed in *Predadores* might materialize. Circumstances may at times be harsh for the bourgeoisie, but it has undoubtedly benefited economically from the changes in political direction that accelerated within the MPLA following the end of the civil war.

Pepetela portrays the bourgeoisie as a cosmopolitan set. Its members are invariably city dwellers, who uncomfortably witness the obscene behaviour of Angola's elites, yet they benefit sufficiently to mute their critiques. For Pepetela, a shared aesthetics binds the bourgeoisie together — an appreciation of global tastes and technologies — that goes hand-in-hand with an aspiration to become the owners of property — a desire signalled in his 1995 *O desejo de Kianda* with Carmina's obsession to acquire prime real estate.

As cosmopolitans, members of Angola's post-conflict bourgeoisie are the cultural inheritors of the frequenters of the Casa dos Estudantes do Império, whose moral demise Pepetela laments in *A geração da utopia* (1992). The difference post-civil war is summed up in the ethical turn, discussed in Chapter 9 in relation to *Jaime Bunda e a morte do americano*, in which characters are more vividly presented as agents with individual choices to make rather than representatives of a collective morality. In the case of the new bourgeoisie, Pepetela asks at what point those who constitute it start making the right individual choices for the greater good of Angola. At what point do they detach from the legacies of a discredited MPLA?

The disillusionment that surfaces in Pepetela's work in the 1990s is more than anything else a profound disappointment with the MPLA's failure to live up to its promise. Party corruption, obscured by a return to the civil war, was at the heart of national malfunction. The nation and the MPLA have always been discursively close for Pepetela. In his earlier works, like *Yaka* (1984), he pushed an isomorphic relation between the two. As a young writer, Pepetela was at the forefront of nation building in the image of the MPLA. He concurred with Agostinho Neto's assertion that 'todos os escritores de Angola estão no MPLA. [...] a literatura em Angola, e podemos estender um pouco mais dizendo a arte em Angola, esteve sempre ao serviço da Revolução' [every writer from Angola is in the MPLA. [...] literature in

Angola, and we can extend this a little to say art in Angola, has always been at the service of the revolution].[18]

For Neto, to be a writer meant to be a member of the MPLA, and more generally, to be Angolan meant to subscribe to the MPLA's vision. The reality on the ground had, however, always been different. There were writers and artists who maintained their distance from the regime, and were kept out of the Angolan Writers Union for much of the civil war.[19] Throughout the civil war, the MPLA painted UNITA as a tribal party, supported by Angola's largest ethnic group, the Ovimbundu. It was cast as a backward, obscurantist project that excluded around two thirds of Angola's population, in supposed contrast to an MPLA narrative of future-facing inclusivity. Didier Péclard challenges that portrayal, pointing to the role of American and Canadian Congregationalists, who arrived in Angola in the late nineteenth century, in recasting tribal identities in a Christian mode.[20]

When UNITA began its struggle against the Portuguese in the colonial era, it did not claim a tribal identity. Only in the late 1970s, once it appeared to have been defeated by the then Cuban-backed MPLA, did it adopt that ready-made, invented tribal identity as a mechanism to sustain itself through years when it could easily have become extinct as an effective force. Then UNITA began to use a Protestant discourse of victimization of the Ovimbundu and of the central highlands that had been pre-rehearsed in the Congregationalist nationalizing project. This offered a counterweight to the MPLA vision of what it meant to be Angolan, at least in the huge swathes of the country that UNITA came to control in the 1980s. The counterweight may have appeared tribal, but it actually drew on the rhetoric of Protestant missionaries operating in Catholic territory.

A clear distinction between the visions of UNITA and the MPLA was their differing attitudes towards urban life. The polis is in the MPLA's DNA. It is also the terrain of the bourgeoisie, with their often scarcely concealed suspicion of rural life. The MPLA under Neto viewed the city as a dialectical locus of ideas, driving humanity forward. Under his successor, the party's aspirations remained channelled towards city life. To a UNITA mindset, that MPLA vision was a neo-colonial imposition of a paradigm that rendered the rural synonymous with underdevelopment. To some degree, the MPLA's vision of the centrality of Luanda was learned in the cosmopolitan milieu of the Casa dos Estudantes do Império in the 1960s and transferred back to Angola's capital, which symbolically gained metropolitan rights over the nation after independence. Pepetela has always seen that flaw in MPLA thinking, and attempted to recuperate a voice for the ignored rural citizens of Angola, even when basing his narratives in cities. The honesty of rural characters, who are depicted as inclusive and diverse, often offers a counter-narrative to the avarice of self-serving urban elites.

As a native of Benguela, Pepetela has consistently maintained a critical gaze on Luanda. His gaze became more accusatory as the capital transformed into a megalopolis, drawing in every class and ethnicity from across the land — a process he depicts vividly in *Se o passado não tivesse asas*. It is a process that exposes the vulnerable to multiple forms of exploitation. Angola was historically predominantly rural yet, in recent years, it has accelerated a developmental model that foregrounds the big city as the cultural and economic melting pot of the future. The effects of the civil war sped up that process, as residents from the countryside fled the fighting and sought refuge in the capital. The trend has not declined since the end of the civil war. With it, the geographical stratifications of class have become more pronounced within Luanda with peripheral shantytowns replicating colonial-era *musseques*, as they are known in Angola.

From his early short stories published in the 1960s under his legal name to his treatise on urban sociology,[21] Artur Carlos Pestana has demonstrated an abiding interest in cities. Writing as an academic in 2014, Pepetela argued that, in countries like Angola, 'a aceleração do crescimento urbano com um ritmo muito superior ao dos países industrializados não vem acompanhada de crescimento económico, facto novo na História' [the acceleration in urban growth at a much faster pace than that of industrialized countries is not accompanied by economic growth, for the first time in history].[22] In his 1962 short story, 'As cinco vidas da Teresa', his native Benguela emerges, in the words of Phyllis Peres, 'as a major character in the text, and supports a reading of geographical conquest and colonization'.[23] From the beginning of his work, the city is a nexus of unequal relations and domination — in contrast to the socially levelling force of the jungle in *Mayombe*. Over the years, the characters enacting that domination change, but their underlying disciplining of the urban space remains the same.

Pepetela returns to Benguela in his later works, most particularly in his 2011 historical novel, *A sul. O sombreiro*, and also in the second of his Jaime Bunda detective parodies, *Jaime Bunda e a morte do americano* (2003). Overwhelmingly, however, the city he most depicts is Luanda, at various stages in its history. He always describes it with the critical eye of an outsider — someone who knows Angola's capital intimately but never feels they completely belong there. Stephen Henighan argues that Luanda represents, for Pepetela, a 'Creolized paradigm' that 'acts as a nucleus that disseminates Angolan national identity'.[24] In other words, Luanda operates as the source of MPLA consciousness in the author's universe. In part, the city created its urban elite and a national bourgeoisie, who inherited their worldview from their former colonial masters.

Pepetela acknowledged in 2014 that 'there continues to be a paucity of literature written about the world outside the city'.[25] Few canonical writers beyond Ruy Duarte de Carvalho have attempted to engage meaningfully with the realities of non-urban life in Angola.[26] Pepetela did use a rural setting as the literary cauldron for a unified national identity, in *Mayombe*, set in the Cabinda enclave where he fought during the struggle for independence. As already discussed, the Mayombe forest acts as a Garden-of-Eden backdrop for multiple ideological and tribal positions to come together for the common good. The utopian future the novel heralds may have proved unobtainable but it was nevertheless a strategically desirable goal.

Where the countryside functions as a catalyst for utopia, cities — and Luanda in particular — are an all-consuming motor of corruption. In them, dreams of a better future are thwarted. The privileged in the city may, over time, be different personalities with different ideologies — or in the case of post-independence Angola with its switch from Marxism to capitalism, the same characters with different ideologies — but the ways in which they frame the city's architecture of power remain remarkably constant. The modern city of Luanda, as a global marketplace that enforces social classes, seems to repeat the patterns of colonialism — patterns that Pepetela's fiction makes clear.

Pepetela claims contemporary Luanda has 'transformada em metrópole ingovernável' [transformed into an ungovernable metropolis].[27] It is a type of 'black hole' — 'a distribution centre that draws people in and continues to draw people in'.[28] In comparison with other African cities, he deems it to be less organized and less law-abiding. From colonial city, to MPLA stronghold during the various stages of the civil war, to post-conflict web of inequality, the monumental transformations in Luanda have been reflected in his evolving fictional representations. Asked to comment on how Luanda has changed, Pepetela asserted:

> There are differences, in the fabric of the city itself — in the new districts being built, in the middle-class suburbs, in the upper-middle-class suburbs, and in those areas where the poorest of the poor lived, in other words, the *musseques*. New things are constantly appearing. That's what's happening on the one hand. On the other hand, the way people relate to each other is constantly changing — businesses and economic life are constantly changing.[29]

From *O cão e os caluandas* (1985) onwards, Pepetela has attempted to capture the urban fabric of those constantly changing relations as manifested in and through Luanda. In *Predadores* (2005), the city operates as a focal point for corruption. It seduces those drawn into its 'black hole', as they attempt to replicate European customs, and then export those tastes to their rural estates. In the plot, the city represents the worst excesses of capitalism. The only hope for the future comes in the form of rural resistance to the unbridled excess of an economic system of exchange, now wholeheartedly endorsed by the urban regime.

Luanda's association with capitalism and its precursors is a leitmotif in Pepetela's work. In his 1997 historical novel, *A gloriosa família*, a novel set during the seventeenth-century Dutch occupation of Angola, Luanda, in the words of Ineke Phaf-Rheinberger, 'is as important a "character" as the van Dum family itself'.[30] The city becomes a nodal point that allows Baltazar van Dum and his family to bridge the gap between a world of European aspiration and a universe of abjection through slavery that financially underpins that world. Luanda's characterization as an Atlantic port evokes its 'underlying social hierarchy and mercantile philosophy'.[31] As Ineke Phaf-Rheinberger points out, 'the readers of Pepetela's novel can almost draw the town plan of Luanda from the information provided in his text'.[32]

Among the various meticulously grounded geographical references to emerge is Kinaxixi, a locale Pepetela repeatedly references, often linking it to a critique of capitalism or its precursor 'mercantile philosophy'. Kinaxixi's association with an otherworldliness, or water spirits who refuse to become part of a global system of exchange, challenge the pure materialism of capitalism in all its stages. In *A gloriosa família*, the narrator declares that in 'a lagoa do Kinaxixi, [...] não havia apenas leões e hienas, mas também as almas injustiçadas, os afogados que ficaram sem sepultura, kiandas de humor imprevisível' [Kinaxixi lagoon, there were not just lions and hyenas, but also wronged souls, those drowned without a burial, kiandas of unpredictable humour].[33]

Kinaxixi is a protagonist in Pepetela's 1995 novella, *O desejo de Kianda*. It serves a similar purpose to its role in *A gloriosa família*. It acts as a foil to the worst excesses of a mercantile mindset. Those overrunning its territory are sucked into voracious capitalism, and can no longer think through any other epistemology. The place — Kinaxixi — represents the latent residue of a mindset that predates mercantile philosophy.

In the novella, Carmina marries João Evangelista in Kinaxixi Square. On the same day, the so-called Luanda syndrome that causes buildings to collapse without harming anyone brings down the office where their wedding ceremony had taken place. The rubble of Kinaxixi represents a challenge to what the square's buildings and their affluent occupants represented in 1990s Luanda: namely the shamelessness of privatizing elites occupying a space previously designated as that of the people. The naked protests that break out in Kinaxixi Square towards the end of *O desejo de Kianda* are a rejection of what the MPLA vision of Angolan civilization was becoming: little more than state-sanctioned self-interest.

Kinaxixi was important in the cultural imaginary of MPLA from the 1960s, when Arnaldo Santos, who would go on to be a founding member of the Angolan Writers Union, published a collection of short stories through the Casa dos Estudantes do Império, entitled, *Quinaxixe*.[34] The opening short story, which gives its name to the volume, depicts the daily life of the square, particularly through the activities of the youngsters who frequent it. It ends with the young Mário dreaming amongst other things of the mermaids of Kinaxixi, and of the freedom of childhood.

Pepetela directly references Arnaldo Santos in *O desejo de Kianda*,[35] alongside the other great writer of Luanda, Luandino Vieira, whose early short stories described the daily experiences of life in the capital's shantytowns, or *musseques*.[36] Both Santos and Luandino, while writing during the struggle for independence, opted to describe the everyday in their stories, seeking to show a universal normality in the lives particularly of youngsters who lived at the urban peripheries under the burden but not the control of colonialism. The writers' narratives were full of hope. The city they described was not a colonial creation but a place that brought together younger generations in solidarity with their neighbours, and nurtured collective dreams for a better, freer future. In other words, they refused to allow colonial power structures to define daily, urban life.

In referencing Santos and Luandino in *O desejo de Kianda*, Pepetela imbues Kinaxixi with nostalgia for something lost in Luanda, first at the hands of the colonizers' 'civilizing' project and later as a result of the MPLA's high modernist project. As the novella draws to a close, Kinaxixi heralds a spreading desire to be free of the constraints of both those projects as water breaks forth and reclaims liberty by coursing through the city. In pre-colonial times, a lagoon had occupied the area of Kinaxixi, only to be enclosed by colonists in an imperial act that attempted to alter the city's geography, and disregarded local folklore about the sacred nature of the site. The area has recently taken a more post-modern form with the post-conflict decision to invest $1 billion in a shopping centre there. The mall is slated to hold 220 shops, seven cinemas, twin twenty-five-storey towers of accommodation, plus a third tower. The complex also benefits from a range of tax exemptions and state subsidies.[37]

There was a prescient irony in Pepetela's 1995 depiction of Kinaxixi — a realization that elite skyscrapers and consumerism were becoming part of the MPLA project for Angola. He juxtaposes the sham of that high modernist urban development with the voices excluded by it, to redefine the city through the actions and lives of the marginalized in the way that Luandino and Santos had done, writing under colonialism.

Kinaxixi is not the only area of Luanda that has acted as a topographical palimpsest in Pepetela. The author shows how the city's history cannot be erased by the practice of renaming streets in line with new ideologies. He also repeatedly references in his later novels how, as the twenty-first-century real estate boom led to speculative construction across the capital's conurbation, the supporting infrastructure failed to keep up. Luanda's basic urban design remained that of the colonial city, a city that was not planned with cars in mind.

In *Jaime Bunda, agente secreto*, the city is, once again, a protagonist. The eponymous bumbling overweight detective shuttles around Luanda in his newly acquired official car, complete with driver. An image of gridlock emerges, resonating with Aubrey Graham and Anne Pitcher's portrait in their 2005 study of cars in the post-conflict capital. For Graham and Pitcher, 'like other cities whose origins predate the invention of motorized transport, parts of Luanda reflect the aesthetic conventions of earlier periods when the urban elite was expected to see and be seen — to stroll through the city as spectators and learn from it'.[38] They argue that the arrival of cars thwarted the practice of the *flâneur*. At the same time, cars became a commodity and a status symbol as much as a means of transportation. Graham and Pitcher draw on Mia Couto's critique of 'cardolatry' — the particularly male fetish for luxury cars and its effect on the economies and social fabric of developing countries — to point to the extent to which cars became a primary marker of a macho class difference in twenty-first-century Luanda.[39] The Marxist New Man was, by the turn of the millennium, replaced by the chauffeur chauvinist.

For Bunda, the acquisition of a car to navigate Luanda's potholes and peripheries represents his upward mobility. With his pastiche and citation from American films and detective fiction, and his desire to graft European and American mores over the Angolan national mindset, Bunda embodies the MPLA's vision of the city at the turn of the century. With the end of the civil conflict in sight, Luanda became an international node, increasingly paralyzed by the globalized taste for personal mobility of an aspiring middle class.

Traces of the history of the colonial city remain, even when an altered political climate enforces changes to the names of its locations. Bunda's driver, Bernardo, races impatiently around Luanda's renamed streets. The capital's fluctuating toponyms reflect the ideologies of the moment. The Avenida do Brasil [Brazil Avenue] in colonial times later became the Avenida Hoji ya Henda (a hero of the liberation struggle), although among the local population it was also known as Avenida dos Massacres [Massacre Avenue], after the FNLA captured and killed opponents there in the early years of independence. For the chauffeur, facing traffic jams and potholes, 'a mudança do nome é que provocou essas desgraças' [the name change caused these problems].[40] There is a subtle nostalgia in Bernardo's position for a (colonial) time when the Avenida do Brasil 'era boa de andar, larga, via rápida' [was good to go along, wide, a fast route] — when Luanda was a city of *gentils flâneurs* rather than rabid road ragers.[41] He questions the ideological impositions of the MPLA on the post-colonial city, with its creaking infrastructure and chronic underinvestment. Renaming streets does not erase the memory of an infrastructure that worked better before the urban demographic explosion, when cars were few and far between, and consumerism limited to a colonial elite.

The MPLA's mismanagement of Angola's urban infrastructure and the betrayal of its revolutionary promise resurface in Pepetela's 2013 novel, *O tímido e as mulheres*. The novel is an ideological sequel to *O desejo de Kianda*. Genoveva, a corrupt MPLA woman politician, inherits the traits of Carmina. She is the post-conflict version of her 1990s incarnation — an MPLA stalwart and Member of Parliament who prefers to go shopping rather than attend an election rally.

Once again, in *O tímido e as mulheres*, Luanda is a protagonist. Pepetela portrays the city's traffic jams and poorly maintained streets, alongside the grotesque distortions of a boom in property prices that have catapulted it into the category of one of the most expensive places in the world. The perverse situation of a 'cidade conhecida pelos preços dignos de Primeiro Mundo' [city known for prices worthy of the First World] is one of the primary concerns of Pepetela in his 2013 novel.[42] How has the city, under the MPLA, become unaffordable for the vast majority of its inhabitants? Why does the city now replicate the colonial paradigm of centres and peripheries, of the *musseque* and exclusive luxury, of abject poverty and obscene wealth?

The relocation of the presidential palace in the 1990s to the former Portuguese governor's mansion replicated the trappings of an imperial monarchy, symbolizing a reclaimed geographical continuity in the nation's architecture of power. For Pepetela, the president was attempting to become a divinely ordained agent of absolute power. In *Jaime Bunda, agente secreto*, Pepetela satirises the 'sanctity' of the terrain on which the president lives, describing the people's need (and legal obligation) to avert their gazes and change their routes away from the palace, 'pelo perigo de ficarem ofuscados pela intensa luz do Poder de Estado' [because of the danger of being dazed by the intense light of State Power].[43]

Through his portrayal of Luanda's spatial reconfigurations, Pepetela continues his career-long analysis of the continuities of power. Luanda was colonized, nationalized and then privatized. It is a location where hierarchies are enforced but also undermined. It is a city where the global has long been present — from the seventeenth-century slave trading of the Van Dums to the twenty-first-century luxury cars of Bunda. At the same time, it is, for Pepetela, a constant home of resistance — through the water spirits of Kinaxixi or the chaos of Roque Santeiro, 'a verdadeira bolsa de valores de Angola, onde se estabelecia o curso real das moedas e o preço dos produtos' [Angola's true stock market, where the currency's real value and the price of goods were established].[44]

Rather like Kinaxixi's transformation into a shopping mall, Roque Santeiro assumed a different value when it was closed in 2010, to the outrage of its traders. It had grown up in the 1980s at a time when only MPLA apparatchiks had access to supermarkets with well-stocked shelves. Its informality and mayhem are captured in *Jaime Bunda, agente secreto*. It was a market beyond state and MPLA control. Officially closed on public health grounds, cynics (and Pepetela) have noted how quickly it became prime real estate in the hands of luxury property developers.[45]

Pepetela's later fiction repeatedly suggests that, regardless of what urban developers and a corrupt government might think, Luanda cannot be controlled. Amidst its chaos, a vibrant and anguished middle class has emerged, and become, nearly four decades after Agostinho Neto authorized their representation, a focus in Pepetela's novels, as we see in *O tímido e as mulheres* (2013) and *Se o passado não tivesse asas* (2016).

In *O tímido e as mulheres*, the emerging middle class shares the tastes of the Creole elites who were the backbone of the MPLA and who looked beyond Angola to Europe and Latin America for their aesthetics. In the novel, Pepetela turns his caustic humour on the bourgeoisie in the midst of a Luanda property boom that has created immense speculative wealth from nothing, and given rise to new mechanisms of corruption and extortion.

The novel is Pepetela's first in which a writer is the protagonist. Heitor is hopeless with women, unable to make the first move. Various women enter his life, stimulate his fantasy, and ultimately, with the exception of the last one, Orquídea, leave him unfulfilled. His mother, Dona Genoveva Barbosa, is a parliamentarian who reaps the personal benefits of her position. Like Carmina in *O desejo de Kianda*, Genoveva dominates her husband, and commits all the gauche style blunders of the upwardly mobile. Her son, Heitor, seeks to avoid living in her shadow, choosing instead to rent a remote plot of land that may soon fall under the sway of property developers, and their constant quest for new opportunities. There, he tries to recover from being dumped by a nameless girlfriend, who is the reflection of Tatiana, Heitor's earlier, childhood crush. Because of the interference of Heitor's meddling mother, who disapproved of Tatiana's lower social standing, any intimacy between Heitor and Tatiana was thwarted before it could come into being.

The fraught relationship between Heitor and his mother helps to explain the writer's inability to relate easily to women. It also represents the MPLA's relationship with Angola's twenty-first-century youth. Genoveva symbolizes the MPLA in post-conflict power. She is part of a cadre that prefers the benefits of privileged consumerism to political action, yet refuses to cede ground to younger generations.

Heitor spends his days writing and rewriting a manuscript entitled 'Para lá das ondas' [Beyond the Waves]. The title references Manuel Rui's 1982 humorous critique of the disconnect between MPLA rhetoric and praxis, *Quem me dera ser onda* [I Wish I Were a Wave].[46] Rui's text is also about the (then incipient) Luandan middle class. As Luís Madureira points out, *Quem me dera ser onda* is an inflection of a famous line of Agostinho Neto's poetry.[47] It echoes a verse from 'Desfile de sombras' [A Succession of Shadows] in which the desire to be a wave is linked to the desire for independence.[48] The title and rewriting of Heitor's manuscript signals independence has arrived, and it is time to 'move on' from whatever that has come to mean. In some ways, for Luanda's twenty-first-century middle class, 'moving on' implies writing over a series of wrongs that the MPLA has perpetrated in the name of the nation and within its own ranks.

The characterizations in *O tímido e as mulheres* attest to the recent possibility of supporting different political parties, while living in a negotiated if fragile harmony within the same household. Luanda's middle classes are now united in a shared 'post-ideological' aspiration for personal improvement in material circumstances. Their aspirations still include an outward-looking aesthetic cosmopolitanism that characterised the Creole elites, but it is devoid of any revolutionary political dimension.

'Cuando calienta el sol' — an Argentinian song, from a 1963 film starring the Chilean Antonio Prieto — features repeatedly in the novel. It embodies the transnational, translingual, and nostalgic tastes of Luanda's middle class. It also becomes a means of communication between the seductive radio broadcaster Marisa and Heitor, alongside his book manuscript, with its twice-written world, 'Para lá das ondas' [Beyond the Waves]. With each rewriting of Agostinho Neto's verse, its political meaning is diluted until it becomes little more than a marker of refined taste.

Marisa is married to Lucrécio, an ideologically pure polio survivor, whose commitment to the revolution never stopped him seeing how independence and the MPLA failed to deliver everything promised. Lucrécio identifies the fundamental problem with Marxism as the constraints it imposes on individual liberty. Unlike other characters in Pepetela's work who become disabled through maiming or the effects of war, Lucrécio's incapacity was caused by a childhood disease. As the bearer of the purest form of ideology — the true utopian visionary who realizes there is no utopia — he is flawed and withered from his infancy. No one outside their marriage can understand why Marisa is faithful to Lucrécio. While she flirts with other men, including Heitor, she does not follow through. Eventually, Lucrécio senses he is holding Marisa back, and determines to commit suicide in order to set her free. However, due to a series of unlucky coincidences, his death points to possible foul play. Marisa is arrested, and her reputation is ruined.

In metaphorical terms, the relationship between Lucrécio and Marisa mirrors Genoveva's relationship with Heitor. Each relationship references the commitment of a different generation of MPLA leaders to the Angolan people. Lucrécio's generation was full of good intentions, and brought a wealth of ideological experience into Angola's service with the goal of setting its people free. However, Marisa's life is ruined by a misinterpretation and mismanagement of Lucrécio's liberating, if suicidal, gesture. So too, it seems, the well-meaning liberating actions of Lucrécio's generation have given rise to the unintended establishment of one of Africa's most perverse income distributions and most corrupt regimes.

In contrast, Genoveva represents a different MPLA mindset — one that followed the liberators, and no longer understood progress in terms of the Internationale and the Marxist New Man, but in terms of the shopping malls of Kinaxixi, Hollywood films and the right to exist beyond Angola. Both are urban projects. As much as it pains Pepetela to write Lucrécio out of Angola's future, his ideals, based on the purity of class struggle, are doomed. In their stead, a world in which the middle classes feed off each other and are pawns in larger capitalist games appears to be the future depicted by the novel.

Despite the middle-class angst his later writing reveals, Pepetela does not portray an irredeemable contemporary Angola. He never lurches into wholesale 'saudades', or pained nostalgia, for a blissful existence ascribed retroactively to the colonial regime — although characters like Bernardo in *Jaime Bunda, agente secreto* do pine for a time when there was less traffic on Luanda's streets and some of Pepetela's short stories reveal a yearning for the moral certainties of the past. Precisely because of his keen understanding of history, Pepetela avoids the trap of idealizing a history that was not. The words of Lucrécio shortly before his suicide remind us: 'Reclamamos todos os dias contra o que está errado. Muita coisa, na verdade. Mas esquecemos como viviam os nossos pais, e eu próprio quando era pequeno. Com medo, com vergonha, sem possibilidade de afirmação' [Every day, we complain about what is wrong. A lot is, no doubt. But we forget how our parents lived, how I lived when I was small. In fear, in shame, with no possibility of affirmation].[49] The revolution may have malfunctioned and not delivered what it promised but colonialism made Angolans 'bons meninos' [good boys] who could not 'aspirar a mais' [aspire to more].[50]

The MPLA version of high modernity essentially changed the rhetoric from dependency to affirmation. For all the flaws that came with its project, including those Pepetela bears and acknowledges, the writer also shows how that change of rhetoric opened up conditions of possibility for the generations that followed to seize.

How subsequent generations seized those possibilities in less than desirable ways is a theme in Pepetela's 2016 novel, *Se o passado não tivesse asas*. In it, he critiques the stratifications of contemporary Luandan society. The narrative follows two interspersed story lines that fuse together in 2002 — the year the civil war ended. The first story begins in 1995, during a particularly violent phase of the conflict. At the time, waves of refugees fled from the central highlands to the capital as UNITA and the MPLA viciously fought each other for control of Angola's natural resources.

The narrative follows the experiences of Himba and Kassule, orphaned street children, subject to multiple instances of violence and hunger. They survive and eventually transform into Sofia — an increasingly successful restaurateur — and Diego — a naïf artist who struggles to find a soul in his painting. Sofia and Diego are the protagonists of the second plot line that begins in 2012, but the reader only discovers that Himba is Sofia and Kassule is Diego towards the end of the novel.

Kassule's first words to Himba are, in fact, 'não és Sofia' [you are not Sofia].[51] Sofia is the name of Kassule's lost sister. For much of the novel, the reader assumes his sister is the Sofia of the second plot line but she is never found. Instead, Himba elects to become known as Sofia and effectively adopts Kassule (who chooses the new name Diego) as her brother in an effort to erase the traumas of their past.

One of Pepetela's darker novels, *Se o passado não tivesse asas* interrogates how Angola's national memory and identity have evolved over the last two decades. It references the enforced amnesia prevalent within the MPLA about the recent past. It portrays the violence endured by children on the streets of Luanda alongside the opulence of the 'jet-set' (p. 174), a group of princelings who 'nunca deixam o seu espaço para os outros, qualquer dia tudo está reservado, terras, praias, até o céu' (p. 306) [never leave any of their space for others, one day everything will be reserved for them, lands, beaches, even heaven].

The central narrative tension of the novel is the evolving relationship between Himba/Sofia and Kassule/Diego. The ordeals they endure in Luanda bring them together and eventually tear them apart. Sofia transforms into a successful businesswoman whose loss of moral compass leads her 'brother' Diego no longer to recognize her. Kassule's initial words to Himba ('you are not Sofia') thus presage how their relationship will end.

Sofia acquires effective ownership of the restaurant in which she works through a series of dubious choices she makes that essentially disinherit its rightful owners and betray the trust placed in her by Dona Ester, who has recognized her talent and offered her a job. Pepetela subtly demonstrates how each time Sofia makes a choice that furthers her interest in the restaurant, she justifies her actions in pseudo-ethical terms. She appears to be innocent until it becomes clear she is shrewd and ruthless. She aspires to be accepted by the elite clientele the restaurant increasingly attracts. However, she always fears that at any moment she will be put back in her place as a 'mulher vinda do musseque ou da rua, sem direito portanto a entrar na intimidade dos eleitos' (p. 320) [woman from the shantytown or the street, and thus without any right to be close to the chosen ones].

Pepetela characterizes those chosen ones as the offspring of Luanda's elite. They have unlimited credit cards, fuelled by the nation's oil wealth, and are 'gente elegante, habituada a fugacidade do interesse' (p. 215) [elegant people, with short attention spans]. They drink in excess and indulge in orgies. They are oblivious to the suffering on the streets of Luanda, and view philanthropy as a pastime to fill their essential vacuous lives. To them, 'o mundo do trabalho lhes era absolutamente estranho' (p. 54) [the world of work was absolutely unknown]. Pepetela's depiction of this parasitic class is as damning as it was in *Predadores*. They are not, however, the focus of the novel. Instead, Pepetela is more interested in portraying the contradictions that create Sofia out of Himba — the way Angola, and Luanda in particular, turns rural innocence into unethical agency, and community spirit into alienated solitude.

Himba's experiences explain Sofia's actions. As she strives towards the end of the novel to 'rasgar o passado' (p. 361) [rip up the past], Sofia cuts links with all those who helped her to escape from the streets and to enter Luanda's aspiring middle class. Diego, the only remaining contact from her life on the streets, challenges her for the self-interested, corrupt capitalist she has become. How could she steal the restaurant? Her reply is 'Eu sou o que fizeram de mim. O teu país' (p. 371) [I am what they made of me. Your country]. Sofia is the product of modern Angola. The country alone now bears responsibility for what its inhabitants have become. It can no longer blame colonialism or the Cold War. *O tímido e as mulheres*'s Lucrécio made clear before his suicide that Angolans were given the opportunity for self-affirmation beyond the constraints of colonialism thanks to the intervention of his generation. Sofia, who is young enough to be his granddaughter, is the embodiment of that affirmation in a country that because of multiple and complicated, but nevertheless, sometimes avoidable and preventable factors, lost sight of her generation's humanity.

Se o passado não tivesse asas has two epigraphs that intimate a contradiction about where responsibility lies for the condition of contemporary Angola. The first is 'o país é de todos e não deve ser culpado pelos erros dos seus filhos' (p. 7) [the country belongs to everyone and it should not be blamed for its children's mistakes]. The second is 'as terras exigem muito das pessoas. Mais do que elas podem dar. Quando as pessoas falham, as terras nunca se sentem culpadas. Talvez tenham razão. Mas como se devem as pessoas sentir?' (p. 7) [the lands demand a lot of the people. More than they are able to give. When the people fall short, the lands never feel guilty. Maybe they are right. But how are the people supposed to feel?].

Much of Pepetela's writing has invested in bringing a sense of Angolan nationhood into being. He conspicuously does not use the word 'nation' in either of the epigraphs or in Sofia's explanation of what she has become, yet, behind the 'lands' and 'country', vestiges of the nation lurk. By 2016, the nation had become so morally bankrupt after years of MPLA abuse that it was little more than a compromised blame game with terminological avatars now standing in for the word itself. As in *A gloriosa família*, epigraphs once again serve the role of pointing to absence and sustaining ambiguities. *Se o passado não tivesse asas* ultimately asks who or what is responsible for all that has gone wrong. Was it those who inherited the country or were the demands of the lands' legacies and expectations too much for anyone to bear?

Pepetela maintains that ambiguity throughout the novel. As Phyllis Peres points out in relation to his twentieth-century writing, 'resistance in Pepetela's texts almost always resides in the narrative refusal of closure. His works end in questions that open the narrative discourse to strategies of resistance'.[52] In *Se o passado não tivesse asas*, the novel begins with an interrogative epigraph and ends with a question, too, articulated by Diego: 'é este o nosso futuro, a ditadura da ganância?' (p. 372) [is this our future, a money-grabbing dictatorship?]. Everything narrated between those two questions points to the historical complications undergirding ethical choices taken on a daily basis in contemporary Luanda.

In the 1990s, when Himba's story begins, Luanda was 'a mítica capital onde tudo acontecia' [the mythical capital where everything happened], full of 'sonhos e temores' (p. 10) [dreams and fears]. Its streets were increasingly filled with children from across Angola. As Pepetela portrays them, these new arrivals lost contact with their native languages, and began to speak like Luandans, losing the underlying Umbundu nasalization typical of certain dialects of rural Angolan Portuguese (p. 114). The loss of contact with their cultural roots was accompanied by a change in moral values, exemplified by Himba's loss of faith in God, and Sofia's subsequent acquisition of a sole belief in the market place. The primary lesson she learns through her experiences of being repeatedly raped and hungry on Luanda's streets is voiced by Kassule: 'o mal de uns é o bem de outros' (p. 158) [the harm of some is the fortune of others]. Himba's sense of right and wrong is replaced by Sofia's degree in marketing and her transactional mindset centred on a zero-sum game. Himba's identity based on an upbringing in the 'ar fresco e puro do Planalto' (p. 10) [fresh, pure air of the highland] is replaced by Sofia's identity based on an ATM card and the elimination of any link to her parents or her past. Ultimately, she blames her parents (her father in particular) for failing to protect her, and for presiding over Angola's dehumanization.

Leonor Simas-Almeida and Patrícia Martinho Ferreira read orphanhood in *Se o passado não tivesse asas* as a metaphor for the generalized suffering of a post-conflict population that 'continua atormentada por traumas e fantasmas de um passado afinal ainda presente'[53] [continues to be tormented by traumas and ghosts of a still-present past]. Those traumas may have begun in the countryside (where the effects of the civil war were fiercest and where Himba lost her parents and siblings), but the city aggravated the loss, destroying the dignity of the children on its streets as it transformed into a playground at the service of the idle rich. As Diego decries, Luanda in 2012 was 'onde só o dinheiro era dono e senhor' (p. 22) [where money alone was owner and lord]. It was a place where bank branches proliferated like 'os cacussos se multiplicam nos lagos' (p. 29) [tilapia multiply in lakes].

Himba learns from the city that she can depend on no one. Like Pepetela's depiction of Americans in the noughties, Luanda's inhabitants in the second decade of the twenty-first century, are fragmented and alienated, riven by class distinctions that create and enforce disconnected worlds. The city's social fabric has disintegrated completely. In the greatest betrayal of what Pepetela's generation set out to achieve, the unprivileged have become discardable objects, who must learn to survive or be destroyed.

As *O tímido e as mulheres*'s Lucrécio recognized before he killed himself, the Marxism that the MPLA tried to impose on Angola in the 1970s placed too many constraints on the individual, failing to take into account the diverse richness of the country's human resources. Pepetela made a similar point in *Mayombe*, when he warned against the movement's tendency to police its members dogmatically, failing to treat them as individuals with differences. However, by the time he wrote *Se o passado não tivesse asas*, concerns about the ideological constraints on individual liberty had given way to despair at the indifferent objectification of the most vulnerable, and abhorrence at the imperial-era stratifications that have returned to Luanda. The city had become a place of atomized individuals, like Sofia, who ends the novel, in the words of Simas-Almeida and Ferreira, 'irremediavelmente só' [irrecuperably alone].[54]

As has repeatedly been the case in his work, Pepetela once again deploys the trope of rape to make a metaphorical point. National innocence is cruelly crushed as Himba is gang-raped. Once again, it is not the depiction of rape that is problematic, but the subsequent feelings the author ascribes to the victim. Himba reaches the conclusion that the only way she can survive is to acquiesce to an older street child Tobias's demand to be his sexual consort. Despite Tobias's occasional violence towards her 'para marcar a sua autoridade' (p. 204) [to mark his authority], Himba learns to enjoy the sex that comes as the price for her protection and to 'sentir um ligeiro prazer' (p. 204) [feel a light pleasure]. She is the latest in a series Pepetela's female characters (from *Mayombe*'s Ondina and *Yaka*'s Chucha to *O tímido e as mulheres*'s Marisa) who, for different reasons, recodify their sexual violation in terms of an awakened enjoyment.

Unlike her predecessors from Pepetela's work, Himba/Sofia squarely lays the blame for what she endures and what she becomes on a society that attempts to dehumanize her, denying her right to a future and obliterating the roots of her past. After she loses Tobias's projection and is again gang-raped, she declares 'o futuro não existe para gente como nós' (p. 247) [the future does not exist for people like us]. Yet Himba/Sofia does carve out a future for herself, learning how to move ahead in a still patriarchal, class-ridden system by weaponizing her sexuality and refusing to allow any man to take advantage of her again. As Himba transitions into Sofia, she exploits the complacent hubris of a teacher known for the sexual harassment of his students in order to blackmail him into giving her prior sight of an exam paper. Then, as she builds up the restaurant in which she works, she flirts with her princeling clients, but never sleeps with them. Her body becomes the one thing she, as Sofia, will not exchange.

Like the country whose lost innocence she embodies, Himba/Sofia is a complex survivor. It is not clear at what point she becomes accountable for her actions but, by the end of the novel when Diego disowns her, she bears some responsibility for what she does. The honest and kind Himba, who was a victim, becomes the wily and calculating perpetrator Sofia, who instrumentalizes others to achieve her goals. Pepetela subtly crafts the continuum of that transition, and maintains its ambiguity. In other words, precisely when Himba's experiences cease to be the sole excuse for Sofia's actions is not a discrete point in time, but by the end of the novel Diego makes clear that the choices his 'sister' makes have become conscious and reprehensible.

Se o passado não tivesse asas is the apotheosis of Pepetela's work. The subtlety of its characterizations and the artfulness of its structure are the product of nearly sixty years of publishing his writing, and a lifetime of studying with the eye of a historian and sociologist the human condition. It is a novel that demonstrates the cultural terrain of complication that Agostinho Neto wanted Angolan authors to explore from the late 1970s. It represents the persistence of Luanda's class structure, foregrounding the changing identity of a bourgeoisie that aspires to forget from where it came. The spirit of solidarity that Luandino and Santos depicted in the quotidian routines of the colonial capital's rebellious youngsters has transformed into the solitude and selfishness of a city and a country that can no longer blame its past for all its current woes.

Notes to Chapter 12

1. James Brooke, 'Angolan Writers Bloom in Independent Climate', *New York Times*, 3 January 1985 <http://www.nytimes.com/1985/01/03/books/angolan-writers-bloom-in-independent-climate.html> [accessed 27 March 2018].
2. Ibid.
3. Neto quoted in Brooke. Brooke dates the speech from 1977. It was actually from 1979. See Agostinho Neto, *Ainda o meu sonho (discursos sobre a cultura nacional)* (Lisbon: Edições 70, 1980), p. 45.
4. Quoted in Brooke.
5. Hamilton quoted in Brooke.
6. Alfredo Margarido, *Negritude e humanismo* (Lisbon: Casa dos Estudantes do Império, 1964).
7. See Pires Laranjeira, 'A poesia de Agostinho Neto como documento histórico', in *Comunidades imaginadas: nação e nacionalismos em África*, ed. by Luís Reis Torgal, Fernando Tavares Pimenta and Julião Soares Sousa (Coimbra: Imprensa da Universidade, 2008), pp. 111–16.
8. Neto quoted in Brooke.
9. Ibid. The original in Portuguese is 'Viver a cultura angolana significa compreender o povo tal como ele é definido. Ser um elemento do povo. Esquecer preconceitos e ultrapassar a classe. Caricaturar a pequena burguesia, ou descrevê-la, é tão válido como exaltar o camponês ou o operário', from Agostinho Neto, *Ainda o meu sonho*, p. 33. This speech was given on 24 November 1977 (in contrast to the later speech which Brooke also cites in his article, conflating the dates of the two).
10. Ali Mazrui, *African Thought in Contemporary Perspective* (Newcastle: Cambridge Scholars Publishing, 2014), p. 43.
11. Ibid.
12. Ibid.
13. Quoted in Lara Pawson, *In the Name of the People: Angola's Forgotten Massacre* (London: Tauris, 2014), p. 105.
14. Ibid., p. 104.
15. 'Angola: Irene Neto critica regime de Eduardo dos Santos e defende modificação da Constituição' in *Africa 21 Digital*, 11 July 2017 <https://africa21digital.com/2017/07/11/29626/> [accessed 27 March 2018]. Irene Neto was originally interviewed by *Novo Jornal*, and her answers reprinted in this article in *Africa 21 Digital*.
16. Ibid.
17. Nuno Ribeiro, '38 anos de equilíbrios e poder', *Público*, 23 August 2017 <https://www.publico.pt/2017/08/23/mundo/noticia/38-anos-de-equilibrios-e-poder-1783023> [accessed 27 March 2018].
18. Agostinho Neto, *Ainda o meu sonho*, pp. 15–16. Speech before the Angolan Writers Union, Luanda, 10 December 1975.
19. One of the most famous examples is Sousa Jamba, whose Angolanness was often challenged because he published novels in English drawing on his experiences in UNITA. See his *Patriots* (London: Viking, 1990).
20. Didier Péclard, 'UNITA and the Moral Economy of Exclusion in Angola, 1966–1977', in *Sure Road? Nationalisms in Angola, Guinea-Bissau and Mozambique*, ed. by Eric Morier-Genoud (Leiden: Brill, 2012), pp. 149–74.
21. Artur Pestana dos Santos, *Sociologia urbana: compêndio* (Mangualde: Edições Pedago, 2014).
22. Ibid., p. 22.
23. Phyllis Peres, 'Colonial Representation and Conquest in Pepetela's "As Cinco Vidas de Teresa"', *Portuguese Literary and Cultural Studies*, 15/16 (2006), 251–57 (p. 53).
24. Stephen Henighan, '"Um James Bond Subdesenvolvido": The Ideological Work of the Angolan Detective in Pepetela's Jaime Bunda Novels', *Portuguese Studies*, 22.1 (2006), 135–52 (p. 135).

25. Quoted in Ana Mafalda Leite et al., *Speaking the Postcolonial Nation: Interviews with Writers from Angola and Mozambique* (Oxford: Peter Lang, 2014), p. 113.
26. See Ruy Duarte de Carvalho, *Vou lá visitar pastores* (Lisbon: Cotovia, 1999) for an attempt to bring rural Angola into the conception of nationhood.
27. Quoted in Luís Ricardo Duarte, 'Pepetela: crónica de uma Angola em mudança' [interview], *Jornal de Letras* 30 October 2013, pp. 8–9 (p. 8).
28. Quoted in Leite, *Speaking the Postcolonial Nation*, p. 116.
29. Ibid., pp. 117–18.
30. Ineke Phaf-Rheinberger, *The 'Air of Liberty': Narratives of the South Atlantic Past* (Amsterdam: Rodopi, 2008), p. 169.
31. Ibid., p. 166.
32. Ibid., p. 169.
33. Pepetela, *A gloriosa família* (Lisbon: Dom Quixote, 1997), p. 317.
34. Arnaldo Santos, *Quinaxixe* (Lisbon: Casa dos Estudantes do Império, 1965).
35. Pepetela, *O desejo de Kianda* (Lisbon: Dom Quixote, 1995), p. 47.
36. See José Luandino Vieira, *A vida verdadeira de Domingos Xavier* (Lisbon: Edições 70, 1974); José Luandino Vieira, *Nós, os do Makulusu* (Lisbon: Edições 70, 1975).
37. 'Portuguese group Somague builds shopping centre in Luanda, Angola' (no byline), *Macauhub*, 12 January 2005, <http://www.macauhub.com.mo/en/2015/01/12/portuguese-group-somague-builds-shopping-centre-in-luanda-angola/> [accessed 27 March 2018].
38. Aubrey Graham and Anne Pitcher, 'Cars are Killing Luanda: Cronyism, Consumerism, and Other Assaults on Angola's Postwar Capital City', in *Cities in Contemporary Africa*, ed. by Martin J. Murray and Garth A. Myers (New York: Palgrave, 2005), pp. 173–99 (p. 175).
39. Ibid., p. 187.
40. Pepetela, *Jaime Bunda, agente secreto* (Lisbon: Dom Quixote, 2001), p. 92.
41. Ibid., p. 92.
42. Pepetela, *O tímido e as mulheres* (Lisbon: Dom Quixote, 2013), p. 23.
43. *Jaime Bunda, agente secreto*, p. 111.
44. Ibid., p. 84
45. Quoted in Leite, *Speaking the Postcolonial Nation*, p. 119.
46. Manuel Rui, *Quem me dera ser onda* (Lisbon: Edições 70, 1982).
47. Luís Madureira, *Imaginary Geographies in Portuguese and Lusophone-African Literature: Narratives of Discovery and Empire* (Lampeter: Edwin Mellen, 2006), p. 233.
48. Agostinho Neto, *Sagrada esperança* (Lisbon: Sá da Costa, 1987), p. 71.
49. *O tímido e as mulheres*, p. 232.
50. Ibid., p. 232.
51. Pepetela, *Se o passado não tivesse asas* (Lisbon: Dom Quixote, 2016), p. 41. Subsequent page references given in the text.
52. Phyllis Peres, 'Traversing Postcoloniality: Pepetela and the Narrations of Nation', *Luso-Brazilian Review*, 40.2 (2003), 111–17 (p. 115).
53. Patrícia Isabel Martinho Ferreira and Leonor Simas-Almeida, 'Os órfãos da Ilha de Luanda em *Se o passado não tivesse asas* — ou a história recente de um vasto segmento da sociedade angolana', *Via Atlântica*, 31 (June 2017), 227–47 (p. 246).
54. Ibid., p. 246.

AFTERWORD

One of Pepetela's earliest works, *Muana Puó*, written in 1969 but published nearly a decade later, is an allegory in which downtrodden bats are forced to eat the excrement of crows for whom they produce honey.[1] The bats fight for their freedom, achieve it, and evolve a humanity. As humans, they experience the challenges of sexual difference. The two protagonists designated as 'Ele' [He] and 'Ela' [She] fall into an ill-fated love. He ends up suicidal in the desert, feeling betrayed. She ends up unsatisfied.

Muana Puó is an early literary manifestation of Pepetela's lifelong commitment to justice and the overthrow of oppression — be it based on class or dubious racial hierarchies. Yet, as Stephen Henighan has noted, among the bats 'the primary division [...] is not one of class, region, or ethnicity, but of gender'.[2] Throughout his writing, Pepetela has repeatedly and effectively challenged the multiple binary axes used to enforce inequality. Yet, he has sometimes struggled in his portrayal of women. Gender remains, for him, the most enigmatic divide — over which he has, on occasions, trodden the clumsy steps of an unreconstructed New Man. He will go down in history as the most important writer during the genesis of an independent Angola. He is a writer who combined political commitment with a wry and knowing gaze on the weaknesses yet beauty of human endeavours. Over the course of his writing, he revealed a profound understanding of where the MPLA revolution went wrong. But he is also a man who, like his male creation in *Muana Puó*, projects his own fantasies onto the desires of his female characters. That, of course, is the prerogative of any writer, which is why the Angolan canon needs to recognize far more women.

Notes

1. Pepetela, *Muana Puó* (Lisbon: Edições 70, 1978).
2. Stephen Henighan, '*Muana Puó* and *Mayombe*: Colonial Pasts and Utopian Futures in Two Early Works by Pepetela', *Romance Quarterly*, 54.2 (2007), 164–77 (p. 165).

BIBLIOGRAPHY

ADORNO, THEODOR W., *The Culture Industry: Select Essays on Mass Culture* (New York: Routledge, 1991)
AGUALUSA, JOSÉ EDUARDO, *A Rainha Ginga e de como os africanos inventaram o mundo* (Lisbon: Quetzal, 2014)
ALVES, NITO, *Discurso no comício de encerramento da campanha eleitoral para os órgãos do poder popular em Luanda* (Luanda: MPLA, 1976)
'Angola: Irene Neto critica regime de Eduardo dos Santos e defende modificação da Constituição' [no byline], in *Africa 21 Digital*, 11 July 2017 <https://africa21digital.com/2017/07/11/29626/> (reprinted from *Novo Jornal*)
ANISTIA INTERNACIONAL BRASIL, 'AÇÃO URGENTE: Jovens ativistas presos arbitrariamente em Angola', 3 July 2015 <https://anistia.org.br/entre-em-acao/carta/acao-urgente-6/> [accessed 27 March 2018]
ARENAS, FERNANDO, *Lusophone Africa: Beyond Independence* (Minneapolis: Minnesota University Press, 2011)
ARENDT, HANNAH, *Eichmann in Jerusalem: A Report on the Banality of Evil* (New York: Viking, 1963)
BAKHTIN, MIKHAIL M., *The Dialogic Imagination: Four Essays*, trans. by Caryl Emerson and Michael Holquist (Austin: University of Texas Press, 1981)
—— *Problems of Dostoevsky's Poetics*, trans. by Caryl Emerson (Manchester: Manchester University Press, 1984)
BARNETT, DON, and ROY HARVEY, *The Revolution in Angola: MPLA, Life Histories and Documents* (New York: Bobbs-Merrill Company, 1972)
BARTHES, ROLAND, *Mythologies* (Paris: Éditions du Seuil, 1957)
BHABHA, HOMI, 'Of Mimicry and Man: The Ambivalence of Colonial Discourse', *October*, 28 (Spring 1984), 125–33
BIRMINGHAM, DAVID, *A Short History of Angola* (London: Hurst, 2015)
—— *The Portuguese Conquest of Angola* (Oxford: Oxford University Press, 1965)
BORGES, AMARÍLIS, 'Grande Entrevista com Júlio de Almeida', *Rede Angola*, 17 March 2017 <http://www.redeangola.info/especiais/nossa-administracao-e-muito-mediocre/> [accessed 27 March 2018]
BORGES TEIXEIRA, VALÉRIA MARIA, 'A ruptura com o discurso do colonizador em *Lueji (o nascimento dum império)*', in *Actas do IV Congresso Internacional da APLC-Relações Intraliterárias, Contextos Culturais e Estudos Pós-coloniais*, 3 vols (Évora: Universidade de Évora, 2001), I, 1–10
BOULANGER, DOROTHÉE, 'Fiction as History? Resistance, Complicities and the Intellectual History of Postcolonial Angola' (unpublished doctoral thesis, King's College London, 2017)
BRITTAIN, VICTORIA, *Morte da diginidade: a guerra civil em Angola*, trans. by Tânia Sofia Rocha, intro by Pepetela (Lisbon: Dom Quixote, 1999)
BROADHEAD, SUSAN H., *Historical Dictionary of Angola*, 2nd edn (Metuchen, NJ: Scarecrow Press, 1992)

BROOKE, JAMES, 'Angolan Writers Bloom in Independent Climate', *New York Times*, 3 January 1985 <http://www.nytimes.com/1985/01/03/books/angolan-writers-bloom-in-independent-climate.html> [accessed 27 March 2018]

BROOKSHAW, DAVID, 'Narration and Nation-Building: The Angolan Novels of Pepetela', in *Fiction in the Portuguese-speaking World: Essays in Memory of Alexandre Pinheiro Torres*, ed. by Charles M. Kelley (Cardiff: University of Wales Press, 2000), pp. 107–16

BROWN, NICHOLAS, *Utopian Generations: The Political Horizon of Twentieth-Century Literature* (Princeton, NJ: Princeton University Press, 2006)

CADORNEGA, ANTÓNIO DE OLIVEIRA DE, *História geral das guerras angolanas*, 3 vols (Lisbon: Agência Geral das Colónias, 1940–42)

CALAFATE RIBEIRO, MARGARIDA, 'Literary Voices of Luanda and Maputo: A Struggle for the City', *Journal of Lusophone Studies*, 1.1 (2016), 88–106

CARLOS, JOÃO, '"Não houve nenhuma Comissão das Lágrimas em Angola", diz Pepetela' [Interview], *DW.com*, 14 May 2012 <http://www.dw.com/pt-002/não-houve-nenhuma-comissão-das-lágrimas-em-angola-diz-pepetela/a-15949744> [accessed 27 March 2018]

CARROLL, RORY, DUNCAN CAMPBELL, JO TUCKMAN and RORY MCCARTHY, 'The British Do the Diplomacy and the Americans Write the Cheques', *The Guardian*, 28 February 2003 <https://www.theguardian.com/world/2003/feb/28/iraq.unitednations> [accessed 27 March 2018]

CASTRO, ROBERTO, 'A dura luta para escrever' [interview], *Jornal da USP*, 30 June 1997, p. 12

CHABAL, PATRICK, *Amílcar Cabral: Revolutionary Leadership and People's War* (Trenton, NJ: Africa World Press, 2003)

CHILDS, GLADWYN MURRAY, 'The Peoples of Angola in the Seventeenth Century according to Cadornega', *The Journal of African History*, 1.2 (1960), 271–79

COLLINGWOOD, R. G., *The Idea of History: Revised Edition with Lectures, 1926–1928*, ed. by Jan van Der Dussen (Oxford: Clarendon Press, 1994)

CORRADO, JACOPO, *The Creole Elite and the Rise of Angolan Proto-Nationalism, 1870–1920* (Amherst, NY: Cambria, 2008)

COSTA ANDRADE, FRANCISCO FERNANDO DA, *Literatura angolana: opiniões* (Lisbon: Edições 70, 1980)

COUTO, MIA, *A varanda do frangipani* (Lisbon: Caminho, 1996)

—— *Pensatempos* (Lisbon: Caminho, 2005)

—— *Vozes anoitecidas* (Lisbon: Caminho, 1987)

CRISTÓVÃO, AGUINALDO, 'O escritor é um ditador no momento da escrita', União dos Escritores Angolanos website (2015) <http://www.ueangola.com/entrevistas/item/384-o-escritor-é-um-ditador-no-momento-da-escrita> [accessed 27 March 2018]

CUSACK, IGOR, 'Perfomance and the Mobilization of Identity in Pepetela's *Lueji. O Nascimento de um Império*', *Portuguese Studies*, 25.2 (2009), 169–81

DAVIDSON, BASIL, *In the Eye of the Storm: Angola's People* (London: Longman, 1972)

DAVIES, NORMAN, 'The Deep Stains of Dictatorship', *New York Review of Books*, LX.8, 9 May 2013, p. 51

DECKARD, SHARAE, 'Deformed Narrators: Postcolonial Genre and Peripheral Modernity in Mabanckou and Pepetela', in *Locating Postcolonial Narrative Genres*, ed. by Walter Göbel and Saskia Schabio (New York: Routledge, 2012), pp. 95–107

DIAS DE CARVALHO, HENRIQUE AUGUSTO, *Etnographia e história tradicional dos povos da Lunda* (Lisbon: Imprensa Nacional, 1890)

DOLAN, KERRY A., 'Daddy's Girl: How an African "Princess" Banked $3 Billion in a Country Living on $2 a Day', *Forbes*, 2 September 2013 <http://www.forbes.com/sites/kerryadolan/2013/08/14/how-isabel-dos-santos-took-the-short-route-to-become-africas-richest-woman/> [accessed 27 March 2018]

DUARTE, LUÍS RICARDO, 'Pepetela: crónica de uma Angola em mudança' [interview], *Jornal de Letras, Artes e Ideias*, 30 October 2013, pp. 8–9
DUARTE DE CARVALHO, RUY, *Vou lá visitar pastores* (Lisbon: Cotovia, 1999)
ESTEVES, JUNNO AROCHO, 'Pope Francis Meets with President of Angola', *Zenit*, 2 May 2014 <http://www.zenit.org/en/articles/pope-francis-meets-with-president-of-angola> [accessed 27 March 2018]
EVANS, DYLAN, *An Introductory Dictionary of Lacanian Psychoanalysis* (New York: Brunner-Routledge, 1997)
FANON, FRANTZ, *The Wretched of the Earth*, trans. by Constance Farrington (New York: Grove Press, 2005)
FERNANDES, FILIPE S., *Isabel dos Santos: segredos e poder do dinheiro* (Alfragide: Casa das Letras, 2015)
FERREIRA, MANUEL (ed.), *No reino de Caliban: antologia panorâmica da poesia africana de expressão portuguesa*, 2nd edn, 3 vols (Lisbon: Plátano, 1988)
FOUCAULT, MICHEL, *Discipline and Punish: The Birth of the Prison*, trans. by Alan Sheridan (London: Penguin, 1991)
FREEDMAN, ESTELLE B., *The Essential Feminist Reader* (New York: The Modern Library, 2007)
FREUD, SIGMUND, *Civilization and its Discontents*, trans. by Joan Riviere (New York: Jonathan Cape and Harrison Smith, 1931)
FRIEDAN, BETTY, *The Feminine Mystique* (New York: Norton, 1963)
FUKUYAMA, FRANCIS, *The End of History and the Last Man* (London: Hamish Hamilton, 1992)
GATINOIS, CLAIRE, 'Portugal Indebted to Angola after Economic Reversal of Fortune', *The Guardian*, 3 June 2014 <https://www.theguardian.com/world/2014/jun/03/portugal-economy-bailout-angola-invests> [accessed 27 March 2018]
GOMES, MANUEL CABELEIRA, *Literatura e estudos interculturais: uma leitura imagológica do romance YAKA de Pepetela* (Lisbon: Universidade Aberta, 1996)
GORJÃO HENRIQUES, JOANA, 'Activistas angolanos libertados da prisão', *Público*, 29 June 2016 <https://www.publico.pt/2016/06/29/mundo/noticia/jornal-angolano-diz-que-17-activistas-vao-aguardar-decisao-em-casa-1736689> [accessed 27 March 2018]
GRAHAM, AUBREY, and ANNE PITCHER, 'Cars are Killing Luanda: Cronyism, Consumerism, and Other Assaults on Angola's Postwar Capital City', in *Cities in Contemporary Africa*, ed. by Martin J. Murray and Garth A. Myers (New York: Palgrave, 2005), pp. 173–99
GUIMARÃES, FERNANDO ANDRESSEN, *The Origins of the Angolan Civil War: Foreign Intervention and Domestic Political Conflict* (New York: St Martin's Press, 1997)
HAMILTON, GRANT, 'Pepetela's Proposal: Desire and Anarchy in *The Return of the Water Spirit*', *African Identities*, 11.4 (2013), 343–52
HEGEL, GEORG W. F., *Lectures on the Philosophy of World History*, trans. by H. B. Nisbet (Cambridge: Cambridge University Press, 1975)
HENIGHAN, STEPHEN, '*Muana Puó* and *Mayombe*: Colonial Pasts and Utopian Futures in Two Early Works by Pepetela', *Romance Quaterly* 54.2 (2007), 164–77
—— '"Um James Bond Subdesenvolvido": The Ideological Work of the Angolan Detective in Pepetela's Jaime Bunda Novels', *Portuguese Studies*, 22.1 (2006), 135–52
HERCULANO, ALEXANDRE. *Eurico, o Presbítero* (Amadora: Bertrand, 1979)
HEYWOOD, LINDA, *Contested Power in Angola, 1840s to the Present* (Rochester, NY: University of Rochester Press, 2000)
—— *Njinga of Angola: Africa's Warrior Queen* (Cambridge, MA: Harvard University Press, 2017)
HEYWOOD, LINDA M. & JOHN K. THORNTON, *Central Africans, Atlantic Creoles, and the Foundation of the Americas, 1585–1660* (Cambridge: Cambridge University Press, 2007)

HOBSBAWM, ERIC, and TERENCE RANGER, *The Invention of Tradition* (Cambridge: Cambridge University Press, 1983)
HODGES, DAVID, *From Afro-Stalinism to Petro-diamond Capitalism* (Bloomington: Indiana University Press, 2001)
HORECK, TANYA, *Public Rape: Representing Violation in Fiction and Film* (New York: Routledge, 2004)
HUNGWE, ELDA, and CHIPO HUNGWE, 'Nationhood and Women in Postcolonial African Literature', *CLCWeb: Comparative Literature and Culture*, 12.3 (2010) <http://docs.lib.purdue.edu/clcweb/vol12/iss3/1> [accessed 27 March 2018]
IRELE, ABIOLA, 'Negritude or Black Cultural Nationalism', *The Journal of Modern African Studies*, 3.3 (1965), 321–48
'Irmãos de José Van Dunem respondem a réplica de Pepetela' [no byline], *Semanário Angolense*, 27 November 2005 <http://www.angonoticias.com/Artigos/item/7243> [accessed 27 March 2018]
JAMBA, SOUSA, *Patriots* (London: Viking, 1990)
JAMESON, FREDERIC, *Postmodernism, or, the Cultural Logic of Late Capitalism* (Durham, NC: Duke University Press, 1991)
JORGE, HUGO, 'Pepetela: o estado da cultura e literatura angolana por uma das suas maiores referências', *Rede Angolana*, 8 June 2015 <http://www.redeangola.info/especiais/cultura-foi-substituida-pelo-interesse-de-enriquecer/> [accessed 27 March 2018]
KANDJIMBO, LUÍS, 'Angolan Literature in the Presence of an Incipient Canon of Literatures Written in Portuguese', *Research in African Literatures*, 38.1 (Spring 2007), 9–34
LABAN, MICHEL, *Angola: encontro com escritores*, 3 vols (Porto: Fundação Eng. António de Almeida, 1991)
—— *Mário Pinto de Andrade, uma entrevista* (Lisbon: João Sá da Costa, 1997)
—— *Moçambique: encontro com escritores*, 3 vols (Porto: Fundação Eng. António de Almeida, 1990)
LARANJEIRA, PIRES, 'A poesia de Agostinho Neto como documento histórico', in *Comunidades imaginadas: nação e nacionalismos em África*, ed. by Luís Reis Torgal, Fernando Tavares Pimenta and Julião Soares Sousa (Coimbra: Imprensa da Universidade, 2008), pp. 111–16
—— *Ensaios afro-literários* (Lisbon: Novo Imbondeiro, 2001)
—— *Literaturas africanas de expressão portuguesa* (Lisbon: Universidade Aberta, 1995)
LEITE, ANA MAFALDA, 'Angola', in *The Postcolonial Literature of Lusophone Africa*, ed. by Patrick Chabal (Evanston, IL: Northwestern University Press, 1996), pp. 103–64
LEITE, ANA MAFALDA, SHEILA KHAN, JESSICA FALCONI and KAMILA KRAKOWSKA (eds), *Speaking the Postcolonial Nation: Interviews with Writers from Angola and Mozambique* (Oxford: Peter Lang, 2014)
LEMISKO, LYNN SPEER, 'The Historical Imagination: Collingwood in the Classroom', *Canadian Social Studies*, 38.2 (Winter 2004) < https://canadian-social-studies-journal.educ.ualberta.ca/content/articles-2000–2010#ARhistorical_imagination_collingwood202> [accessed 27 March 2018]
LOPES, FERNÃO, *Crónicas*, ed. by Maria Ema Tarracha Ferreira (Lisbon: Verbo, 2005)
LUANDINO VIEIRA, JOSÉ, *A vida verdadeira de Domingos Xavier* (Lisbon: Edições 70, 1974)
—— *Nós, os do Makulusu* (Lisbon: Edições 70, 1975)
MACEDO, HELDER, *Partes de África* (Lisbon: Presença, 1991)
—— *Parts of Africa*, trans. by Phillip Rothwell (Dartmouth, MA: LAABST, 2015)
—— *Tão longo amor tão curta a vida* (Bacarena: Presença, 2013)
MACEDO, HELDER, and FERNANDO GIL, *Viagens do olhar: retrospecção, visão e profecia no renascimento português* (Porto: Campo das Letras, 1998)

MacAskill, Ewen, John Henley and Rory Carroll, 'Scramble for Africa as Britain and France Go Head to Head for Key Votes' *The Guardian*, 11 March 2003 <https://www.theguardian.com/world/2003/mar/11/iraq.foreignpolicy> [accessed 27 March 2018]

Madureira, Luís, *Imaginary Geographies in Portuguese and Lusophone-African Literature: Narratives of Discovery and Empire* (Lampeter: Edwin Mellen, 2006)

Marcuse, Herbert, *Eros and Civilization: A Philosophical Inquiry into Freud* (New York: Vintage, 1961)

—— *One Dimensional Man: Studies in the Ideology of Advanced Industrial Society* (London: Routledge, 1964)

Margarido, Alfredo, *Negritude e humanismo* (Lisbon: Casa dos Estudantes do Império, 1964)

Marques de Morais, Rafael, 'Religion and the State in Angola', *Maka Angola*, 27 April 2014 < https://www.makaangola.org/2014/04/religion-and-the-state-in-angola/> [accessed 27 March 2018]

Martinho Ferreira, Patrícia Isabel, and Leonor Simas-Almeida, 'Os órfãos da Ilha de Luanda em *Se o passado não tivesse asas* — ou a história recente de um vasto segmento da sociedade angolana', *Via Atlântica*, 31 (June 2017), 227–47

Mata, Inocência, *Ficção e história na literatura angolana: o caso de Pepetela* (Luanda: Mayamba, 2010)

Mateus, Dalila Cabrita, and Álvaro Mateus, *Purga em Angola: o 27 de Maio de 1977* (Lisbon: Texto, 2007)

Mazrui, Ali, *African Thought in Contemporary Perspective* (Newcastle: Cambridge Scholars Publishing, 2014)

Mbah, Jean Martial Arsene, *As rivaldades políticas entre a Frente Nacional de Libertação de Angola (FNLA) e o Movimento Popular de Liberatação de Angola (MPLA) [1961–1975]* (Luanda: Mayamba, 2010)

Messiant, Christine, '"Em Angola até o passado é imprevisível": a experiência de uma investigação sobre o nacionalismo angolano e, em particular, o MPLA: fontes, crítica, necessidade actuais de investigação', in *Actas do II seminário internacional sobre a história de Angola: construindo o passado angolano: as fontes e a sua interpretação, Luanda 4 a 9 de Agosto de 1997* (Lisbon: Comissão Nacional para as Comemorações dos Descobrimentos Portugueses, 2000), pp. 808–11

Mignolo, Walter D., *The Darker Side of Western Modernity* (Durham NC: Duke University Press, 2011)

Milhazes, José, *Angola: O princípio do fim da União Soviética* (Lisbon: Vega, 2009)

Miller, Christopher L., 'The (Revised) Birth of Negritude: Communist Revolution and "the Immanent Negro" in 1935', *MLA*, 125.3 (2010), 743–49

Miller, Joseph C., *Kings and Kinsmen: Early Mbundu States in Angola* (Oxford: Clarendon Press, 1976)

Mohanty, Chandra Talpade, Ann Russo and Lourdes Torres (eds), *Third World Women and the Politics of Feminism* (Bloomington: Indiana University Press, 1991)

Mondlane, Eduardo, *The Struggle for Mozambique*, intro. by John Saul and biographical sketch by Herbert Shore (London: Zed Books, 1983)

Moorman, Marissa J., *Intonations: A Social History of Music and Nation in Luanda, Angola, from 1945 to Recent Times* (Athens: Ohio University Press, 2008)

MPLA, 'José Eduardo dos Santos, o modelo de angolano', 28 August 2012 <http://www.mpla.ao/mpla.6/artigos.14/jose-eduardo-dos-santos-o-modelo-de-angolano.a403.html> [accessed 27 March 2018]

—— *História de Angola* (Algiers: MPLA, 1965)

Nama, Charles A., 'Art and Ideology in Angolan and Afro-American Fiction: Pepetela's

Mayombe and Richard Wright's *The Long Dream*', in *On the Road to Guinea: Essays in Black Comparative Literature*, ed. by Edward O. Ako (Ibadan: Caltop Publications, 1992), pp. 20–34

NETO, AGOSTINHO, *Ainda o meu sonho (discursos sobre a cultura nacional)* (Lisbon: Edições 70, 1980)

—— *Sagrada esperança* (Lisbon: Sá da Costa, 1987)

—— *Speeches* (Luanda: Department of Politico-Ideological Education, Propaganda and Information, 1980)

NEWITT, MALYN, *A History of Mozambique* (London: Hurst, 1995)

NGUGI WA THIONG'O, 'Born of Violence: Pepetela's Narrative of the National Question in the Postcolonial Era', in *Transplanted Imaginaries: Literatures of New Climes*, ed. by K. T. Sunitha (Trenton, NJ: Africa World Press, 2007), 9–27

NNAEMEKA, OBIOMA, *The Politics of (M)Othering: Womanhood, Identity and Resistance in African Literature* (New York: Routledge, 1997)

OLIVEIRA PINTO, ALBERTO, *A oralidade no romance histórico angolano moderno: A gloriosa família de Pepetela, A casa velha das margens de Arnaldo Santos* (Lisbon: Novo Imbondeiro, 2003)

ONDJAKI, *Bom dia, Camaradas* (Lisbon: Caminho, 2003)

—— 'Let's Share the Dream: Stories for Children in Angola', *Bookbird*, 2 (2009), 46–52

ORNELAS, JOSÉ, 'Pepetela', in *Dictionary of Literary Biography, Volume 367: African Lusophone Writers*, ed. by Monica Rector and Richard Vernon (Detroit, MI: Gale, 2012), pp. 131–48

OWEN, HILARY, *Mother Africa, Father Marx: Women's Writing of Mozambique, 1948–2002* (Lewisburg, PA: Bucknell University Press, 2007)

PACAVIRA, MANUEL PEDRO, *Nzinga Mbandi* (Lisbon: Edições 70, c. 1979)

PACHECO, CARLOS, *Agostinho Neto: o perfil de um ditador* (Lisbon: Vega, 2016)

—— *Angola: um gigante com pés de barro e outras reflexões sobre a África e o mundo* (Lisbon: Vega, 2014)

—— *Repensar Angola* (Lisbon: Vega, 2000)

PADILHA, LAURA CAVALCANTE, *Novos pactos, outras ficções* (Porto Alegre: EDIPUCRS, 2002)

PAREDES, MARGARIDA, *Combater duas vezes: mulheres na luta armada em Angola* (Vila do Conde: Verso da História, 2015)

PAWSON, LARA, *In the Name of the People: Angola's Forgotten Massacre* (London: I. B. Tauris, 2014)

PEARCE, JUSTIN, *An Outbreak of Peace: Angola's Situation of Confusion* (Claremont, South Africa: David Philip Books, 2005)

—— *Political Identity and Conflict in Central Angola, 1975–2002* (Cambridge: Cambridge University Press, 2015)

PÉCLARD, DIDIER, 'UNITA and the Moral Economy of Exclusion in Angola, 1966–1977', in *Sure Road? Nationalisms in Angola, Guinea-Bissau and Mozambique*, ed. by Eric Morier-Genoud (Leiden: Brill, 2012), pp. 149–74

PEPETELA, *A geração da utopia* (Lisbon: Dom Quixote, 1992)

—— *A gloriosa família* (Lisbon: Dom Quixote, 1997)

—— *A montanha de água lilás* (Lisbon: Dom Quixote, 2000)

—— *As aventuras de Ngunga* (Lisbon: Edições 70, 1977)

—— *Crónicas com fundo de guerra* (Lisbon: Nelson de Matos, 2011)

—— *Jaime Bunda, agente secreto* (Lisbon: Dom Quixote, 2001)

—— *Jaime Bunda e a morte do americano* (Lisbon: Dom Quixote, 2003)

—— *Lueji, o nascimento de um império* (Lisbon: Dom Quixote, 1990)

—— *Mayombe* (Lisbon: Edições 70, 1980)

—— *Mayombe*, trans. by Michael Wolfers (Oxford: Heinemann, 1996)

―― *Muana Puó* (Lisbon: Edições 70, 1978)
―― *O cão e os caluandas* (Lisbon: Dom Quixote, 1985)
―― *O desejo de Kianda* (Lisbon: Dom Quixote, 1995)
―― *O planalto e a estepe* (Lisbon: Dom Quixote, 2009)
―― *O quase fim do mundo* (Lisbon: Dom Quixote, 2008)
―― *O sul. O sombreiro* (Lisbon: Dom Quixote, 2011)
―― *O terrorista de Berkeley, Califórnia* (Lisbon: Dom Quixote, 2007)
―― *O tímido e as mulheres* (Lisbon: Dom Quixote, 2013)
―― *Parábola do cágado velho* (Lisbon: Dom Quixote, 1996)
―― *Predadores* (Lisbon: Dom Quixote, 2005)
―― *Se o passado não tivesse asas* (Lisbon: Dom Quixote, 2016)
―― *The Return of the Water Spirit*, trans. by Luís R. Mitras (Oxford: Heinemann, 2002)
―― *Yaka* (São Paulo: Ática, 1984)
―― *Yaka*, trans. by Marga Holness (Oxford: Heinemann, 1996)
PERES, PHYLLIS, 'Colonial Representation and Conquest in Pepetela's "As Cinco Vidas de Teresa"', *Portuguese Literary and Cultural Studies*, 15/16 (2006), 251–57
―― *Transculturation and Resistance in Lusophone African Narrative* (Gainesville: University of Florida Press, 1997)
―― 'Traversing Postcoloniality: Pepetela and the Narrations of Nation', *Luso-Brazilian Review*, 40.2 (2003), 111–17
PHAF-RHEINBERGER, INEKE, *The 'Air of Liberty': Narratives of the South Atlantic Past* (Amsterdam: Rodopi, 2008)
'Pope takes African pilgrimage to Angola' [no byline], *Philstar Global*, 20 March 2009 <http://www.philstar.com/breaking-news/450000/pope-takes-african-pilgrimage-angola> [accessed 27 March 2018]
'Portuguese group Somague builds shopping centre in Luanda, Angola' [no byline], *Macauhub*, 12 January 2005 <http://www.macauhub.com.mo/en/2015/01/12/portuguese-group-somague-builds-shopping-centre-in-luanda-angola/> [accessed 27 March 2018]
PRATT, ANNIS, *Archetypal Patterns in Women's Fiction* (Bloomington: Indiana University Press, 1982)
RAVENSTEIN, E. G. (ed.), *The Strange Adventures of Andrew Battell of Leigh in Angola and the Adjoining Regions, Reprinted from 'Purchas His Pilgrimes,' Edited with Notes and a Concise History of Kongo and Angola* (London: Hakluyt Society, 1901)
Rede Angola, 'Presos políticos proibidos de ler Pepetela', 14 July 2015 <http://www.redeangola.info/presos-politicos-proibidos-de-lerem-pepetela/> [accessed 27 March 2018]
REZA, ALEXANDRA, 'African Anti-colonialism and the *Ultramarinos* of the *Casa dos Estudantes do Império*', *Journal of Lusophone Studies*, 1.1 (2016), 37–56
―― 'African Literary Journals in French and Portuguese, 1947–1968: Politics, Culture and Form' (unpublished doctoral thesis, University of Oxford, 2018)
RIBEIRO, NUNO, '38 anos de equilíbrios e poder', *Público*, 23 August 2017 <https://www.publico.pt/2017/08/23/mundo/noticia/38-anos-de-equilibrios-e-poder-1783023> [accessed 27 March 2018]
RIBEIRO, RAQUEL, 'Angola, a Nation in Pieces in José Eduardo Agualusa's *Estação das chuvas*', *Journal of Lusophone Studies*, 1.1 (2016), 57–72
ROGERS, SEAN, 'Imagining Revenge: The Adoption of Violence by *Mayombe's* Fighters', *Transformation: Critical Perspectives on Southern Africa*, 62 (2006), 118–29
RUI, MANUEL, *Quem me dera ser onda* (Lisbon: Edições 70, 1982)
SÁ, ANA LÚCIA, 'Vozes na narrativa da história de Angola', *The Scientific Journal of Humanistic Studies*, 1.1 (2009), 35–41
SANTOS, ALEXANDRA DIAS, 'Nação, guerra e utopia em Pepetela (1971–1996)' (unpublished doctoral thesis, University de Lisbon, 2011)

Santos, Arnaldo, *Quinaxixe* (Lisbon: Casa dos Estudantes do Império, 1965)
Santos, Artur Pestana dos, *Sociologia urbana: compêndio* (Mangualde: Edições Pedago, 2014)
Santos, Carlos, 'Quem são os ativistas presos desde 20 de junho e as acusadas que não estão detidas', *Esquerdanet*, 21 October 2015 <http://www.esquerda.net/dossier/quem-sao-os-ativistas-presos-desde-20-de-junho-e-acusadas-que-nao-estao-detidas/39200> [accessed 27 March 2018]
Scheub, Harold, *A Dictionary of African Mythology* (Oxford: Oxford University Press, 2002)
Schurmans, Fabrice, *O trágico do estado pós-colonial: Pius Ngandu Nkashama, Sony Labou Tansi, Pepetela* (Coimbra: CES-Almedina, 2014)
Scott, Joan W., 'Gender: A Useful Category of Historical Analysis', *The American Historical Review*, 91.5 (December 1986), 1053–75
Serrano, Carlos, 'Angola: a "Geração de 50", os jovens intelectuais e a raiz das coisas', União dos Escritores Angolanos [Web Essays] <http://www.ueangola.com/criticas-e-ensaios/item/157-angola-a-geracao-de-50-os-jovens-intelectuais-e-a-raiz-das-coisas> [accessed 27 March 2018]
Silva, Rodrigues da, 'Da utopia à amargura' [Interview], *Jornal de Letras, Artes e Ideias*, 29 March 1995, pp. 14–16
Soares de Oliveira, Ricardo, 'Illiberal Peacebuilding in Angola', *Journal of Modern African Studies*, 49.2 (June 2011), 287–314
—— *Magnificent and Beggar Land: Angola since the Civil War* (London: Hurst, 2015)
Sousa Pinto, Paulo Jorge de, 'Em torno de um problema de identidade: os 'Jaga' na história do Congo e Angola', *Mare Liberum: Revista de História dos Mares*, 18/19 (1999–2000), 193–243
Sousa Santos, Boaventura de, 'Os sociólogos não sabem andar de boleia', in Manuel Rui, *O Kaputo Camionista e Eusébio* (Lisbon: Guerra e Paz, 2017), pp. 95–99
Stockton, Sharon, *The Economics of Fantasy: Rape in Twentieth-century Literature* (Columbus: Ohio State University Press, 2006)
Talaia, Júlia Massoxi da Costa, *O neo-realismo na poética de Agostinho Neto* (Luanda: União dos Escritores Angolanos, 2009)
Tali, Jean-Michel Mabeko, *Dissidências e poder de estado: o MPLA perante si próprio (1962–1977): ensaio de história política*, 2 vols (Luanda: Nzila, 2001)
Tanner, Laura, *Intimate Violence: Reading Rape and Torture in Twentieth-Century Fiction* (Bloomington: Indiana University Press, 1994)
Tavares, Ana Paula, 'Contar Histórias', in *Lendo Angola*, ed. by Laura Cavalcante Padilha and Margarida Calafate Ribeiro (Porto: Afrontamento, 2008), pp. 39–50
US Department of State, Office of the Historian, 'A Guide to the United States' History of Recognition, Diplomatic, and Consular Relations, by Country, since 1776: Angola' <https://history.state.gov/countries/angola> [accessed 27 March 2018]
Venâncio, José Carlos, *Literatura e poder na África lusófona* (Lisbon: Ministério da Educação, 1992)
—— *Literatura versus sociedade* (Lisbon: Palavra Africana, 1992)
Vitanza, Victor J., *Sexual Violence in Western Thought and Writing: Chaste Rape* (New York: Palgrave, 2011)
Wall, Kathleen, *The Callisto Myth from Ovid to Atwood: Initiation and Rape in Literature* (Montreal: McGill-Queen's University Press, 1988)
Walker, Alice, *In Search of our Mother's Gardens: Womanist Prose* (San Diego, CA: Harcourt Brace Jovanovich, 1983)
Wesseling, Elisabeth, *Writing History as a Prophet: Postmodernist Innovations of the Historical Novel* (Amsterdam: John Benjamins, 1991)

Willis, Clive, '*Mayombe* and the Liberation of the Angolan', *Portuguese Studies*, 3 (1987), 205–14

Woolley, Benjamin, *Savage Kingdom: The True Story of Jamestown, 1607, and the Settlement of America* (New York: Harper Collins, 2007)

INDEX

A geração da utopia 49, 76–77, 79, 81, 114, 145
A gloriosa família 5, 49, 54, 57, 65 n. 1, 86, 92, 94–105, 148–49, 156
Adamichin, Anatoli 11
Adorno, Theodor 122 n. 11
Africa 1, 4, 12, 23, 58, 60, 68, 97, 112, 118–20, 134–36, 138, 140–41, 143–44, 154
    Francophone 127
    as mother 139
    post-colonial 2, 5
African American 70
Afro-Stalinism 77
'Agarra que é polícia' 113–14, 119
Agostinho Neto University 47 n. 1
Agualusa, José Eduardo 16, 46, 68
Algiers 3, 16
alienation 130–31, 155, 157
Almeida, Júlio de 14–15, 42
Alves, Nito 35, 42–43, 46, 51
    protester with same name 126
Alps 136
Amado, Jorge 9, 89
American Dream 129
American imperialism *see also* colonialism 70, 125, 127, 132
amnesty 5
Amnesty International 10, 44, 47 n. 4, 126
Amos, Valerie 119
anarchy 82
Andrade, Mário Pinto de 10, 17 n. 4, 17 n. 9, 36
Angola 1, 3–5, 8, 12–14, 24–25, 27, 29–30, 36, 38, 46, 49–51, 59, 64, 68, 70, 77, 80–82, 86, 88–91, 93–94, 98, 101, 104, 109, 112–15, 125, 127, 130, 134, 144–48, 153–57, 161
    government of 22, 34, 37, 126, 136
    on UN Security Council 118–19
Angolan Writers Union (UEA) 143–44, 146, 149
angolanidade (Angolanness) 4, 19, 35, 37, 44, 50, 52, 58
anti-semitism 130
Arenas, Fernando 3, 76, 86, 129
Arendt, Hannah 40, 100, 126
arms trade 80
As aventuras de Ngunga 19, 35, 89–90, 118
'As cinco vidas de Teresa' 147
assimilado 10
atheism 108–09
Aviz, House of 2, 15

Bakhtin 24, 110
Bakongo 36
Baku 77
Bantu 127
Barnett, Don 8
Barthes, Roland 67
Battell, Andrew 53–57
BBC (British Broadcasting Corporation) 39
Benedict XVI (pontiff) 109
Benguela 2, 15, 49, 53, 89, 110–11, 114, 123, 146–47
Berkeley, University of California 115, 127, 130, 140
Berlin Conference 67
Berlin Wall, fall of 4, 11–12, 16, 52, 74, 77–78, 81, 94, 98, 107
Bhabha, Homi 110
Bicesse peace accord 12, 77
Birmingham, David 56, 66 n. 36
Borges Teixeira, Valéria 67
Boulanger, Dorothée 3, 46
bourgeois intellectuals 144
bourgeoisie 5, 20, 24, 44, 93, 115, 138, 143–45, 147, 152, 158
Brazil 1, 90
Britain 119
British Empire 57
Brittain, Victoria 18 n. 26, 45–47
Broadhead, Susan 55
Brooke, James 143
Brookshaw, David 3, 77
Brown, Nicholas 33 n. 31
Brownmiller, Susan 28
Brutentz, Karen 11
Bush, George W. 5, 38, 110, 112, 116, 119, 123, 125–26, 128, 132

Cabinda 19, 30, 78, 147
Cabral, Amílcar 11, 118
Cadornega, António 54–57, 97, 100–02
Calafate Ribeiro, Margarida 97
California 126
Calomboloca Prison 126, 132
Calpe 134–36
Cameroon 119
Caminha, Pêro Vaz de 1
Candomblé 27
canon of Angolan literature 50, 161
Cão, Diogo 57

Cape Verde 11, 22, 113
capitalism 1, 44, 46, 61, 63–64, 77, 79–81, 89, 91, 93, 97, 101, 112, 118, 125, 129, 132, 139, 148, 154, 156
  in Angola 14, 88, 136
  as law 5, 134–35, 137–39, 141
cars 150–51
Carvalho, Henrique Augusto Dias de 67, 73
Casa dos Estudantes do Império 12–13, 15–16, 67, 143, 145–46, 149
Castro, Fidel 11, 16
Catherine the Great 68
Catholic Church 20, 24, 93, 108
  in Angola 53, 124, 146
Catholicism 25–26, 76
  conversion to 108–09
Centre for Angolan Studies 16, 67, 94–95
Cerveira Pereira, Manuel 53
Césaire, Aimé 9
Chabal, Patrick 11
chauvinism 22
Che Guevara 76, 108
Cheney, Dick 119
Chicago 127
Childs, Gladwyn Murray 66 n. 21
China 13
Chitunda, Jeremias Kalandula 86
Chiziane, Paulina 27
Chungara, Domitila Barrios de la 139 n. 6
Christianity 19, 61, 108
  and colonialism 2
  and morality 26
  in Angola 146
  repetition of 16, 20, 23–25, 81, 108
CIA (Central Intelligence Agency) 39
circumcision, female 140
city 5, 143, 145–47, 150–51, 157–59
civil war 2, 5, 10, 12, 37, 44, 51, 77–81, 84, 86–87, 90–93, 104, 112, 116, 123, 129, 143, 145–48, 150, 154
  aftermath 5, 109, 112, 126, 145
clientelism 4, 44, 74, 87, 91, 145
Cleopatra 68
Cold War 2, 8, 10–12, 14–15, 37, 43–44, 74, 77–78, 87, 118–20, 156
Collingwood, R.G. 99
colonialism 21, 23, 29, 89, 120, 134, 136, 139, 148
  American see also American imperialism 124–25
  Portuguese 1, 4, 7, 10, 13–14, 20, 36, 52, 57–58, 60, 77, 80, 98, 114, 119, 125, 146, 149–50, 154, 156
  French 20
coloniality 5, 97–98, 101
Comissão das Lágrimas 38–41, 46
communion (between men) 26
communism 8–9, 44, 76, 81, 88, 125
Concordat 20
Congo (Angolan region) 36, 55–56

Congo River 134
Congregationalists 146
Conrad, Joseph 135
consumerism 122–23, 150–52
Corrado, Jacopo 18 n. 30
corruption 28, 31, 44, 47, 65, 67, 73, 81–82, 84, 87, 104, 112, 134, 145, 148, 151–54
cosmopolitanism 8, 13, 143, 145–46, 153
Costa Andrade, Francisco Fernando da (Ndunduma) 39–40, 89–90
coup 35, 41, 43
Couto, Mia 90, 109–10, 120 n. 8, 150
Creole elites 1, 12, 21, 30, 34, 36, 107, 109, 112–13, 119, 127, 131–32, 134, 145, 147, 152–53, 155
Crónicas com fundo de guerra 114
Cruz, Viriato da 10, 13–14
Cuba 10, 44
  in Angola 11, 43, 78, 118, 146
'Cuando calienta el sol' 153
Cusack, Igor 68–69
Cuvale 35

Dante 113
Dark Continent 135
Davidson, Basil 8, 17 n. 4
Deckard, Sharae 104
dehumanization 87, 157–58
democracy 30, 45
Democratic Republic of the Congo 69
desire 25–26, 28, 31, 138, 141, 161
detective fiction 104, 110, 122
dialectic 76, 96–97, 146
dialogism 4, 21, 24, 110–11, 134
didacticism 29, 35, 89–90
disillusionment 15, 51, 76, 113, 145
Dokolo, Augustin 94 n. 12
Dokolo, Sindika 94 n. 12
drive 130
Duarte, Luís Ricardo 106
Duarte de Carvalho, Ruy 147
Dunem, Francisca van 39, 41, 43
Dunem, João van 39, 41, 43
Dutch occupation of Luanda 5, 49, 97–100, 102, 148

Eiffel Tower 93
El Dorado 129
elections 2, 12
  multiparty in Angola of 1992: 77–79, 86
Elizabeth I of England 68
emasculation 63–64, 124
Empire 45–46, 110, 118–19, 121, 123, 125–26, 129
epic 4–5, 28, 49, 53
  family epics 49–50
epigraphs 101–04, 156
epistemology, Angolan 24, 38, 127–28, 131–32
ethical subject 5

ethical turn 2, 88, 93, 95
ethics 5, 29, 49, 94–97, 99, 102, 104, 110, 115, 155–56
ethnicity 2, 9, 35, 56, 63, 69, 161
eurocentrism 8, 98
Europe 4, 15, 45, 134, 137, 140, 152
   nineteenth-century 49
Europeanized 13
exceptionalism:
   Angolan 45
   Portuguese 13
extortion 152

factionalism 36, 44
Fanon, Frantz 19–21
fantasy 130, 140, 161
father 86, 89–94
   of the nation 92
FBI 111, 114, 122, 129
fellow travellers 8, 44
feminism 135, 139, 141
Fernando I of Portugal 95
Ferreira, Manuel 32 n. 8
Flanders 97
flâneur 150
FNLA 9–10, 14, 36–37, 151
Foucault 20, 96
forgiveness 5, 24, 108, 110, 112–13, 115
France 119
Francis I (pontiff) 109
Frankfurt School 122–23
free-market economics 1, 4–5, 29, 70, 79–80, 92, 98, 120, 138
FRELIMO 11, 24, 138
Freud 28, 93, 120, 136
Friedan, Betty 139 n. 6
Fukuyama, Francis 81, 107, 113, 115
fundamentalism, religious 135, 137, 139

Gamboa, Zézé 90, 129–30
GDR (German Democratic Republic) 44
Ginga, Queen *see also* Jinga 68, 70
globalization 80–81, 110, 118–19, 121, 135
Golden Gate Bridge 128
Gomes, Manuel Cabeleira 63
Graham, Aubrey, & Anne Pitcher 150
Greek mythology 59, 61
Guimarães, Fernando Andressen 17 n. 17
Guimarães Rosa 9
Guinea 119, 144
Guinea-Bissau 11, 22
Gulf War 119

Halloween Massacre 86
Hamilton, Grant 80, 83
Hamilton, Russell 46, 143
Harvey, Roy 8

Hatshepsut 140
Hegel 95–96
   and Africa 97
Henighan, Stephen 3, 107, 115, 147, 161
Herculano, Alexandre 50
heterosexuality 26
Heywood, Linda 18 n. 18, 68
Heywood, Linda M. & John K. Thornton 66 n. 26
História de Angola, MPLA 68
historian, role of 3
historical novel 49–50
History 3, 94–97, 100, 106, 114–15
   as imagination 99–100, 102
   in Marxism 8, 94–95, 107, 113
   objectivity of 5
Hobsbawm, Eric & Terence Ranger 71
Hodges, David 1, 77
Hollywood 114, 122, 154
homophobia 130
homosexuality 26
homosociality 26
Horeck, Tanya 28
humanism 3, 9, 143
Hungwe, Elda and Chipo Hungwe 33 n. 31
Hutcheon, Linda 49

idealism 81
identity politics 132, 135
ideology 2, 13, 15–16, 20, 25, 35, 37, 41, 50, 52, 67, 76, 80, 88, 102–03, 106, 134–35, 140–41, 148, 150–51, 153, 157
Imbangala 52, 55–56, 58, 69
impotence 63, 124
incest taboo 136
independence 1, 31, 34, 36, 38, 46, 49, 69, 86, 89, 93, 114, 118, 125, 127, 138, 143
   movements 15–16, 50, 138
   as project 46
   struggle for 13–14, 19, 21, 29–31, 76, 90, 106, 134, 140, 149, 153
Inês de Castro 95, 103
infanticide (among Jaga) 54–56
Internationale 154
Iraq, invasion of 119
Irele, Abiola 9

Jaga 50, 52–58, 65
Jaime Bunda, agente secreto 5, 37, 49, 65 n. 1, 77, 87, 100, 104, 109–11, 150, 152, 154
Jaime Bunda e a morte do americano 5, 37, 49, 65 n. 1, 70, 100, 104, 107–16, 118–26, 129, 132, 145, 147
Jamba, Sousa 46, 146 n. 19
James Bond 5, 104, 107
Jameson, Frederic 84 n. 16
Jesus Christ 76
Jinga, Queen *see also* Ginga 101

João I of Portugal 95–96
jouissance 141

Kandjimbo, Luís 35 n. 2, 50
Kant 109
Kimbundu 100
Kinaxixi 79, 82, 148–50, 152, 154
King, Martin Luther 132
Kinsey, Alfred 140
Kruse, Hanne 94 n. 12
Kukanova, Tatiana 78

Laban, Michel 17 n. 9, 23, 46
Lacan, Jacques 136
Lara, Lúcio 16, 17 n. 4, 42, 144
Laranjeira, Pires 3, 20, 35, 50 n. 7, 51, 51 n. 8, 59, 159 n. 7
Latin America 152
Leite, Ana Mafalda 22
Lenin 15
lesbian 70, 111, 123, 125, 128–29
  as fetish 132
liberal democracy 5, 98–99, 107
liberation 8
Lisbon 2, 8, 13, 16, 53
Lopes, Fernão 1–2, 15, 95–96, 103
Lourenço, João 77
Luanda 1, 10, 12, 27, 35–36, 44, 49, 53, 77, 79–80, 83, 86–87, 89–91, 97, 99, 107, 109–10, 115, 118, 124, 146–51, 153–58
  property boom 152
Luandino Vieira, José 149–50, 158
Lubango 15, 144
Lueji, o nascimento de um império 4, 49, 65, 67–74, 81, 83, 94, 96, 108, 134, 139
Lunda 9, 68–69, 71, 73, 96, 139
  Empire 4, 67, 71
Lunda-Norte 126
lusotropicalism 57, 61

Macedo, Helder 54, 96, 106–07, 116
Machel, Samora 139
Machiavellian 67, 72, 139
Madureira, Luís 153
Manichean 21, 114, 123
Monimambu, Spartacus 13 n. 35
Maoist faction 43
Marcuse, Herbert 120–23
Margarido, Alfredo 54, 143
Marques de Morais, Rafael 108
Martinho Ferreira, Patrícia Isabel & Leonor Simas-Almeida 157
Marx 15, 79, 93
Marxism 9, 19–20, 26, 29–31, 70, 87, 108–09, 118, 131, 138–39, 144
  as religion 23

Marxist-Hegelianism 94–95
Marxist-Leninism 1, 8, 16, 47, 76, 78, 80, 120
masculinity 89–91
Mata, Inocência 3, 46, 96
Mateus, Dalila Cabrita & Álvaro Mateus 42–43
May 1977 (27 de Maio) 11, 24, 32, 34–48, 120, 126–27, 132, 144
Mayombe 4, 16, 19–34, 36–37, 49, 59, 65, 68, 71, 76–77, 83, 94, 96, 108, 111–12, 118, 134, 138, 141, 147, 157–58
Mazrui, Ali 144
Mbah, Jean Martial Arsene 17 n. 4, 17 n. 19
Mbundu 9, 68
McCarthy, Joseph 132
Medici of Florence 93
mediocrity 3, 5, 49, 59, 62, 86–87, 93, 100, 145
Messiant, Christine 7
mestizo 7, 9–10, 20–21, 35–36, 123, 139
Mexico City 139 n. 6
Mignolo, Walter 97
Miller, Christopher 9
Miller, Joseph 56
misogyny 3
Mitras, Luís 79
Mobutu 14
modernity 97–98, 101, 135, 138, 141, 154
Mohanty, Chandra Talpade, Ann Russo & Lourdes Torres, 139 n. 4
Mondlane, Eduardo 11
Moorman, Marissa 13
moral relativity 114–15
moral void 1–2
morality 2, 25–26, 29, 31, 93, 95–97, 101, 104, 112, 145, 157
Moscow 47
mother as trope 22, 57, 73, 139
Mozambique 22, 139
MPLA 1–2, 4–6, 19–21, 23–24, 27–31, 35–38, 40–42, 44–45, 51–52, 58–61, 68, 70, 73–74, 76–79, 83–84, 86, 88, 90, 92–94, 104, 106–07, 112–13, 116, 118, 120, 126, 136, 138–39, 144–46, 148–57, 161
  Central Committee 43–44
  dogma 50
  history of 7–17, 34, 36, 46
  propaganda 92
Muana Puó 19, 52, 161
musseque 148–49, 151
myth 4, 55, 67–69, 73
  of Lueji 70, 108

Nama, Charles 33 n. 35
Namibia 44
Nascimento, Lopo de 144
nation 2, 13, 15, 19, 62, 145, 156
  Angolan 9–10, 13–14, 23, 30, 35, 37, 44, 50, 52, 57–58, 65, 69, 79, 106, 112, 138

National Assembly of Angola 144
nationalism 13–15, 37, 68
nationhood 2, 14, 21, 27–28, 30, 50, 106, 156
NATO 119
negritude 7, 9, 143
neo-colonial language policy 30, 157
neo-liberalism 1, 29, 79–81, 91, 93, 104
Neto, Agostinho 2–4, 7–11, 13, 15–16, 19–20, 25–26, 31, 34–44, 46–47, 50–52, 60, 65, 73, 92, 106, 109, 118, 120, 138–39, 141, 143–46, 152–53, 158
Neto, Irene 144–45
New Jersey (USA) 112
New Man, Marxist 3, 10, 22, 26–29, 63, 68, 76, 89–91, 104, 138, 140, 150, 154, 161
New State (Portuguese) 8, 83, 118–19, 126
Newitt, Malyn 24
Ngugi wa Thiong'o 4, 30–31
Nile River 134
Nito, *see* Alves, Nito
Nnaemeka, Obioma 139 n. 5

O cão e os caluandas 135, 148
O desejo de Kianda 49, 70, 79–84, 86, 93, 108, 112, 115, 139, 145, 149, 151–52
O planalto e a estepe 116, 134
O quase fim do mundo 5, 38, 51, 109, 132, 134–42
O sul. O sombreiro 50, 53–57, 147
O terrorista de Berkeley, Califórnia 5, 38, 51, 109, 112, 116, 119, 126–34
O tímido e as mulheres 27, 77, 116, 142, 145, 151–54, 156–58
Obama, Barack 132
objectivity 95–96, 100, 102–03
'objet petit a' 136
obscenity 51
Ogun 27
oil 77, 79, 89, 118–20, 126
Oliveira Pinto, Alberto 49
oligarchs 5
Ondina 19, 22, 24–28, 30–31, 63, 65, 68, 71, 138, 141, 158
Ondjaki 14, 42, 44 n. 32, 89
Organization for African Unity 10
Orientalism 134
original sin 12, 23, 34, 37
Ornelas, José 104, 135
orphanhood 157
Ovimbundu 146
Owen, Hilary 139 n. 7

Pacavira, Manuel Pedro 68
Pacheco, Carlos 17 n. 4, 33 n. 36, 37, 39–41, 47
Padilha, Laura Cavalcante 49, 79
pan-Africanism 9, 13
Parábola do cágado velho 135
Paredes, Margarida 33 n. 34

Paris 16
parody 5, 79, 104, 109–10, 132
patriarchy 22, 26–28, 31, 72–73, 79, 91, 100, 123, 158
Pawson, Lara 45–46
peace process 77–79
Pearce, Justin 12, 18, 78
Péclard, Didier 146
Pedro I of Portugal 95, 103
Peres, Phyllis 3, 19, 23, 46, 69, 147, 156
Pessoa, Fernando 9
Phaf-Rheinberger, Ineke 148
phallocentrism 19
Pitcher, Anne 150
Pleasure Principle 136
Plymouth University 126
pope 76
Portugal 13, 15
Portuguese Communist Party 1, 8, 16
Portuguese language in Angola 14
positivism 135
post-colonial historian 3
post-colonialism 30, 49, 65 n. 1, 76, 93, 108, 118, 124, 135–36
post-communism 12, 15, 77
post-ideology 153
post-imperial 1
post-modernism 49, 79, 107, 110, 113, 115, 121–23, 125, 132, 150
post-racial 4, 9–10, 61
power structure 1, 3–4, 15–16, 19–22, 26–27, 29–31, 49, 64, 67, 69–74, 80–81, 87, 92–93, 97, 106, 108, 110, 112, 115, 120–22, 125, 127, 132, 134, 136, 138, 148, 151
Pratt, Annis 22
praxis 21, 23, 108
Predadores 4, 37, 41, 49, 65 n. 1, 78, 84, 86–94, 98, 100, 109, 115, 127, 145, 148, 155
Prieto, Antonio 153
primal scene 28
Prometheus 27
Protestantism 146
Proudhon 137
Purchas, Samuel Vicar of Eastwood 53–54
purges of 1977: 2–4, 12, 35, 37–38, 42–43, 51, 60, 97, 145

race 7–10, 17 n. 3, 20, 50–51, 60, 62–65, 129, 132, 135, 161
racism 7–9, 15, 35–36, 58–65, 78, 129–30, 135–36
Rádio Eclésia 109
Ranger, Terence 71
rape 19, 22, 26–30, 60–61, 63–64, 103, 158
rape fantasy 29
Ravenstein, E.G. 53
Redol, Alves 9
Return of the Water Spirit see also *O desejo de Kianda* 79

revenge 29
Revolta Activa 36
Revolta do Leste 36
revolution 2–3, 13, 16, 20, 22–23, 31, 38, 44, 60, 64, 73–74, 76, 81, 83, 86, 90, 93–94, 107, 113, 136, 140–41, 143, 145–46, 153–54, 161
    sexual 120
Reza, Alexandra 9, 13
Ribeiro, Nuno 145
Ribeiro, Raquel 16
Rogers, Sean 29
Romanticism 57
Roque Santeiro 152
Rui, Manuel 3, 39, 46, 152–53
Rumsfeld, Donald 110
rural 90, 146–48, 157

Sá, Ana Lúcia 97
Salazar 8, 16, 20, 54, 92, 125
Sambizanga 77
San Francisco, California 129
Santos, Arnaldo 149–50, 158
Santos, Alexandra Dias 51
Santos, Isabel dos 78, 84 n. 7, 92–93
Santos, José Eduardo dos 4–5, 7–8, 15, 22, 34, 36–37, 44, 47, 74, 77–79, 86, 92, 108–09, 118–20, 126–27, 144–45
Santos Lima, Manuel dos 46
São Tomé e Príncipe 22
satire 5, 52, 81
Savimbi, Jonas 77–78, 88, 111–12, 120
schisms 36
Schurmans, Fabrice 65 n. 1
science fiction 132
Scott, Joan 101
Scramble for Africa 67, 119
Se o passado não tivesse asas 27, 145–46, 152, 154–59
Second World War 11, 74
self-criticism (in Marxism) 24–25, 76, 108, 112
Semanário Angolense 38, 40
Senegal 9
Senghor 9
September 11 (terrorist attack) 110, 119–20, 123, 126, 132
Shore, Marcia 99
Simas-Almeida, Leonor 157
Soares de Oliveira, Ricardo 78–79
social contract 28, 115
socialism 30–31, 81, 114, 138–39, 141
    in Angola 115, 121, 134
socialist realism 143
socialist transformation 144
Sociologia urbana: Compêndio 147 n. 21
sociology 3, 29, 62, 69, 94, 131, 147
Somague 150 n. 37
Soromenho, Castro 50

Sousa Pinto, Paulo Jorge de 66 n. 26
Sousa Santos, Boaventura de 3
South Africa 10, 12, 111, 121, 143
    invasion of Angola 44
    occupation of Namibia 43–44
    and racism 78
Soviet Communist Party 11
Stewart, Justice Potter 51
Stockton, Sharon 28
subjectivity 29, 88, 97, 130
Supreme Court of Angola 126
surplus repression 120, 122

Talaia, Júlia Massoxi da Costa 17 n. 8
Tali, Jean-Michel Mabeko 18 n. 40
Tanner, Laura 28
Tanzania 144
Tavares, Ana Paula 65, 68 n. 5
Teixeira, Ildeberto 144
terrorism as discourse 38, 98, 110, 112, 116, 121, 124–25, 127–30
Thing (in Lacanian psychoanalysis) 134–38, 140
third-way politics of 1990s: 98
Thornton, John 66 n. 26
tradition 71–74, 90–91, 135, 138, 140–41
transition to market economy 1
tribalism 15, 19–20, 22, 36–37, 146
Troni, Alfredo 50
Trump, Donald 132

UEA, *see* Angolan Writers Union
ultimatum, British 58
Umbundu 157
UN Security Council 119
UNITA 9–10, 12, 14, 77–78, 84, 86–88, 92, 111–12, 146, 146 n. 19, 154
United States of America 5, 11–12, 78, 89, 110–11, 115–16, 118–21, 123, 125–32, 157
universalism 13
UPNA (Northern Angolan People's Union) 36
urban 13, 45, 84, 149, 154
urban development 152
USA, *see* United States of America
USSR 11, 43–44, 52, 77–78, 92, 143
    in Angola 12, 44
utopia 2–3, 7, 29, 81, 100, 109, 114–15, 147

Vamos Descobrir Angola movement 13–14
Van Dunem, *see* Dunem, van
vanguard 2, 10, 23, 36, 50–51, 60, 77, 83, 93
Vansina, Jan 66 n. 26
Vatican 20, 109
Vecchi, Roberto 102
Venâncio, José Carlos 52, 58 n. 35
Vieira, António 9, 13
Vieira da Cruz, Tomás 50

Vieira Machado, Francisco José 54
Vitanza, Victor 28
Voice of America 40
voyeurism 103

Wall, Kathleen 22
Walker, Alice 139 n. 4
war on terror 119, 124, 126
Wesseling, Elisabeth 49
West India Company 98, 103
white supremacists 38
Willis, Clive 32 n. 4
Wizard of Oz 122
Wolfers, Michael 18 n. 26, 32 n. 7

women:
   in Angola 16–17
   bodies of 4, 19–33, 63, 71, 87, 139
   Pepetela's characterization of 3–4, 138–39, 161
   as womb 70–71, 73, 140–41
Woolley, Benjamin 55–56

Yaka 4, 24, 27, 34–35, 37, 47, 49–53, 57–65, 68–69, 76, 83, 86, 91, 96, 108, 145, 158

Zaire 14
Zambezi River 134
Zambia 36, 43
Zimbabwe 144

www.ingramcontent.com/pod-product-compliance
Lightning Source LLC
LaVergne TN
LVHW061252060426
835507LV00017B/2025